PERSPECTIVES ON
CONTEMPORARY MUSIC THEORY

PERSPECTIVES
ON CONTEMPORARY
MUSIC THEORY

Edited by

Benjamin Boretz and Edward T. Cone

W · W · NORTON & COMPANY · INC ·

NEW YORK

Published simultaneously in Canada by
George J. McLeod Limited, Toronto

Library of Congress Cataloging in Publication Data

Boretz, Benjamin, comp.
  Perspectives on contemporary music theory.

  (The Perspectives of new music series)
  Essays, principally by composers, reprinted from
various periodicals.
    1. Music—Theory—Addresses, essays, lectures.
  2. Music—History and criticism—20th century.
  I. Cone, Edward T., joint comp. II. Title.
  ML197.B65   781'.08   72-269
  ISBN 0-393-02162-9
  ISBN 0-393-00548-8 (pbk.)

The emblem on the cover is a reproduction of a drawing made by Igor
Stravinsky as a visual representation of his "recent music." Used by
permission.

PRINTED IN THE UNITED STATES OF AMERICA

3 4 5 6 7 8 9 0

ACKNOWLEDGMENTS

Ars Viva Verlag (B. Schotts Söhne, Mainz). Westergaard: Quartet, Copyright 1960.

Belmont Music Publishers, Los Angeles. Schoenberg: *Klavierstück*, Op. 33a, Copyright 1929.

Bote and Bock, Berlin. Westergaard: Five Pieces for Small Orchestra, Copyright 1959.

C. F. Peters Corporation, New York. Schoenberg: *Phantasie,* Op. 47, Copyright 1952.

G. Schirmer, Inc., New York. Schoenberg: Fourth String Quartet, Copyright 1939; Violin Concerto, Op. 36, Copyright 1938.

Theodore Presser Co., Bryn Mawr. Boulez: *Structures I,* Copyright 1955. Pousseur: *Characters,* Copyright 1962. Schoenberg: *Six Little Piano Pieces,* Op. 19, Copyright 1913; Suite, Op. 25, Copyright 1925. Webern: Three Pieces for Cello and Piano, Op. 11, Copyright 1924; Symphony, Op. 21, Copyright 1929; Concerto, Op. 24, Copyright 1948; Variations, Op. 27, Copyright 1937. All by Universal Edition, Vienna.

PREFACE

THIS BOOK, the first of several devoted to aspects of contemporary music theory, celebrates in particular the engagement by composers in fundamental music-theoretical explication, although not only composers are represented among its contributors. The recognition of music-theoretical questions as critical compositional ones is not, of course, unique to the twentieth century, nor to composers. But the uniquely explicit, uniquely consequential, and uniquely exposed contemporary involvement of composers in theory as writers and system builders has given the theoretical-compositional connection unprecedently wide, if not always benign or even accurate, publicity: we live, as every reader of the public musical print knows, in an age of "theoretical composition." Yet this characterization seems oddly skew to the actual singularities of the contemporary theory-composition relation: it is scarcely that compositions have become in any observable way more "theoretical," but rather that theory has become radically more "compositional." Surely the unique "theoreticalness" of the musical present is not to be found in any of those anciently familiar phenomena of conformity in composition to the supposedly transcendent authority of externally imposed theoretical principles, be they those of a Zarlino, a Fux, a Rameau, a Sechter, a Gedalge, a Hindemith, or a Schillinger. On the contrary, the demand of contemporary composers has been for the formulation of *adequate* theoretical principles, principles in conformity with what they know and need empirically, and capable of accounting for and supporting all the complexity, depth, and scope of what is musically actual, potential, and problematic.

That such a demand should be the particular child of our century is plausible, in view of the musical crisis precipitated by the appearance of extraordinary compositional events following a long habituation to a stable and powerful tradition. For the very inexplicability of these events at the moment of their appearance exposed brutally the inadequate conceptual and empirical scope of existing traditional theory, even in its function as the theory of the existing musical tradition, by revealing its powerlessness to render them explicable, to account for them as departures by extension rather than discontinuity from that tradition. To the composers thus left stranded by what was supposedly the intellectual foundation of the very tradition in which their own compositional thought had matured, and to which it was still com-

mitted, the issue must have hardly seemed one of ideological or pedagogical nicety, but of sheer musical survival. The virtually "metaphysical" problem that the failure of their own theory must have represented
to them is probably inconceivable to composers of the pluralistic, rela-
tivistic 1970s. But surely there has never been a more heartfelt need
in the history of music than that of composers like Schoenberg for an
adequate theory of musical structure.

Schoenberg in particular, and by his own account, felt himself utterly
abandoned to conceptual isolation and empirical self-reliance by the
failure of any available account of traditional music to provide a coherent reference for the developments taking place within his own
work. And since Schoenberg, like Schenker, had grown up in a world
where the precepts of tonality were the only musical "universals," it is
natural that his theoretical preoccupation should, like Schenker's, have
been the elucidation of still deeper universals which, in being derived
from a searching re-examination of the traditionally unimpeachable
literature, would serve to "justify" a given compositional context. That
this context was tonality, for Schenker, may suggest that, say, Brahms's
enthusiasm for his work had a deeper compositional relevance than the
mere communing of shared traditionalist prejudices. And that for
Schoenberg it was the supposed "motivicism" of all music served his
obviously profound need to have the history of music come out "inevitably" his way.

In this, Schoenberg, despite the deterministic surface of his prose,
behaved theoretically, as he continued to behave compositionally, in a
truly empiricist spirit. To be sure, the effort was metaphysical "justification"; but it was justification sought for the affirmation of what was,
rather than its denial, or the legislation of what was to be. Hindemith,
by contrast, for all his vaunted practicality, was as a theorist, and ultimately as a composer, a radical idealist rather than an empiricist. For
the principles Hindemith derived from his own scrutiny of musical
tradition were offered as ideological prescriptives of transcendent authority, immune from empirical correction; and their effect was not
explicative or suggestive but imperative, for both composition and
evaluation.

In Schoenberg's theoretical quest, moreover, one can discern the
spirit of what might be termed the *Bauhaus* mentality, which in turn
reflected, however hazily, the philosophical Vienna Circle's ideal of
"unified science." For the musical Vienna Circle's aspiration to a reintegration of the shattered musical literature into "one music" again
is remote only in verbal surface from the philosophical notions of "one
scientific language," of one mode of representation for all cognitive
human endeavors, and indeed of the very equivalence of "cognitivity"

and "experiencibility" that pervades the writings of Schlick, Neurath, Carnap, and Wittgenstein.

This extraordinary correspondence of intellectual developments on either side of a chasm of mutual ignorance, which were yet almost literally opposite sides of a single street, strenuously tempts nostalgic speculation regarding the amount of conceptual anguish Schoenberg might have been spared had he shared the epistemological and methodological discoveries of his Viennese co-residents. But, in fact, the explicit relation of the study of musical structure to the whole spectrum of contemporary intellectual development was an insight of a later generation of composers. Milton Babbitt, in particular, was the first to suggest that the force of any "musical systems" was not as universal constraints for all music but as alternative theoretical constructs, rooted in a communality of shared empirical principles and assumptions validated by tradition, experience, and experiment. Under such an interpretation, the invention of musical systems is itself seen to be part of the creative resource of composition, rather than its invariant context. And the remarkable structural power of the (Schenker-)tonal and (Schoenberg-)twelve-tone systems, revealed under Babbitt's explicit and implicit analyses of them as empirical-theoretical systems in the classic scientific mold, served not as demonstrations of the universal validity sought for them by Schenker and Schoenberg, but as standards of depth, resource, and relevance against which to assess the music-structural inherences of any hypothesized or presented instances of systematic invention. An even more radical relativism, in which standards of musical cognitivity are still further detached from universals—among others, from those extramusically invoked standards of "unified science" themselves—is suggested in the writings of some younger composers (cf. the essays by Randall and Boretz in the present volume).

Alongside, and often in explicit criticism of, such contextualism, a more strictly "classical" traditionalism has also been developing as a rationalized compositional position. This position, in its contemporary form, was initially inferrable from the early, and influential, critiques by Roger Sessions of the writings of Schenker, Schoenberg, and Hindemith. Its individuating characteristic is the conviction that the continuity of compositional tradition depends crucially on the retention of traditional musical appearances in the surfaces of texture, succession, contour, and sonority, and that the continuity of theoretical tradition requires as well the conservation of traditional models and terms. The fuller articulation and ramification of the consequences of such beliefs for composition, performance, analysis, and pedagogy have been undertaken by some of Sessions's younger colleagues, including Arthur Berger, Edward T. Cone, and Peter Westergaard, among those who have contributed extensively to the prose literature (and to the present volume).

There are, moreover, other uniquely twentieth-century modes of theorizing about music, not necessarily concerned with the predominantly "inward" issues that occupy all the multiple facets of what may be considered the "Brahms-Schenker-Schoenberg" tradition. The most spectacular of these modes, undoubtedly, is a "radical historicism" whose origin may be in Wagner's polemical prose (rather than in his musical practice). Such theory tends to view "tradition" as an ideological position, as a set of merely conventional constraints reflecting an exterior *Zeitgeist*. Musical "progress," then, depends not on renewal and reconstruction but on the wholesale replacement of these conventions by alternative constraints equally, but more "relevantly," ideological in their supposed conformity to a contemporary complex of metaphysical, socio-cultural, political, or psychological dynamics. The scope of this tradition is considerable: its fundamental premises are shared by the speculations and proposals regarding inner musical resources and outer musical "functions" emanating from such manifestly divergent composers as Busoni, Varèse, the Futurists, the Dadaists, Ives, Seeger, Cowell, Partch, and, more recently, the ideologues of "total serialism," "indeterminacy," "microtonalism," and the various "temperaments" (cf., in the present volume, the essays by Boulez and Stockhausen). Although much of the literature associated with this mode of theorizing is polemical rather than rationalized, which seems a natural effect of its deterministic, populistic, and speculative biases, it is in fact defensibly "theoretical" in the sense being employed here, for the reflection of its explicit compositional concerns in correlative characteristics of musical surface and structure is undeniable.

Neither these remarks, nor the collection of essays that follows, reflect any effort to survey exhaustively the "tendencies" or the significant instances of this remarkable theoretical output. The principal point we hope to make, beyond the intrinsic intellectual and musical significance of the essays contained herein, is that the vitality and diversity of contemporary music theory is comparable to, and—more pertinently—closely aligned with, that of composition itself. And while much of this theory has revealed, retrospectively as it were, the extent to which our experience of traditional music itself would have been impoverished in the absence of an adequate theoretical-conceptual framework, it has even more crucially revealed how our experience of and within contemporary music would, in such an absence, have been virtually inconceivable.

B.A.B.
E.T.C.

Princeton, N.J., December 1971

CONTENTS

Metatheory and Methodology

Compositional Theory

METATHEORY AND METHODOLOGY

PAST AND PRESENT CONCEPTS OF
THE NATURE AND LIMITS OF MUSIC

MILTON BABBITT

INASMUCH AS the term *concept* at present is taken to designate "properties, relations and similar entities . . . expressed in language by a designator of nonsentential form"[1] and necessarily to involve "an analysis of the nature of a referent,"[2] the term itself can serve most appropriately as the point of entry for a discussion in which I shall be concerned chiefly with contemporary aspects of the question at issue. For the essential elements of the above characterizations, involving the correlations of the syntactic and semantic domains, the notion of analysis, and—perhaps most significantly—the requirements of linguistic formulation and the differentation among predicate types, beyond strongly suggesting that the proper object of our assigned investigation may be—in the light of these criteria—a vacuous class, and strongly reminding us of the systematic obligations attending our own necessarily verbal presentation and discussion of this presumed subject, provide the important reminder that there is but one kind of language, one kind of method for the verbal formulation of "concepts" and the verbal analysis of such formulations: "scientific" language and "scientific" method. Without even engaging oneself in disposing of that easily disposable, if persistent, dichotomy of "arts" and "sciences" (or, relatedly, "humanities" and "sciences") —that historical remnant of a colloquial distinction[3]—it only need be insisted here that our concern is not whether music has been, is, can be, will be, or should be a "science," whatever that may be assumed to mean, but simply that statements about music must conform to those verbal and methodological requirements which attend the possibility of meaningful discourse in any domain. Although there remain unsolved problems associated with the determination of these conditions for complex and sophisticated cases, no problems accompany the identification of the grossly "meaningless"; it is neither surprising nor singular that, casually and non-controversially, a hypothetical, but cautiously unexaggerated

---

[1] Rudolf Carnap, *Meaning and Necessity* (Chicago, 1956), p. 21.
[2] W. H. Werkmeister, *The Basis and Structure of Knowledge* (New York, 1948), p. 52.
[3] See, for instance, H. Margenau, *The Nature of Physical Reality* (New York, 1950), pp. 17–18.

instance of "musical criticism" is cited on the first page of an elementary discussion of language[4] as "sheer nonsense" when "interpreted 'literally.'" The content of this specific example is of no consequence, except to the extent that it shares with the majority of past and—admittedly—present "statements" about music the property of being at best an incorrigible statement of attitude grammatically disguised as a simple attributive assertion. If it is taken at its grammatical face value, then it creates inevitably a domain of discourse in which negation does not produce contradiction, and in which a pair of such assertions entails, in turn, any statement and its negation. If it is translated into a logically tenable form with a two-place (relational) predicate, then it must satisfy criteria of intersubjectivity, which involve a definitional, reductional prodecure which few, if any, such statements about music have attempted to satisfy.

Present concepts of the limits and scope of music must proceed, then, from an initial concern with the limits and scope of statements about music. Proceeding from this preliminary stage by way of Hempel's statement that "concept formation and theory formation in science are so closely interrelated as to constitute virtually two different aspects of the same procedure,"[5] one arrives at that area, of "theory," which is regarded normally as a legitimate and traditional if ill-defined region of musical inquiry, the one, indeed, most likely to contain statements as to the scope and, complementarily, the limits of musical structure. Progressing from the concept to the law (synthetic generality) we arrive at the deductively interrelated system of laws that is a theory, statable as a connected set of axioms, definitions, and theorems, the proofs of which are derived by means of an appropriate logic. A musical theory reduces, or should reduce, to such a formal theory when uninterpreted predicates and operations are substituted for the terms and operations designating musical observables. That no musical theory yet has been presented in such a formalized manner is not in itself particularly consequential, but the fact that when so formulated, when the imperatives and prescriptives are converted generously to propositional form, musical "theories" (such as, for example, that of Rameau's *Génération harmonique,* which insists upon its "empirical" nature and its "propositional" presentation) emerge as, fundamentally, a collection of usually unsatisfactorily formulated definitions, unconnected protocol sentences containing these defined terms, and superfluous insular constructs; thus, the explanatory, postdictive scope of such "theories" is essentially non-existent. Since a satisfactory

[4]R. B. Kershner & L. R. Wilcox, *The Anatomy of Mathematics* (New York, 1950), p. 7.
[5]C. G. Hempel, *Fundamentals of Concept Formation in Empirical Science* (Chicago, 1952), pp. 1–2.

theory is a satisfactory explanation[6] of aspects of the empirical domain with which the theory is concerned, the contemporary dissatisfaction with the great body of pre-twentieth-century "theory" (and much twentieth-century "theory") is a fundamental one, stemming from the basic inadequacies of this theory in 1. stating its empirical domain and 2. choosing its primitives. More complex methodological questions aside, the first inadequacy makes it impossible to confirm the laws of the theory, since their range of applicability is not indicated; the theory presents the scope (and limits) of what music? The very expression "analytical theory" is current at present merely to identify theory which defines its region of inquiry.

The second inadequacy reflects what has long been an occupational malady of theorists of music: the futile concern with "ultimacy," arising apparently from the belief that to reveal that a theory has its origin in "unprovable" protocol statements is to admit its "arbitrariness"; so, "justificatory" "proof" is sought, necessarily, outside of the frame of the formal system. Thus, Mersenne—pursuing the perennial "why" of the correspondence between the interval content of the major triad and the first six divisions of the vibrating string—supplies a characteristic "justification" for the "use" of but six by citing the numerical indentification with the then known number of planets. Beyond the intimations of the cosmic scope and affinities of music, there is the implication that certain classes of objects hierarchically "justify" others, and the pressure of the still persistent numerological fallacy (the assumption that two different exemplifications of the same number class therefore possess other properties in common). The unclear theoretical status of this admittedly tentative suggestion in Mersenne's theory still leads one to conjecture as to whether, in all seriousness, the discovery of a seventh planet invalidated the theory or the music founded upon the assumption of the "incorrect" number. But, more importantly, the same concerns reappear with those later theorists who attempted and attempt to invoke "the" overtone series as a primitive. The question here is not the fact of overtone structure as the spectral determinant of timbre, but its theoretical status in any theory concerned with explaning the structure of the triadic-tonal system; for even with regard to merely this system, it is necessary to adjoin independent assumptions of octave equivalence, of numerical significance (Mersenne's six or Schenker's five), of the identification of timbrally significant or insignificant partials with explicitly presented fundamentals (leading to the necessary generation of a simultaneity of infinitely many components whose status must be equated with that of the major triad). Add to these the familiar difficulties in the overtone explanation of the independent use of the minor triad, of "consonance" and "dissonance" in triadic practice (not, of course, when the overtone

[6]See, for example, C. G. Hempel and P. Oppenheim, *The Logic of Explanation,* in *Philosophy of Science,* XV (1948), pp. 135–73.

series is used to "define" "consonance" and "dissonance"), and it becomes evident that the overtone series has not functioned and, most probably, cannot function as the object of a significant protocol statement in the formulation of triadic theory. For our immediate purposes, it further indicates that the limits of coherent musical structure are in no sense to be inferred from the properties of an overtone series.

Those theorists who have disdained the seductions of "the chord of nature" and the associated comforts of the—therefore—"natural" system, and started from the concept of similarity classes of simultaneities (founded often, in turn, on a number of unstated further similarity assumptions), although unknowingly posing for themselves an exceedingly difficult methodological task in taking similarity as a primitive,[7] failed also because this concept was not applied beyond this zero-order (or, occasionally, first-order) level of connection. Since no theory of an extended explanatory nature arose from these assumptions, it was impossible to determine the relative fruitfulness of, for example, Mattheson's three classes as opposed to Reicha's thirteen classes, but the notion of similarity is a valuable one to which I shall return.

Today, often in the form of similitude assumptions, it has proven valuable and reasonable to take as primitive, statements that may be described as embodying perceptual "incontrovertibles," and which possess the highest possible degree of theoretical fruitfulness, and thus—implicitly, at least—one limiting boundary is suggested.

Recently, and I need not cite specific instances since a segment of the recent literature abounds with them, the scope of music apparently has been extended to include the interpretation in musical notation of arithmetical expressions. On this scale, at least, this is a new role for mathematics in the history of Western music: as a compositional prescriptive. Although the word "mathematics" has figured prominently in this history as both epithet and encomium, beyond the incidental notational use of number symbols, mathematics and music have been conjoined on the non-compositional level: in a Pythagorean, numerological, Quadrivium-oriented association, or quasi-analytically—as in such a familiar, characteristic case as the *Esthétique musicale* (1876) of Wronski and Durutte. The compositional invocations of "mathematics" which are current pose so many fundamental questions that only one of them will be even stated at this time. This centers around the apparent relationship of a mathematical expression and its musical representation inherent in these procedures, which parallels the relation between a formal theory and an interpretation of it. What, then, determines the choice of the mathematical expression? Usually, a formal theory is chosen or constructed in the light of an intended interpretation; what

[7]N. Goodman, *The Structure of Appearance* (Cambridge, Mass., 1951), p. 220.

properties are possessed by an arithmetical progression, for example, which make it appropriate for interpretation as a metrical or ordinal pitch, or durational, or dynamic, or timbral, or density determinant? What data in the field of musical perception determine the rules of correlation? And what of the possible overpredictability and the assumed separability of the components of even the atomic musical event? All of these questions and others must be probed thoroughly before a decision can be even tentatively reached as to the extent to which such procedures enlarge the domain of music.

The introduction of "random" or "chance" methods into musical composition depends in general upon an informal application of these slippery terms to the method of compositional production rather than to the characteristics of the musical object itself; a proper, or perhaps more correctly, improper choice of rules of correlation between a non-randomly generated succession of numbers and a domain of musical entities may create a more nearly "random" result with regard to a given musical characteristic[8] than will the transfer of a greater area of choice to a performer or a group of performers, who may well be more highly constrained "machines" than is even the composer.

However, the preceding two paragraphs must not be construed as providing support for that often-stated imperative which would impose stringent limitations upon the scope of possible musical construction: "Musical theory must not precede musical practice." Here the term "theory" is used, of course, not in the sense of generalized characterization and explanation, but of a formal theory as hypothesis; in the musical case, primarily the rules of formation and transformation applied to the musical components are formally hypothesized. Even beyond its invocation of the intentional error (for, unless a composer chooses to reveal, and truthfully, whether such a "theory" has or has not preceded his compositional practice, how can it be decided whether his music shall or shall not be disqualified for this possible reversal of "natural" processes), this imperative misinterprets the principle that the logically true is not necessarily empirically true, by overlooking the qualification "necessarily" and the fact that the empirically true *is* necessarily logically true. Informally, in addition to the crucial point of susceptibility to a perceptually feasible interpretation, the potential fruitfulness of such a theory is obviously contingent upon its degree of avoidance of "triviality" both formally and interpretively, in the sense of containing musical interpretations of the logical entailments of the formal system beyond the most immediate consequences of the assumptions, those new cognitions of necessary musical relationships inherent in the logical truths of the formal system.

From the present point of chronological removal, the twelve-tone system,

[8] See, for example, W. R. Ashby, *An Introduction to Cybernetics* (London, 1956), p. 259.

by virtue of its influence and its widespread and varied application, would seem to have passed the "pragmatic test." I attribute this in large part to the simple and demonstrably realistic perceptual assumptions of the system: the capacity to perceive pitch-class identity and non-identity, and interval-class identity and non-identity (only in the memorative domain may it be said to make demands which are new in degree), and to the finite group model which completely characterizes this musical system. That this model was arrived at analytically rather than, presumably, postulated synthetically must be regarded, as indicated previously, as irrelevant. From the conjunction of these two sets of characteristics (the perceptual and the formal) there results a large number of compositional consequences directly derivable from the theorems of finite group theory; for instance, the nonobvious relation between complementary transpositions of the set and the attendant number of order-inversions,[9] a significant general measure of rearrangement in a system in which a defined linear ordering functions as the primary norm.

The recognition of the permutational character of twelve-tone operations suggests their application to orderable non-pitch elements such as duration, dynamics, etc. This extension of autonomous and analogous structuring to non-pitch elements has, to the present writer's knowledge, no precedent in musical history with the possible exception of M. Hauptmann's "dialectical" characterization of rhythm, paralleling his characterization of harmony. The twelve-tone application by analogy demands, for its feasibility, rules of correlation which assure the empirical interpretability of those invariants which inhere under the pitch application of the operations employed; such rules have been defined.[10]

If one of the twelve-tone system's historical roles has been that of demonstrating the adaptability of a structurally new musical system, it has also "suggested" generalizations which, in their abandoning of some of the most determinative properties of the system, return musical composition in many respects to its "contextual" phase, where the closure—and thus, the permutational—properties of the twelve-tone system are not present. Here the basic hierarchical scope of the system is contained essentially in the simple theorem that: given a collection of pitches (pitch classes), the multiplicity of occurrence of any interval (an interval being equated with its complement, since ordering is not involved) determines the number of common pitches between the original collection and the transposition by the interval. This theorem, together with its extension to inversionally related collections, reveals the purely contextual nature of the hierarchical relationships of the selected collection. The inferrable primitives of "con-

[9]M. Babbitt, *Twelve-Tone Invariants as Compositional Determinants*, in *The Musical Quarterly*, XLVI (1960), pp. 246–59.

[10]M. Babbitt, *Some Aspects of Twelve-Tone Composition*, in *The Score*, XII (1955), pp. 53–61.

textual" music suggest the analytical primitives applicable to other musical works, without the *a priori* assumption that such works are instances of a given musical system. These primitives are time—independent binary similarity relations (identity and non-identity) among pitch classes, interval classes, and contours.

Present-day electronic media for the total production of sound, providing precise measurability and specifiability of frequency, intensity, spectrum, envelope, duration, and mode of succession, remove completely those musical limits imposed by the physical limitations of the performer and conventional musical instruments. The region of limitation is now located entirely in the human perceptual and conceptual apparatus, and the discovery and formulation of these constraints fall in the province of the psycho-acoustician. Beyond the atomic and easily determinable physical limits of hearing and aural differentiation, the establishing of "molecular" limits on the memorative capacity, the discrimination between aural quantizations imposed by physiological conditions and those imposed merely by the conditioning of prior perceptions, and the formulation of laws in the auditory domain accurately reflecting the complex interrelationships of the incompatible variables representing the components of the acoustic domain, will be necessary before a statement of even the most general limits of musical perception will be available.

The limits of music reside ultimately in the perceptual capacities of the human receptor, just as the scope of physical science is delimited by the perceptual and conceptual capacities of the human observer. But the recent history of both disciplines, by bearing witness to explosive and decisive extensions of these capacities, constrains us from venturing only into the realm of prediction.

THE STRUCTURE AND FUNCTION
OF MUSICAL THEORY

MILTON BABBITT

I LIKE to believe that a not insignificant consequence of the
proper understanding of a proper theory of music is to assure that a composer who asserts something such as: "I don't
compose by system, but by ear" thereby convicts himself of, at
least, an *argumentum ad populum* by equating ignorance with
freedom, that is, by equating ignorance of the constraints under
which he creates with freedom from constraints. In other words,
musical theory must provide not only the examination of the
structure of musical systems—familiar and unfamiliar by informal conditioning—as a connected theory derived from statements of significant properties of individual works, a formulation of the constraints of such systems in a "creative" form (in
that, as a language grammar does for sentences, it can supply the
basis for unprecedented musical utterances which, nevertheless,
are coherent and comprehensible), but—necessarily prior to
these—an adequately reconstructed terminology to make possible and to provide a model for determinate and testable
statements about musical compositions.

Whether one prefers to declare that a theory must be,
should be, or is a mere symbolic description, or a structured
formulation of statements of relations among observed phenomena, or a collection of rules for the representation of observables,
or an interpreted model of a formal system, or still none of these,
presumably it can be agreed that questions of musical theory
construction attend and include all matters of the form, the
manner of formulation, and the signification of statements about
individual musical compositions, and the subsumption of such
statements into a higher level theory, constructed purely logically from the empirical acts of examination of the individual

compositions. Surely there is no more crucial and critical issue in music today, no more central determinant of the climate of music today, than that of the admittedly complex and intricate problems associated with assertions about music. Perhaps there have been eras in the musical past when discourse about music was not a primary factor in determining what was performed, published, therefore disseminated, and—therefore—composed, and when the criteria of verbal rigor could not be inferred from either discourse in other areas or from the study of the methodology of discourse, when—indeed—the compositional situation was such as not to require that knowing composers make fundamental choices and decisions that require eventual verbal formulation, clarification, and—to an important extent—resolution. But the problems of our time certainly cannot be expressed in or discussed in what has passed generally for the language of musical discourse, that language in which the incorrigible personal statement is granted the grammatical form of an attributative proposition, and in which negation—therefore—does not produce a contradiction; that wonderful language which permits anything to be said and virtually nothing to be communicated. The composer who insists that he is concerned only with writing music and not with talking about it may once have been, may still be, a commendable—even enviable—figure, but once he presumes to speak or take pen in hand in order to describe, inform, evaluate, reward, or teach, he cannot presume to claim exemption—on medical or vocational grounds—from the requirements of cognitive communication. Nor can the performer, that traditionally most pristine of non-intellectuals, be permitted his easy evaluatives which determine in turn what music is permitted to be heard, on the plea of ignorance of the requirements of responsible normative discourse. Nor can the historian, in the sanctified name of scholarship, be allowed such verbal act as the following: "There can be no question that in many of Mendelssohn's works there is missing that real depth that opens wide perspectives, the mysticism of the unutterable." Can one conceive of a possible interpretation and application of those mild Humean criteria so liberal as to save a book containing a sentence such as this from the flames? And what of the more apparently factual scholarly statement that the c-flat of measure 53 of the second movement of the Mozart G Minor

Symphony (K. 550) is "an unexpected c-flat"; overlooking for
the moment the dubious status of such expressive descriptives,
what can the term "unexpected" be inferred to designate when
applied to the succession b-flat, c-flat, which had been stated in
the movement in question at the outset in measure 2? If nothing
else, such verbal phenomena would appear to be instances of the
situation characterized by Quine's conservative observation:
"The less a science is advanced, the more its terminology tends
to rest on an uncritical assumption of mutual understanding."
In attempting to preserve or defend this self-indulgent, unwar-
ranted state, it may be asserted that music is not a science. This,
naturally, is not the point, not even a point. Parenthetically, it
may be said that neither the proclamations of those who work in
what are traditionally termed sciences as to the essentially
artistic nature of their activity, or the proclamations of those far
fewer who work in what are traditionally termed the arts and
humanities as to the appropriateness or necessity of scientific
method in their activity, need be cited to discredit an already
indefensible dichotomy or multichotomy, the perpetuation of a
linguistic fortuity as if it embodied a fundamental and persistent
truth. Whatever such categorizations, if any, of fields of intellectual creation are justified or fruitful must await an investigation
which is not even yet begun, but even were it now completed,
there would remain the still more germane question for us as to
whether the term "musical composition" is accurately applicable to the many apparently diverse activities to which it is now
applied, or—perhaps more importantly—to all of those or any
of those activities and to any activity of, say, a half century ago.
It is at least worth asking whether so generic a description has
survived that revolution in musical thought which has been and
is still in progress.

    Certainly it is tantalizing to conjecture why, far more
violent than the responses to the music of this period, responses
which have ranged usually from patronizing tolerance to
amused tolerance, have been those to the verbal activities. But,
since the subject here is musical theory rather than clinical
psychology, only one such conjecture will be pursued and this
only to return to a temporarily abandoned line of discussion.
The issue of "science" does not intrude itself directly upon the
occasion of the performance of a musical work, at least a non-

electronically produced work, since—as has been said—there is at least a question as to whether the question as to whether musical composition is to be regarded as a science or not is indeed really a question; but there is no doubt that the question as to whether musical discourse or—more precisely—the theory of music should be subject to the methodological criteria of scientific method and the attendant scientific language is a question, except that the question is really not the normative one of whether it "should be" or "must be," but the factual one that it is, not because of the nature of musical theory, but because of the nature and scope of scientific method and language, whose domain of application is such that if it is not extensible to musical theory, then musical theory is not a theory in any sense in which the term ever has been employed. This should sound neither contentious nor portentous, rather it should be obvious to the point of virtual tautology. Assuredly, I am not stating that all of the problems of musical theory can be resolved automatically and easily by our merely embracing the latest formulations of the philosophy of science, for neither music nor the philosophy of science is that simple and static; and the problems of musical theory are, in many ways, so complex as to carry one unavoidably and quickly to still highly contro- versial, still unresolved questions in philosophy and related fields. For instance, functionality in the traditional tonal sense probably can be formulated only as a disposition concept, which may account for the unsatisfactory character of less formal attempts to "define" tonality; musical analysis involves many of the contested problems of explanation, postdiction, and predic- tion, which are regarded by many as the most crucial compo- nents in the construction of a possible musical theory; concept formation in music involves those problems of intersubjectivity and of verbal utterances as empirical data with which psycho- logical theory has been grappling, and for the formulation of which it has been obliged to employ advanced and novel notions and techniques. One need but recall the forbidding appearance, to musicians, of Suppes' partial formalization of the notion of "finite equal difference structure," of which the musical concept of interval is a familiar instance.

But if there are obstacles to the construction of a satisfac- tory musical theory in the form of such systematic difficulties, there are obstacles also in the form of the task being too easy, for if a composition be regarded—as manifestly it can be, completely and accurately—as events occurring at time-points, then there are an infinity of analytical expressions which will generate any given composition, and one moral of this casual, but undeniable, realization is that the relation between a formal theory and its empirical interpretation is not merely that of the relation of validity to truth (in some sense of verifiability), or of the analytic to the synthetic (be this or not an untenable dualism or a dogma of empiricism), but of the whole area of the criteria of useful, useable, relevant, or significant characterizations. Another facet of the same question, a facet which had made possible a great many of the analyses by which we find ourselves confronted at the moment and which perhaps underlies our dissatisfaction with a great deal of traditional theory, is that there are an infinite number of true (or false) statements that can be made about any composition, and—therefore—any collection of compositions. Putting aside formalities, only because the result of not putting them aside is known and herein represented, any theory is a choice from an infinite number of possible theories, and the choice is determined by what can be termed a criterion of significance in the selection, first, of primitives, whatever the linguistic form of these primitives. Whether this significance be expressed in terms of predictive power, explanatory scope, simplicity, or some other criterion, the decision is not easily made or ever surely made, which is only to state that an empirical theory is subject always to revision and reformulation. The question of significance arises as soon as one seeks to formulate concepts for the analysis of an individual piece founded on the notion of, say, pitch. One cannot be at all certain that any concept is necessarily a fruitless or an absurd one; one simply does not know if it is or not until one has tested the results of the application of this concept for correlation with other independent concepts, for invariance under non-vacuous conditions. The musical naive realist impatiently may dismiss concepts involving the conjunction of primitive and logical terms as normally fruitless from his point of view of aural immediacy, so I shall begin with a concept to which he could not possibly take exception, that of "interval" in the usual sense of measure of distance between two pitches or pitch-classes. We can explicate it as the result of applying to two pitch terms (represented in conventional numerical pitch-class notation) the operation of subtraction mod. 12, or by constructing its geometrical isomorph and regarding it as directed distance. Either of these representations should satisfy the realist, for they both entail that characteristic of transposition which must be regarded as primary: the invariance of the interval value under transposition. In terms of its geometrical analog, this is a statement that translation is distance preserving. Still, however immediate the experiential fact of interval may be, it is here not only a concept, but a theoretical construct, a two-place predicate, and if on no other basis than the role it has played in all component statements about musical composition, it is probably generally acceptable as a significant concept. In order to compare it with another, less familiar concept, I shall examine a statement including the concept "interval," that concerning the hierarchical implications of the intervallic characterization of a pitch-class collection. Given n pitches or pitch-classes, the $\frac{n^2 - n}{2}$ non-zero intervals or interval classes they define can be collected in equal interval categories, and the multiplicity of occurrence number associated with each of the categories determines the number of pitches in common between the original collection and the collection transposed by the interval associated with a particular category. That is, in the equivalent geometrical language, a fairly obvious statement of the relation between the distances defined by a point collection, and the distance defined by these points and their images under a given translation. An immediate and simple consequence of this property is the "circle of fifths," a symmetric (because of the equivalence of complements in an unordered collection) hierarchization of major-minor scale content in terms of pitch-class intersection. This property is inferrable therefore from the interval structure of the scale, since each interval occurs with unique multiplicity. It is easily shown that the major scale is a maximal structure possessing this property in the usual equal-tempered division of the octave. The compositional consequences in the tonal system of this property are so fundamental as to require no statement of specifics, but one of the importantly therapeutic values of such a generalized formulation is that of, at least, restraining that pedagogical liberalism which would urge students to "experiment" with other, less familiar, more exotic scales, on the basis that they are just as fruitful as our traditional scales. But in general they are not from a structural point of view, since they do not admit comparable properties of hierarchization.

It may be less obvious that the same concept is equally consequential in twelve-tone composition, since all sets have the same total interval concent. But the utilization of subsets as combinational units within the sets—for example, the hexachord in Schoenberg's and Stravinsky's twelve-tone music—leads to the contextually hierarchical function of this property. Assuming that this is either familiar or can become so by the consulting of the available literature, I shall draw musical examples of this property in those works of Stravinsky which are most efficiently described as serial, but not twelve-tone, where the serial unit is—therefore—in general uniquely characterized, to within transposition—and possibly inversion—by its intervallic content. Perhaps the most general and inclusive basis of relationship in such music resides in pitch-class identification between and among the compositionally defined serial units, since they are not embedded in larger serial units as in twelve-tone works, or associated with concepts of functionality as in tonal music. The pitch collection from which the serial unit of the Gigue of the *Septet* is formed is so constructed that maximum identification of pitch content is achieved by transposition by an interval of 5 or 7; this reflects the compositional design of the movement, with the serial unit employed as a thematic entity in what may be described as a succession of fugal entries. In *In Memoriam* the transpositions effecting maximum intersection are 1 and 11, reflecting the fact that the succession of serial units is in the vocal part, as a linear succession. The concept of interval, and at least this one of its applications would appear to belong to a theory that subsumes traditional tone, twelve-tone, and non-twelve-tone serial theory, but what of another concept closely similar in arithmetical form, represented by, instead of the difference of pitch-class numbers, the sum of pitch-class numbers: $a + b$ (mod. 12), where a and b are pitch class numbers. This may appear to smack of that familiar pedagogical procedure of demonstrating that the analytically valid is not necessarily empirically true or even meaningful. But we are not

dealing here with analytical validity, only with a formal operation which can be performed with great ease, but appears to lack
any interpretation and application in the musical domain. What
could be meant or designated by a sum of pitch numbers? The
difference between such numbers defines what has always been
termed an interval, but the sum represents no traditional
property, and there is no term, no abbreviative definition, for it.
Surely the sum, like the difference of pitch numbers is not a
pitch number, and there appears to be no observation concept
associated with this arithmetical expression. But the $\frac{n^2 + n}{2}$ sums
of set numbers of a collection characterizes such a collection in
terms of its *inverted* forms in precisely the same way as the
differences characterize a collection in terms of its transposition.
Why this is so becomes clear when it is recalled that the sums
defined by order corresponding elements of inversionally related
collections are equal, and that inversion is definable in terms of
complementation. The applicability of this concept to twelve-
tone set construction is generally understood, but—again—I
choose examples from non-twelve-tone serial works of Stravinsky. The Ricercar II of the *Cantata* employs a six note
collection which permits maximum intersection of pitch content
by inversion at the interval 6, which is employed by Stravinsky
in the initial statement of forms of the collection, while the
collection of the *In Memoriam* is inversionally symmetrical,
thus permitting total pitch intersection at the interval of 4.

There is, then, this close analogy between interval and
whatever we wish to call the concept represented by the sum of
pitch-class numbers. And yet, in some musically important
sense, these two concepts would seem to require differentiation
at some level. Surely interval is an "observation concept"; does
the other concept require categorization as "theoretical," in the
usual sense of the term, since it is not apparently translatable
into perceptual terms? Until, if ever, an ultimate disposition is
made of this terminological differentiation, this latter concept,
for all of its hierarchical implications, will be formulable only in
theoretical terms.

The whole question of the status of the notion of the
overtone "system" (surely not a system, but a phenomenon), the
checkered history of this status for two centuries, and that of its

predecessor—the divisions of the string, must occupy a central place in any discussion of musical theory. Naturally, since I am not concerned with normative allegations, I cannot be concerned here with the invocation of the overtone series as a "natural" phenomenon, and that application of equivocation which then would label as "unnatural" (in the sense, it would appear, of morally perverse) music which is not "founded" on it. Now, what music, in what sense, ever has been founded on it? Experimentally, the intensity of harmonic, and non-harmonic, partials in a spectrum associated with a given sound source would appear to be an important determinant, but by no means the sole determinant, of what is ordinarily termed tone color. But what is, what can be, the status of the overtone series in a theory of the triadic, tonal pitch system? For it to furnish the criterion of the structure of the major triad it is necessary—first —to append the independent assumption of octave equivalents, for to assert that the overtone series itself supplies this criterion because the octave is the first interval above the fundamental, or the interval determined by frequencies whose ratio is a power of 2, or etc., obviously is to adjoin independent assumptions of the equivalence priority of the first interval, or of the intervals determined by powers of 2, etc. Then, the independent assumption of the significance of the number 6, or 5 as that which determines the highest partial to be included as a specifically realized pitch, has required "justifications" which have ranged numerologically from the number of planets to the number of fingers on the human hand. And again, the principle which permits one to proceed from the assertion that "associated with a given frequency produced at a given intensity by a given instrument are other frequencies" to the assertion that "such other frequencies always may be explicitly presented on any instrument simultaneously with a given frequency" must be combined with another rule which prohibits this process from continuing, this principle then being further applied to the frequencies so explicitly presented. And still, the structure of the harmonic series does not supply a basis for the status of the minor triad in tonal music. It either dissonantly "contradicts" it or requires the invocation of still further assumptions of intervallic permutability or numerology. And yet, the succession of intervals in the overtone series does not correspond to the categorizations of "consonant" and "dissonant," even in relative terms, whether one asserts the independent assumption of adjacency or of relation to the first partial. Under the former criterion, the fourth would be termed more consonant than the major third; under the latter, the minor seventh and major second would be termed more consonant than the major or minor sixth, or the minor third. The concepts of consonance and dissonance have induced centuries of a comedy of methodological errors, from the rationalistic stage, through the so-called "experimental stage," without its having been clear or inquired at any time as to the object of the rationalizing or the experimentation. Clearly, this is because consonance and dissonance are context dependent tonal concepts; it is impossible to assert that an interval is consonant aurally, since it always can be notated as dissonant, and this notation reflects a possible context.

One can continue with the overtone follies, with what having the overtone series commits one to eat, but perhaps it is necessary only to point out that a theory compounded from statements descriptive of a body of representative works of the 18th and 19th centuries undoubtedly would include the concepts of the major and minor triad as definitional, and as instancing the property of consonance, which, with the property of non-consonance, describe the two basic states of a composition which determine the modes of succession to the next state, octave equivalence classes (identical, in this body of literature, with function equivalence classes) , the major scale (as completing independently the concept of consonance and providing the criterion for proceeding from state to state) . These concepts hardly suggest the postulation of an overtone series as a master concept entailing them.

But from this body of works one probably would formulate, for example, a law regarding the "prohibition" of motion in parallel fifths (not, however, of unisons or octaves, since these scores are packed with such parallelisms; it does not do to say that these are the "same notes," but rather it is this parallelism which suggests the formulation of function class equivalence, and thus octave equivalence, and thus this degree of "sameness") . The formulation surely would not take the form of: "Parallel intervals of the unison, octave, and perfect fifth have been systematically avoided by composers of the 18th and 19th centuries, whenever it has been their intention to write a basic four-part texture," for all that this is the most popular of formulations. Nor would it or could it be explained by some statement such as: "Fifths are too closely related." What does it mean to be too closely related? To be fifths. It is difficult to see how the law can be derived from other, non-tautologically related, more general laws of "tonality," nor should it, if—for example—Debussy's music is to qualify as tonal.

Empirical theory construction to the end of either discovering a known formal theory of which the empirical theory is an interpretation or constructing such a formal theory, serves not only the goal of clarity, precise communication, and efficiency, but of providing knowledge of general and necessary characteristics of the empirical system through the structure of the formal model. It is well known that it can be shown easily that the rules of formation and transformation of the twelve-tone system are interpretable as defining a group element (a permutation of order or set numbers) and a group operation (composition of permutations). There then follows from a deduced property of inverse permutations the following property of twelve-tone sets, a now familiar property whose discovery in all its generality scarcely could have been accomplished—perhaps not even suspected—without such a formal model. The theorem states, in terms of the twelve-tone system, that two transposed set forms which are complementary with regard to a third have the same number of order inversions (and, therefore, permanences) with relation to this third set. This property is explanatory in explaining the compositional use of such related sets, and—by extension in suggesting more general applications of complementation, as in the case of the operation of inversion. This property also functions as predictive in determining possible attributes of future works concerned with exposing this property. So too, for example, the even less intuitively manifest property of the systems of common representatives shared by any two similar partitions of the same collection of, say, pitch-classes reveals what is, in some reasonable sense, a new facet of the possible relation between analytical explanation and creative prediction.

The Schenkerian theory of tonal music, in its structure of

nested transformations so strikingly similar to transformational grammars in linguistics, provides rules of transformation in proceeding synthetically through the levels of a composition from "kernel" to the foreground of the composition, or analytically, in reverse. Since many of the transformational rules are level invariant, parallelism of transformation often plays an explanatory role in the context of the theory (and, apparently, an implicitly normative one in Schenker's own writing). The formulation of this theory in relatively uninterpreted terms (as Kassler is doing), as a partially formalized theory, serves to reveal not only its essential structure but its points of incompleteness, vagueness, and redundancy, and the means for correcting such flaws. The laying bare of the structure of an interpreted theory in a manner such as this is an efficient and powerful way also of detecting false analogies, be they between systems (for example, the "tonal" and the "twelve-tone"), between compositional dimensions (for example, that of pitch and that of timbre), or between compositions (with a composition regarded as an interpreted theory).

Such concerns with and, hopefully, contributions to verbal and methodological responsibility (far more than whether theoretical instruction begins with "tonal," "atonal," or "all" music, with species counterpoint or Webern counterpoint) must be central to the instruction of the student of music theory in the liberal arts college, only a rare one of whom will employ such theory creatively as a composer or professionally as a theorist, if he—as a student of contemporary philosophy and science—is not to dismiss the theory and—therefore, probably—the music as immature and irresponsible, or if he—as a student of predominantly literary orientation—is not to transplant mistakenly the prevalent verbiage of that domain to our, at least, more modest area of activity, and if he is to attain that rarest of all states: that of the concerned and thoughtful musical citizen.

NEW LINGUISTIC MODES AND
THE NEW THEORY

ARTHUR BERGER

I T   I S   N O T   S U R P R I S I N G   that a preoccupation with new terminology among composer-theorists should be encountered with skepticism in certain quarters and that such reaction should unfortunately
deflect attention from the substantive issues. What is, on the other hand,
very surprising indeed is the fact that an aggravation of the problem of
verbal expression should fail to be recognized as an inevitable by-
product of the emergence of PERSPECTIVES OF NEW MUSIC within the
ambience of today's heightened self-awareness and—why be apologetic
about it—persistent self-analysis. That a by-product of this order was
anticipated by the founding editors is apparent from the following
remarks in their statement of objectives in Vol. 1, No. 1 (p. 5):

> Another consequence of the absence of a journal like PERSPECTIVES
> OF NEW MUSIC is that the younger generation of American composers
> has been deprived of a focus for the orderly development of its think-
> ing as well as of a forum in which to evolve linguistic modes for com-
> munication. PERSPECTIVES OF NEW MUSIC will provide such a forum
> and encourage young composers to deal with their perplexing
> problems. . . .

Were the problems resolved, were adequate "linguistic modes" already
crystallized and neatly collated in a reference source within arm's
reach of the editors, these observations would have been superfluous.

A faithful account of current musical thought must necessarily reflect
the diverse ways in which some of us are searching, at times tentatively,
clumsily, or inscrutably, for a new theoretical approach motivated by a
profound reaction against the woolly, otiose attempts at explanation
and the inflexible definitions that have been allowed to achieve the
sanctity of divine law through the sheer inertia of almost everyone concerned with music. What seems to be taking place, in a domain to
which the designation "theory" or even "analytic theory" can only
be applied provisionally, is curiously reminiscent of the gestations that
not so long ago preceded the establishment of musicology as a legitimate
scholarly discipline in our universities. I have in mind not only the

skepticism (directed among other things toward the choice of so stern a label for any pursuit having to do with one of the arts), but also—and mainly—the tendency to equate rigorous method and clear, logical thinking with scientific research.

The recurrence of the old symptoms may be fortuitous. But it may also suggest either that there is a certain parallelism between the problems encountered at their formative stages by the new tendency and the old, or—a possibility that seems to me less likely and not quite consistent with the spirit of the current theoreticians—that a certain affinity maintains between the new theory and musicology, a family relationship, as it were, in which the former figures as an outgrowth of the latter. This second possibility has its attractions for those who would like to fill the slot provided for "music theory," "theory of music," "theory of music theory," "speculative theory" (call it what you will) in Guido Adler's original groundplan for musicology—not in the "historical" part, which has emerged in the course of years as the principal orientation of the field as a whole, but in the "systematic" part, where it makes curious bedfellows with ethnomusicology. Indeed, William Poland has gone so far as to infer that the gradual infiltration of the very concept "science" into musicological thought was in itself something in the nature of an adumbration of those preoccupations with music theory that are nowadays becoming more and more evident as a significant force.[1] Citing the allusion to "scientific methods" in Glen Haydon's *Introduction to Musicology,* Mr. Poland concludes that "considering it was made in 1941," it "approaches the prophetic. Haydon's use of the word science is congruent with current usage." I wonder if Mr. Poland is not overlooking the fact that the earliest attempts to translate *Musikwissenschaft* and *Musicologie* (for which our "musicology" usually did double duty) repeatedly raised the question of a choice of denotations for the suffix of each of them: viz. between "branch of learning" and "science." This must be why Mr. Haydon began his book with an effort to settle the matter, and that he made no claims to being the first to bring up the word "science" with reference to musicology is evident from a footnote (pp. 3f.) deploring the "incongruities" that had resulted from indiscriminately translating *Musikwissenschaft* sometimes as "musicology" and at other times as "musical science." While Mr. Haydon rejects the expression "musical science," he does decide in favor of characterizing musicology as a "science"—only, however, through a bit of legerdemain in which "science" as understood in ordinary language is eschewed for the highly generalized connotation of "research in any given field."

[1] "Theories of Music and Musical Behavior," *Journal of Music Theory,* Winter 1963, p. 164 (originally read at the Symposium on Music Theory at Ohio State University in 1962).

It is natural for those who regard the new theory as (actually or potentially) a branch of musicology to find fault with it for not conforming to specifications of the parent discipline, which is unfortunate, since there are reasons enough of more pertinence for finding fault—the tenderness of so youthful a venture inevitably exposing it to error, lapses of judgment, and a temptation to overreach itself. Moreover, the foregone conclusion that scientific method is endemic to the new theory imposes a needless bugbear between it and those—how shall I put it— who cherish music's sanctity as an "art," an "aesthetic" genus. Now it is perfectly true that mathematics and physical science are tools both in the practice and theory of electronic music; and the advantages of numerical calculations for elucidating and anticipating the results of serial organization have been repeatedly demonstrated. (Let us not forget, too, the tonal theorists with their Information Theory.) But it does not follow from all this that scientific method is the only one open to the new theory, or that the rationale behind electronic or serially organized music prevents it from being apprehended via some of the same perceptual channels through which we apprehend any music. Not all of us who are involved with the new theory or engage in detailed analysis follow Mr. Babbitt's directive that "there is but one kind of language, one kind of method for the verbal formulation of 'concepts' and the verbal analysis of such formulations: 'scientific' language and 'scientific' method."[2] System-construction reveals facets of music that cannot, or only with difficulty can, otherwise be revealed. But other analytic methods effectively cope with facets just as significant, and despite the claims or implications of the system-builders that theirs is the only valid way, I am convinced those methods—rigorous in their own terms—can perfectly well be encompassed by the new theory without coming into irreconcilable conflict with the system-builders.

It might be a good idea to make the establishment of mutual understanding among the different points of view within the territory of the new theory a first step in a larger campaign for peaceful coexistence with the interests exerting pressure at the periphery. Different interests need not impose themselves on one another if it is understood different purposes are being served. For example, there is a type of theory obviously germane to musicology,[3] embracing identification, description, and analysis of style in respect to period and/or conventional form. This is not the aim of the new theory, in which style description, if it

2 "Past and Present Concepts of the Nature and Limits of Music," above, pp. 3-9.

3 Mr. Haydon has been one of its eminent exponents and has also contributed to its definition. See, for example, "Music Theory and Music History," *Journal of Music Theory*, Winter 1963, pp. 249ff. (also read at Ohio State: see footnote 1).

occurs, is mainly incidental to determining how specific relations yield structurally significant points within a work or account for similitude and differentiation within a technique. Unique techniques may demand unique terminology, and in this there is nothing untenable or upsetting to a comprehensive evolutionary plan when the aim is not to classify techniques as to period-style or works as to conventional form, nor to relate one instance to the whole of music literature. Elsewhere I have demonstrated how the loose application of the term "tonality" leads to conceptual confusion; and it also, I might add, can lead to irrelevant associations damaging to proper apprehension of heard relations: e.g. where there is a tone center but no tonal functionality.[4] Neither is the term "atonality" suitable here, normally implying, as it does, absence of tone center (i.e. of "pitch class" of "priority"). The following statements are not only mutually contradictory, but both are at odds with the work to which they refer: 1) "the harmony of *Sacre* . . . emphasizes a definite tonality";[5] 2) "When Stravinsky used the language of atonality in his middle period, particularly in his *Sacre du printemps,* he seemed to take his place alongside Schoenberg as a pioneer of a new type of language."[6]

Here are instances where a work is misrepresented by being forced into available categories and where both errors might have been avoided by treating it *sui generis*. The musicologist may argue that the error is due not to the intention itself (i.e. of placing *Sacre* in perspective), but to the poor historical method employed in carrying it out. His preoccupations lead him quite understandably to keep on insisting that any discussion of a musical composition be attentive to historical context. But in that case neither, in a certain sense, can we ignore the physical source (acoustics), the listener's nervous reactions (neuropsychology) and bodily states (physiology), the reflection of social forces (sociology), etc.

None of us has the right to legislate a priori that this branch of knowledge or that dimension of phenomena must be taken into account by every theoretical speculation. If anything beyond the pure quest for knowledge conditions the speculation of composers, it is the incentive to satisfy such of their own needs as are not satisfied by the speculative endeavors of others. This, I realize, is ammunition for those who complain that composers (not only in their music but also as theorists)

---

[4] "Problems of Pitch Organization in Stravinsky," PERSPECTIVES OF NEW MUSIC, Fall–Winter 1963, pp. 11–42. An example of what I have in mind would be provided by someone listening to Stravinsky's *Serenade en La* with strong tonal bias that would introduce the extraneous association of F major to such a degree that he would crave a resolution in that key.

[5] Alexander Tansman, *Igor Stravinsky: the Man and His Music,* New York: G. P. Putnam, 1949, p. 187.

[6] Ernst Krenek, *Music Here and Now,* New York: W. W. Norton, 1939, p. 72.

address no one but themselves and one another. But it should be obvious that while some things will be clinically interesting to composers alone as craftsmen, the quest for understanding of what they accomplish as creators will also yield conclusions of concern to anyone who aspires to such understanding. (Was it not E. M. Forster who once observed, speaking as a novelist, "How can I know what I think before I see what I say?") At the same time it is important not to ignore the fact that they are not averse to having their needs for better understanding satisfied by others. The most verbally articulate composers are dominated by ultimate allegiance to expression in a nonverbal medium and should welcome someone else to represent their viewpoints, to help solve their problems: the theorist, for example, who has special insight into the creative process without being a practising composer himself. Such a theorist, alas, is rare, and rather than settle for anything less, composers may prefer to turn out their own hasty, incipient statements of their ideas at the price of moments jealously guarded for writing music. How is such a practice to be reconciled with the disciplined, rigorous method posited as a condition of the new theory? If our yardstick is the vague treatment so often accorded individual works, especially when contemporary (though composer-theorists are not limited to the latter), concrete treatment of the musical entity from within by those with direct experience of how it is made, even when leaving something to be desired, may seem by comparison quite "rigorous" indeed.

It is idle to predict that composers would abstain from theoretical speculation if the kind of theory they now produce were sufficiently provided by thinkers in other branches of the music field. Perhaps there would be less of it on their part, but the current predilection for self-searching that was mentioned earlier is for some composers more than an adjunct: it stimulates creativity and may be essential to their successful functioning *qua* composers. Yet, whether they present their theoretical ideas well or lamely, composer-theorists are liable to be viewed with suspicion, their creativity seriously placed in doubt in the eyes of those— among them some of their most distinguished composer colleagues— who believe that an absorption in directly apprehended qualities is upset beyond repair by any digression into discursive thinking or talking about these qualities, and above all by the type of analysis productive of those writings that are summarily dismissed as "technical" (implying by this dismissal that the most penetrating critico-structural investigation is on the same level as, say, a handbook on trumpet fingering). To avariciously guard the creative experience as an "intuitive," indivisible, and mysterious affair is the prerogative of some composers; and virtually to boast of total lack of interest in the "technical" studies not only is their prerogative, but in the case of the older generations may even be a justifiable necessity, since very likely their most disturbing compositional problems have by now finally been worked through to their satisfaction, and to a point where doubt may actually be inhibiting. Neither the exercise of the prerogative, however, nor the submission to necessity can justify bringing in its wake, as it too often does, the aspersion that the composer-theorist's behavior is unbefitting to the truly creative spirit. The "intuitive" composer (I call him this for convenience) is not alone in regarding every activity that splinters experience as something incalculably poorer than the experience itself. An intelligent analyst is aware that to call attention to a single tone or configuration is to dwell on an experience different from, yet relevant to, the totality of which the tone or figure is a part, somewhat in the same way that, were I to say of a person (X) entering the room that he wears a smile, scant information about X would be conveyed—e.g. whether X is man, woman, or child—nevertheless what we would now know about X's disposition is not without significance (even were the smile later to be found to have been pasted on). What so often passes for "mystery" is nothing more than our inability (aided though we may be by a powerful computer) to stipulate the whole complex of relations in an art work, which is no reason not to try to stipulate some of them.

Rational man (I assume this includes composers) is naturally inclined to verbalize experience, not only for practical purposes, but also to ask gratuitously "how," "why," and, beyond the surface level of the descriptive, "what." The insistence that there is but one valid type of composer, a nonanalytic type, places the "intuitive" composers in the company of the most prescriptive reactionary, though they would be indignant if they were accused of sharing the latter's belief that there is but one way to write music: the traditional one. The skeptical attitude toward the composer-theorist is an aspect of a familiar attitude toward analysis in general: the art work is inviolable and the composer who attempts to violate it commits what amounts to a self-destructive act. In line with this attitude, the only way an art work should be discussed, whether in analysis or what is usually taken to be criticism, is by communicating the totality, the music's flow and excitement, its "color"—what impressionist critics attempted by means of empty, often embarrassing rhetoric.

Beliefs such as these do nothing so much as betray a serious failure to distinguish between "concept" and "percept," as Arnold Isenberg has pointed out—between the "idea *of* a quality" and the "quality itself."[7] Mr. Isenberg's subject is the critic's task of communication, and since the

[7] "Critical Communication," *Aesthetics and Language,* ed. William Elton, Oxford: Basil Blackwell, 1959, p. 141.

new theory, as I envisage it, is essentially a form of criticism, and since communication looms among its primary concerns, his line of reasoning should be of interest to us:

"What can be said" and "what cannot be said" are phrases which take their meaning from the purpose for which we are speaking. The aesthetics of obscurantism, in its insistence upon the incommunicability of the art object, has never made it clear what purpose or demand is to be served by communication. If we devised a system of concepts by which a work of art could be virtually reproduced at a distance by the use of language alone, what human intention would be furthered? . . . Now if we set up as a condition of communicability that our language should *afford* the experience which it purports to describe, we shall of course reach the conclusion that art is incommunicable. But by that criterion all reality is unintelligible and ineffable, just as Bergson maintains. Such a demand upon thought and language is not only preposterous in that its fulfillment is logically impossible; it is also baneful, because it obscures the actual and very large influence of concepts upon the process of perception . . . (pp. 141f.).

We have been considering concept and percept as, in a very important sense, distinct from one another, and we observed that the confusion between theorizing and creating not only instilled fears in the "intuitive" composer, because he could only think in terms of one type of behavior arrogating the place of the other, but also put the practice of music criticism or of any writing on music in constant danger of being used as an excuse to get rid of frustrated creative drives. Now, however, it would appear (from the last thought expressed in the above quotation) that there *can* be a transaction between concept and percept, an "influence" of the one on the other. Everyone has had the experience of seeing a new relationship or pattern in a familiar object, or hearing a new aspect in a familiar constellation of tones, *after* someone else has elucidated it and explained its presence (and I don't mean simply pointing, since it may be intricately woven into the whole). Obviously, such experience is possible only if we correlate concept and percept. "Reading criticism, otherwise than in the presence, or with the direct recollection, of the objects discussed," Mr. Isenberg admonishes, "is a blank and senseless employment—a fact which is concealed from us by the cooperation, in our reading, of many non-critical purposes for which the information offered by the critic is material and useful" (p. 139). Music, especially if it is unpublished and unperformed, creates insuperable obstacles in establishing this "presence," but we can go far toward achieving the ideal by supplying at least some of the context in as many music examples as practicable, much as we may regret excluding intelligent readers who cannot decipher notation. How very odd it is that those who object most vociferously to the atomization of music by the analyst should be most voluble in decrying music examples (that which ostensibly makes the writing more "technical") when these examples aim precisely at restoring the reader to the musical entity.

The examples, besides refreshing the memory, enable the reader to reassemble the dissected parts (which is not, and in a very real sense cannot be, the analyst's job), to check details against context, to assess new concepts which "place a frame upon the object and upon its parts and features . . . by an unnatural use of words in description."[8] Instead of the disapproval voiced nowadays because the strange new language fails to summon up at once the musical sensations associated with its nomenclature, what we really want is at least the willingness to allow that the new concepts may conceivably be significant enough to broaden, and alter our auditory experience. For intelligent disagreement there is ample room, but only after careful and tolerant correlation of concept and percept. It is through such a process that "tonality" was questioned apropos of *Sacre,* and though I shudder to bring up such a fighting word, it might also serve for a re-examination of "modulation." When currently used for those progressions represented with greater precision by a newer concept like "tonicization," the word "modulation" so distresses some theorists that one would think it as damaging in its way to the proper apprehension of the heard relations as "tonality" was found to be in quite another way when applied to *Sacre.* I am not convinced the cases are parallel as long as the listener who thinks to himself the concept "modulation" perceives something resembling the *Ursatz* (the horizontalized tonic triad as basic shape), though he may never have encountered Schenker's term.

This matter, so badly in need of exploration, is mentioned as a warning that some new concepts which yield clearer methodology may not modify direct auditory perception as much as it is supposed. The relationship between concept and percept is not one to one, and among the first challenges to the new theory is the study and evaluation of this relation. Clarification of basic terms is also on the priority list: the word "theory" itself; the distinction between theory and analysis, analysis and description, technique and structure, structure and form, form and conventional formula, as well as the relevance of them all to criticism. Also, it devolves upon the system-builders to explain what I take to be their artificial

[8] Stuart Hampshire, "Logic and Appreciation," in *Aesthetics and Language,* p. 167.

language which aims at "simplified" constructs,[9] though the complaint
we hear from readers is that the going is anything but simple. I cannot
help feeling this is something easily rectified and that the key was perhaps provided in the seminars where the subject matter was first brought
to light. If I am mistaken and the definitions are provided *passim* in the
earlier essays, then it is still not too much to ask for some more cross
reference.

At the risk of lapsing into cliché, I should like to suggest, as conclusion
to these ruminations, that the vicissitudes of the new theory are of the
general variety of those to which any innovations are prone: the most
significant tend to seem like nonsense, and others that may later turn
out to have been nonsense now pass for significant. "If you have had
your attention directed to the novelties in thought in your lifetime,"
Whitehead remarked somewhere, "you will have observed that almost all
really new ideas have a certain aspect of foolishness when they are first
produced, and almost any idea which jogs you out of your current
abstractions may be better than nothing." If what I believe to be the
new theory has accomplished anything at all, it has been precisely to jog
us out of our proverbial abstractions, and this is certainly better than
any of the varieties of nothing to which our field has for so long been
subjected.

---

[9] Above I indicated there is more than one viewpoint represented within the new theory but
I did not mean there are only two. Different approaches are naturally found among the
"scientifically" oriented, and as a matter of fact, when I recently heard the view expressed
that some new terms need no explanation because they are used in a literal, ordinary
language sense, I did not know how representative I could assume it to be of the system-
builders as a group. In any case, I seriously question it. If I came across the following
sentence: "The letter-sequences 'boy' and 'lad' are synonymous and each letter-sequence has
one syllable," I would have no difficulty understanding it, but I'd be full of curiosity to know
why one of our most commonplace expressions was being replaced. Of an adequate explanation of new terminology we require not only a definition but a *reason why* a new term is
necessary or useful.

NELSON GOODMAN'S *LANGUAGES OF ART* FROM A MUSICAL POINT OF VIEW

BENJAMIN BORETZ

To MANY OF us in music, the virtues of a confluence of rational inquiry and art have long been evident, if rarely exhibited. So the existence of a book explicitly devoted to the epistemology of art by the author of *The Structure of Appearance* seems to us not only an imposing benefice, but an entirely appropriate one as well. We do not, moreover, share the surprise of some of Professor Goodman's philosophical colleagues that he, in particular, should have become engaged in such an enterprise; for, from our vantage point, Goodman's contribution to the metalanguages of art had already seemed a considerable one, long before the publication of his most recent book. And that it was an indirect contribution, a use to which his work was put rather than one it specifically proposed, in no way diminished for us the scope and explicitness of that contribution's significance to our art-theoretical concerns. Thus, before turning to the matter of *Languages of Art* directly, it might be useful to elaborate briefly on the nature of this antecedent contribution, so that the Goodmanian influence on the music-conceptual scheme out of which my remarks about *Languages of Art* emerge will be apparent.

Quine has pointed out that "the less a science has advanced, the more its terminology tends to rest on an uncritical assumption of mutual understanding." Given this observation, it is hardly surprising that the customary inadequacy of meta-artistic communication has resulted in the usual, though erroneous, attributions of cognitive indeterminateness to the manifestations of the object-domains of art themselves, an attribution which is evident in the prevalent practice, in the philosophy and theory of art, of identifying as the salient aspects of art almost anything other than the con-

* Delivered at the Sixty-Sixth Annual Meeting of the American Philosophical Association, Eastern Division, on December 29, 1969, at a symposium devoted to Nelson Goodman's *Languages of Art*.

textually observable properties of those manifestations. Here another remark of Quine comes to mind: that "what counts as observation sentences for a community of specialists would not always so
count for a larger community." The converse of this sentence is,
of course, frequently also true, for many other domains as well as for'
art; but the particular failure of nonartists to recognize, and
of artists to explicate, the intersubjectivity of the entities the observation of which constitutes the contemplation of something *as*
a work of art of a particular kind, has made this fact a particular
burden to the theory of art, as it is not in science, linguistics, or
mathematics, in all of which the authority of competence is assert-
ible in a metalanguage that is culture-wide recognizable.

But it is the *explicative* theory of art—*not* the theory of structure which may be understood as what is unfolded by a set of
perceptual data selected and contemplated in a certain way which
we may call "making a musical (or visual-artistic, or literary) structure of that data"—that has been in the primitive state characterized in Quine's remark. And therefore, those of us who have observed the cognitivity of music as a highly developed medium of
thought within its empirical object-language have attended with
increasing urgency to contemporary epistemology, philosophy of
science, philosophical linguistics, and the study of formal and
interpreted systems, to derive an explicative theory of music that
might do justice to what may be called the "empirical theory of
music" of which it would be a model.

Now the special character of art entities *as* entities has lent a
particular art-explicative relevance to the literatures of nominalis-
tic epistemology and rational reconstruction, quite apart from the
positions in specifically intraphilosophical controversy they represent. Such relevance resides in particular in what Quine concedes
to rational reconstruction: that "imaginative construction can afford hints of actual psychological processes." And since "actual
psychological processes" are all there are in the entification of things
as works of art, such reconstructions have obvious epistemic value in
these cases. The nonimperativeness of the construal of any slice of
sensory experience as determining an art entity and the determinacy
of the entities derived from such a construal, as well as the variability of that determinacy with respect to the supposedly "same"
entities within the range delimited by the "field"-term involved, are
all aspects of artistic cognition that correlate with the methodological attitude toward entification adopted in Goodman's epistemological investigations.

Thus the replacement of the Given by the Chosen, or at least by the choosable-in-principle, is an indispensable *practical* concept in the perception and composition of art entities. What this concept enables, principally, is the awareness that the structure, or the identity, of a work of art is in the mind's eye or ear of the perceiver. And this consequence of Goodman's earlier epistemology is significant in that of *Languages of Art* as well; for example, in the explication of the dependence of representation on what Goodman calls the "non-innocent eye." But a further consequence of this dependence, namely the necessary presence, in the cognition of something as an art entity, of a *theory*, however internalized, of that entity's structure, is not explicitly engaged in the book; and this is a matter to which much of the sequel will be addressed.

The kind of analysis undertaken in connection with such constructional systems as those of Carnap's *Aufbau* and *The Structure of Appearance* also represents an intensely practical matter for art, since the very identity of an art entity *is* a theoretical construct quite remote from the pragmatics of object-identification in the physical world. Art entities, in fact, may be said to *have identity as entities of their types* just by virtue of being identifiable as interpretations of a general notion of *entityhood within that type*. Therefore, the extent to which they can be determinately recognized as *particular* entities of their types depends first of all on the *generality* of the concept of entityhood they are regarded as interpreting. And secondly, the degree of their particularity depends on the number of intervening concepts that can be, or that are, invoked between the atomic and the global levels, concepts which distinguish and order subentities as the ultimate determinants of the global structure. Thus the salient characteristic of an art entity may, most generally, be considered to be its "coherence"; and the *extent* of its coherence, and hence of its particularity as a work of art, may be considered to reside in the degree of determinate complexity exhibited in the ordered structure of subentities of which it is a resultant.

Moreover, in speaking of artworks as such we denote entities which, though they are *inferred from* observable characteristics of particular slices of the physical-entity world, *are not* themselves, as art entities, *composed of* those slices. Rather, these art entities are, so to speak, purely phenomenal things, intersubjective in the sense of thoughts rather than in that of sounds and sights. Now here I may appear, contrary to my assurances, to be raising strictly philosophical issues of the nature of reality; but this is not so. For I mean to suggest that art entities are purely phenomenal not in the *pre-objective* sense that has vexed constructional systems with the problems of abstraction from particulars or of concretion from qualities, but rather in a *post-objective* sense, as constructions placed on intersubjective aspects of entities that have been *previously* identified as concrete, *however* that prior identification is understood. The component elements of such constructions are indeed *qualia,* which are indeed *with* one another in concreta, in Goodman's senses. But as qualia they are retreads of previously identified qualities, and the entities they determine are not concreta at all, but structures of selected, discriminated, and quantized relations of qualia *in* ordered successions of distinct concreta. In this sense, our phenomenalistic constructions of works of art would begin where Carnap's and Goodman's constructions of the world would terminate, had they been completed.

Sounds, then, are not part of music, however essential they are to its transmission. And neither are paint, pigment, or canvas parts of paintings, nor masses of bronze parts of sculptures, nor pages and letters parts of poems. Sounds, in fact, are not even what musical notation specifies, a matter which Goodman seemingly overlooks in his discussion of such notation in *Languages of Art.* What scores do specify is information about music-*structural* components, such as pitches, relative attack-times, relative durations, and whatever other quale-categorical information is functionally relevant. Thus it may be said that the notations of scores determine their interpreting musical works, and the performances thereof, to varying degrees and in varying respects, depending on the identity of the functioning quale-categories and on quantization thresholds that are functional within each category.

So the varying determinacies of score-notations with respect to various quale-categories at different music-historical junctures, which Goodman engages in his chapter on music in *Languages of Art,* simply correspond to the degrees of structural functionality that are at maximum assignable to those categories in those compositions, at least on the evidence of their scores. "Precision" of notation is, of course, relative to inferred "thresholds"; and a piece whose pitch notation specifies only "relative height" may be one where pitch-relational characteristics function only to within "higher-than" determinations. Thus such a notation would constrain the appropriate interpretations just to within the "higher-than" boundary criterion without any lack of music-structural "precision." For *any* interpretation conforming to such a criterion contains precisely "the" correct pitch-structural information for that piece.

Now this means that our present pitch notation is not necessarily *more precise* relative to the piece it notates than, say, that of pre-Gregorian chant, but only that what counts as compliance to it of interpreting sounds may be inferred as being more highly constrained with respect to their pitch components, and thus that our music *may* be interpreted as invoking *discriminable* pitch differences more *determinately* than just in terms of "higher than."

But even so, what will count as compliance to even a supposedly "precisely" notated score is relative to a theory of the structure of the work with reference to which the score-performance relation is evaluated. It is in the nonrecognition of this *music*-structural theory-dependence of compliance that I think Goodman goes wrong in his explication of musical notation. For whatever the *notation* involved, a listener to early church music conditioned to more precisely quantized pitch-functional music such as our own might infer that he was hearing *two different pieces* in successive performances that, under the pitch-quantizational concepts being used by the performers, were also noticeable as being performances of the *same piece*. One reason for this perplexity is, of course, that it is *sound-successions* rather than *notations* that are the real symbolic languages of music; and notes require prior music-structural interpretation to be regarded as *music-determinately* symbolic of sounds.

Thus a listener from an Eastern culture, learning that a given notation represented two attacks of the same pitch, might hear a Western-culturally "correct" realization of that notation as an "incorrect" succession of *two different pitches,* because his background pitch-structural vocabulary was more finely quantized than ours. For pitch-function assignments are *contextual,* and take place within thresholds that in practice enable such apparent anomalies as the assignment of discriminably different pitches to identical pitch functions, and of indiscriminable pitches to different pitch functions, depending on the *structural* context.

Similarly, the difference of a G♯-versus-A♭ notational problem as it arises with respect to a piano score and as it arises in connection with a violin score is not, as Goodman seems to believe, a question about pitch-function difference, but only an observation of the inflectional room left by our traditional quantizations of pitch-functional thresholds. Similar differences *within* a piano-score realization are assigned the status of "out-of-tuneness," which can be determinately distinguished from "wrong-pitchness" only by the operation of a background pitch-function reference.

Thus the notational question raised by Goodman of the relation of "wrong pitches" to "genuine instances of a musical work" is tied to the structural question of what constitutes a "wrong note" with respect to a given work. For the theory of the structure of that work, which is, first of all, requisite to determine what that work's *identity* is, will interpret some wrong notes as wronger than others, disenabling any correlation of "degree of nongenuineness as an instance of a work" with "number of noncompliant sounds presented." To give a crude example, say that one's theory of some work's pitch structure constructs it by means of just three pitch functions, which we may call "high," "middle," and "low." Then the *structural* limits within which notation-determinably wrong notes may still be part of a "wholly correct" performance of *that piece* might be considerably wider than the notationally determined limits; but such structural limits would still be non-*indifferent* to the question of "wrong-note" determination, even after that question had passed out of the range of the notational limits.

Moreover, the compliances determined by a figured-bass notation and a free-cadenza notation are similarly theoretical. By Goodman's purely notational criterion, only a failure to observe actually notated "facts" counts as a "mistake"; but a music-structural theory will extend from what is notated to what is interpolated, and, for any given performance, will determine how *what is not specified* is constrained by what *is* specified such that literal compliance to the *specified* entities is no more or less determinate of "correctness of realization" than is the appropriateness of what is *chosen* to intervene between them.

Thus I would argue that Goodman's avoidance of music-structural questions in talking of musical notation is not so much frivolous as impracticable; and in fact his own discussion does not fail to *be,* however inadvertently, music-theoretical. For what he tells us about the limits of determinability of compliance-classes for John Cage's notations is pure music criticism, since it really tells us what the limits of music-structural determinacy in Cage's compositions are likely to be, with predictable consequences for the *particularity* those compositions are likely to be able to exihibit *as* musical structures.

On the other hand, Goodman's allographic-autographic distinction is obviously useful; indeed, the problem of pure "autographical-ness" has already arisen in connection with some forms of electronically performed music, although computer-synthesized electronic performances use a numerical, musically interpretable, allographic notation.

Now if my account of musical structure can be taken as art-typical, it implies that the "actual psychological processes" which Quine allows that rational reconstructions may "hint at" are, in the case of art entities, in fact *crucially determined by* those reconstructions. The path and content of a hierarchical construction of an art entity, through progressive subentity articulation, determine the content of that entity in the only sense in which it may be said to have a content as a work of art. And the more such a construction proceeds through relational concepts defined in a maximally *open* way, consistent with the retention of the intuitive concepts involved, the more different-appearing things may be subsumed as interpretations of the same concepts, and, hence, the more works may be commensurable at the more levels of their construction. For a perceiver, this engenders the capacity both to "understand" a greater number of more unlike-appearing things as instances of a single art-entity domain, and to regard each such thing as a more individuated thing within its domain.

This consideration engages the most general art-theoretical aspects of *Languages of Art*. For it is crucial to the argument of *Languages of Art,* as to the above remarks, that what the observer brings to his perception of a work in the way of predisposition is a crucial determinant of what he perceives therein. But my remarks raise the additional question whether some aspects of what a given perceiver might bring to such a perception might not count toward the *competence* of that perception, as a perception *of* a, or in particular of that, work of art, and whether some other aspects of what such a perceiver might bring might not count as *irrelevant* thereto. A rough analogy may be the relevance of English-understanding to the perception of an utterance as an English sentence, as against the relevance to that perception of a disposition to regard English utterances as "sad-sounding."

This suggests that some kinds of "non-innocence" may be more sophisticated than others, where art-perceptual competence is concerned; and although Goodman and I seem to agree that relevant non-innocence involves previous experience *of* artwork perception, I would insist additionally that it also requires that such experience *of* artworks be of them *as* artworks.

Thus, in analyzing ascriptions made to artworks, we might distinguish between those which are relevant to them as artworks and those which are not. The issue is related to that of the interpretability and applicability of theoretical terms. Sometimes, for example, it might seem from the form of an ascriptive discourse that evidence of a certain type—for example, observations on the perceptual data of a work of art—could influence the determination of a truth-value assignment of a given use of a predicating term, when in fact it could not. In other words, we might distinguish terms whose uses *make a difference* to our perception of a thing from a *certain* point of view, from those whose uses matter only in the context of some *other* point of view.

To take a simple example, compare the ascriptions to, say, something identified as "Beethoven's Eighth Symphony" of 'This is sad' and 'This is in F major'. Now it would be as absurd to decide the question "This is in F major" by an audience poll as it would be to decide "This is sad" by surveying the musical data.[1] In which case, then, are we making a statement "about" Beethoven's Eighth Symphony? A popular way to resolve the issue has been to say that the referents in the two cases are different, as those of 'book' might be in two possible uses of 'This is a weighty book'.

But here the problem is deeper; for how is the "this" being *identified* in the first place in the case of "This is sad"? The "book" model breaks down here, for no observation comparable to that which could confirm a porter's report that something was a weighty book could be brought to bear. And to bring the point closer to Goodman's investigations, how does an ascription like 'high note' differ from one like 'sad piece'? Goodman methodologically equates the 'is a red book''–''is a novel' type of disjunction of our earlier example with this latter case: he suggests that "Calling a picture sad and calling it gray are simply different ways of classifying it." But what competence is invoked in declaring a picture "sad"? Not "psychological," since that would have to do with making assignments by observing correlations with other people's

---

[1] Goodman describes me (in his "Reply to Benjamin Boretz," *Journal of Philosophy*, LXVII/16 [August 20, 1970], 567) as a "formalist" to whom "the actual structure of the work is all that matters." But since what I call "musical structure" is just the coherent juxtaposition of *everything* relevant to the identity of a musical work, I can't see what an "exclusive concern with musical structure" excludes. And I cannot imagine, as a practitioner of music, what significance might be attributed to a property of which it could be said that "works differing widely in detail may have the *same* property of sadness" (568, emphasis mine); the notion of "details that don't matter" in the ascription of properties to a work would seem to have a legitimate place only in an aesthetics of the immediate, such as is disclaimed by Goodman in the first paragraph of his reply, or in a study of art as inattentively or casually observed.

assignments, not by observing as they do. I find a clue to this perplexity in our musical example: a "high note" is understandable
as a hypostatization of observable relations of "higher than";
whereas "sadder than" is just as inscrutible as "sad." Another clue
may be that such predications as 'sad', of pieces, are invariably restricted to familiar musical domains, such as tonal pieces, whereas
the pieces in unfamiliar domains like, for example, twelve-tone
pieces, are more often described as "noisy" or in some other way
that simply reports failure to ascribe identity.

The latter case seems to provide the better clue; for I think that
the "this"-identification underlying the "This is sad" ascription is
just a hidden music-theoretical one of the "This is in F major" type,
just as the "picture" referred to in the activity of "calling a picture sad" is in a *prior* sense the picture that was called gray.

Now this means that the *whole* act of identification that underlies
a "this-is-sad"-type ascription' to works of art is, in fact, located
in the data-discriminative domain relevant to the particularization
of things as entities of certain types. As predications *in those domains,* the status of such ascriptions is thus as mere "proper
names." For they are intelligible only as ascriptions to things to
which prior, if hidden, recognition has been given as entities of the
structural kind; but as ascriptions with regard to those structures,
they are *empty,* in that they make no discernible difference.

Whether these ascriptions are metaphorical or not is, moreover,
immaterial in the same sense; as defined predicates, they are systematically indifferent under explication: "higher than" could be
called "lower than," as it was by the ancient Greeks, or "greener
than," or "greater than," or "left of," without affecting the *music-*
identifying question. The etymologies of metaphors, their "schema-
transferring" attributes investigated by Goodman, are *heuristically*
useful just to the degree that the transferred term-names can be
determinately correlated with observables. Thus Goodman's explication seems essentially to enable the *elimination* of metaphors
as special "types" of ascriptions to works of art. And in this light,
the only problem with 'sad' is that we simply have nothing observational to tie it to in either music or painting, and so it makes no
difference to the music- or painting-identity of anything. In use,
however, such "proper names" have *negative* value, since they serve
to perpetuate the internalization of a perceiver's theoretical scheme
and, hence, to minimize his competence. The world of the average
listener contains very little music and a great deal of noise, a gap
which he tends to cover by the invocation of picturesque place-

holding slogans.

But to a sophisticated observer, the space thus straddled is filled with so many determinate particulars producing such particular identities that the sloganizing terms actually do seem hopelessly inapplicable. Like prescientific attributions, to natural phenomena, of anthropomorphic and volitional characteristics, predications like 'sad' of art simply symptomatize an underprivileged *stage* of cognition, not a *category* thereof. How cogent, I wonder, would philosophers find the assertion about *The Structure of Appearance* that it was "colorful"?

But to call such predicates "supervenient terms" or "slogans" is only to characterize their inapplicability to art, not to explicate their cognitivity in *any* respect. To understand their cognitive status, however, I believe it is necessary to look to those domains where metaphorical schema transfer is part of the determinate identity of structures, namely, to the arts of language, as exemplified in literary structures. For paintings are represented by predicates like 'sad' in literary works as objects are represented by color-patch structures in paintings, not as paintings *are* objects.

This last observation invites a confrontation with Goodman's notion of *representation*. Here again, I think that the epistemological interest of the explication is quite independent of its relevance to art-theoretical concerns. For the problem in ascribing representation to works of art as a primary attribute thereof is not uninterpretability or inapplicability, but grossness. Most of the attributes that distinguish a painting as a *particular* painting lie below the level at which representation is predicable of it; the situation is rather like that of predicating 'a gas' of something where what was important was *how* it was a gas, whether it was *helium* or *oxygen*, for example. Hence I suspect that Goodman's principal interest was to explicate representation, rather than paintings. Otherwise I cannot understand why he would take such a complex "fact" about a painting as that it "represents something thus" as virtually "atomic" for it, without investigating what particularizes, determinately, that representation with respect to any other. For to say just that "awayness up" and "awayness forward" are "differently represented" from each other in a given *literature* of paintings is not to characterize what constitute the palpable determinants of even the observation that in a given *single* painting "things receding upward are represented as parallel and things receding forward are represented as convergent." That is, is not the level at which color areas articulate the visual space itself a distinctive determinant—for each single case

—of the particular identity which is only loosely classified as "parallelism" or "convergence"?

Music's failure to represent, of course, has happily always been an embarrassment to the art-as-representational thesis. On the other hand, traditional music does reveal, at a comparable level of grossness, an observational characteristic that corresponds to representation in painting; namely, "thematicism." In both cases, it seems to me, such entities as "themes" and "represented things" are best understood as subglobal structural frameworks that enclose complex sets of quale-relations in mnemonically convenient form, as advantageous strategies in the optimal communication of the often highly complex structural identities of the global structures they articulate.

As to the predicate 'picture of x', this, like the "theme" of a symphony or the fact that it is in "Sonata Form," can be eliminated altogether as a special stage in the subentity ascension. As part of such an ascension, it is merely a "proper name" for a defined predicate, with more or less heuristic value; as such, it may also function as a conceit, constraining the limits of what would count as an appropriate resultant, much as the "Mickey-Mousing" of literary texts in songs provides such external constraints. But as a significant individuating term for paintings, 'picture of x' seems to me only slightly beyond the level of 'oil painting', 'landscape', 'portrait', or 'abstraction'. Thus, again, I find that Goodman's explication enables rather the *elimination* of a notion than its invocation as a significant factor in the construction of art entities.

What, then, *do* art entities *express*? Ideas of relation, I think, *particular* coherences, in analog form; and what they *exemplify* are their structures. That is, works of art may be regarded as analog models of closed formal-systematic structures whose interpreting entities express the relations of the formal-systematic entities through patterns of relative quantity of perceptual qualities, such qualities being quantitatively articulated by scales of measurement chosen by a perceiver. A "scientist" constructs an experiment to test "his" structure of the world against the measurable facts of observation, on the scales of magnitude relevant to the properties being tested for. The experimental complex is strategically designed to extrude optimally those properties regarded as critical. The composition of works of art may be described as the definition and creation of relational "universes" of elements in whose interrelations are embedded hypothetical properties of relational behavior; hypotheses, that is, of "what can be learned to be observed" on the basis of what has already, by appropriate receptors, been learned to be observed. And, ultimately, it is the reasonable possibility that, from the data he specifies, the relational properties he has embedded will be the "most favorably inferrable" things, that justifies the artist's "experiment." In art, of course, all the "measuring instruments" are perceptual, not physical; but their measurements, on the quantizational scales needed to infer all the significatively embedded properties, are as precise and unambiguous as those of the scientist—which is not surprising, since the data relations were designed in the first place to be measured by perceptual instruments.

Moreover, the relation of the "analog" state of non-art-theoretical quality perception to a syntactically and semantically interpreted perception of those qualities as components of art entities seems to me to explicate the relation between what may be termed "aesthetic experience," on the one hand, and "art," on the other. I would liken an "aesthetic experience" to an informal act of "quasi-analysis," in which the component qualities of concrete entities rather than their gross entityhood are what is being taken note of. Noticing the sunset *as* a certain confluence of a certain red over a certain spatial extension, etc., is an activity of the "aesthetic" type.

Art, on the other hand, uses these quasi-analytically derived qualities as materials with which to build structures, whose syntactically differentiated and discontinuous elements are semantically interpreted by qualia that are degree-ordered into differentiated and discontinuous *vocabularies*. Here, of course, I am engaging Goodman's explication of the digital-analog relation (157–173), which is for me not only the most enlightening passage of *Languages of Art,* but that which seems most directly to enable the connection of art-entity construction with the constructions of *The Structure of Appearance.* But Goodman does not specify how the connection is to be made, nor does he otherwise take note of it.

The final question that I want to engage with respect to *Languages of Art* is the analogy between verbal and art-symbolic languages proposed by Goodman. Again, we seem to invoke quite disparate desiderata and, accordingly, to arrive at quite different conclusions. Goodman locates the analogy in the problematic area of *reference,* the *aboutness* of language. This assignment seems entirely consistent with his concern, throughout *Languages of Art,* with representation, expression, and the "comprehension of our worlds" to which he refers. He replaces Oscar Wilde's epigram about art and life with a stronger one of his own: "Nature is the product of art and discourse." And throughout the book, the discussion centers on what is *in* works of art, while never once addressing the question of what works of art *are*.

Although he never says so explicitly, I wonder whether, as a non-specialist, Goodman felt constrained to attempt a cognitive explication of what is commonly *said about* art rather than one of art itself, limiting himself to a rational analysis of popular notions about art, as reflected in traditional aesthetics and the critical and journalistic literature, rather than attempting to explicate the identities of artworks from a rational analysis of their perceptual attributes directly.

In any case, the trouble with regarding works of art as primarily *about* the world is that they are in the first place *of* the world. And in the sense that the world is what communicates through language-dependent perception, art works surely *add themselves to* the world and *use* the *ways* that the world communicates to communicate themselves.

The issue of the languageness of the languages of art clears, moreover, if we turn from the aboutness of language to the special entityness of verbal-linguistic things, which, like art things, are entities just by virtue of being inferred as such from aspects of concreta filtered through a syntax and a semantics. As such, they may be mentally experienced as *thought;* the same, I believe, is true of art entities. And the absence of "aboutness" in the languages of the musical and visual arts, at least, frees them from the constraints of conventional norms of syntactical and lexical formation and association. As a result, they are free to create their own norms contextually from much simpler perceptual-assumptive bases. Hence, for example, works of music are constructable from a general notion of "music" without the *essential* intervention of stages identified as, say, "tonal" or "twelve-tone," which would be analogous to the construction of a particular English utterance wholly from a system that defines "language" in general, without the essential intervention of an English dictionary or grammar.

Thus the structures of the "contextual" arts are like man-made possible "mini-worlds," perceivable and palpable, and yet not constrained by the exigencies and recalcitrances of the physical, constrained only by the bounds of human perceptual and intellectual capacities, which are thereby both demonstrated and expanded. This, it seems to me, is essentially the awareness that the epistemology of *The Structure of Appearance* has contributed to the theory of art, locating the relevant focus of such theory in the activity of entification and particularization by means of conceptually guided systematic construction.

Therefore, that art has fed back into the epistemology, of *Languages of Art* mainly in the form of a *referential* theory is something I find deeply perplexing, and earnestly hope that Professor Goodman's remarks will help to explain. For even linguistic entities *refer* only by virtue of linguistic interpretation, so that, like art entities, they *are* something before they *do* anything. And I thought it was from Goodman himself that we had learned most lucidly that just *being* something is *doing* plenty already.

ALEA

PIERRE BOULEZ

SEVERAL COMPOSERS of our generation show currently a constant preoccupation with chance—you might even say they are obsessed by it. This is, at least as far as I know, the first time such a notion has assumed a place in Occidental music, and the fact surely deserves to be examined at length, for it is too important a bifurcation in the idea of composition to be either underestimated or rejected unconditionally.

Is it possible to trace this obsession to its origin? Outwardly, one could suggest various causes that seem to have a certain solidity, changing in accordance with the temperament of the different creators. The most elementary form of the transmutation of chance would lie in the adoption of a philosophy tinged with Orientalism that masks a basic weakness in compositional technique; it would be a protection against the asphyxia of invention, the resort to a more subtle poison that destroys every last embryo of craftsmanship; I would willingly call this experiment—if experiment it be, since the individual does not feel responsible for his work, but merely throws himself by unadmitted weakness, by confusion, and for temporary assuagement into puerile magic—I would call this experiment chance through inadvertence. In other words, the result comes about any which way, uncontrolled (an absence that is voluntary though not praiseworthy, through impotence), *but* within a certain network of probable results, for chance must have at its disposal some kind of eventuality. Therefore, why choose the network so meticulously, why not leave this network itself up to inadvertence? That is something I have never been able to clear up. The game is played only partly aboveboard, but at least no one pretends otherwise, which is creditable. It is a nicely laid out artificial paradise where, I think, dreams are never very miraculous; this kind of narcotic indeed constitutes protection against the goad inflicted upon you by all inventiveness; it is to be observed that its action is exaggeratedly soothing, sometimes mirth-provoking, like what hashish fanciers describe. Peace to these angelic creatures; we can be sure they run absolutely no risk of stealing any thunder, since they wouldn't know what to do with it. Inadvertence is amusing at the beginning, but one gets tired of it very quickly—all the more quickly because it is condemned to never renew itself. This being so, we incontestably prefer natural inadvertence, which doesn't require *instruments* for its existence. "Non-art," "anti-art" still take as their point of reference "art." And in the search we are engaged in, what people agree to call by this name is not at all the focus of our efforts. Some decades have passed since Beauty was found to be bitter. Let's put together with that enchantress A-Beauty, Anti-Beauty, etc., and throw a few shovelfuls of earth. Chance will do the rest!

However, there exists a more poisonous and more subtle form of intoxication. I have already spoken of it on several occasions, for this form dies hard and arises once again every time it seems to have been overcome. Composition chooses to approach as closely as possible the most perfect, smooth, untouchable objectivity. And by what means? Schematization, quite simply, takes the place of invention; imagination—an auxiliary—limits itself to giving birth to a complex mechanism which takes care of engendering microscopic and macroscopic structures until, in the absence of any further possible combinations, the piece comes to an end. Admirable security and a strong signal of alarm! As for the imagination, it is careful not to intervene after things are under way: it would disturb what is absolute in the development process, introducing human error into such a perfectly deduced ensemble; a fetishism of numbers, leading to pure and simple failure. We plunge into statistical lists that have no more value than other lists. In its Omni-Objectivity, the work represents—here we are again—a fragment of chance that is just as justifiable (or just as unjustifiable) as any other fragment. The difference between the form described earlier and this new, equally pernicious temptation is evident: there is more trickery in this one, and the spontaneous confession of weakness is transformed into a hopelessly sterile search for combinative devices, into an aggressive refusal of arbitrariness, that new "diabolus in musica." Paradoxically, however, the result is that this hated and repudiated arbitrariness is, on the contrary, most often encountered when most shunned. Objectivity recedes at every instant in front of your eyes, like a kind of irritating and fragile mirage that exhausts and dries up all vital energy; these slices of chance are unfit for consumption because, first of all, one wonders *why* they should be consumed!

Once this overt objectivity had failed, they hurled themselves like madmen into a search for arbitrariness. They went looking for the devil and brought him back with a suitable escort, imprisoned, bound by a thousand nets, in a work that he was supposed to vivify by his omnipresence. The devil will be there, shamefaced, or will not be anywhere. Were there complaints about the lack of subjectivity? There'll be some at each note, within each structure; this ferociously dislocated, dismembered, scattered subjectivity is going to force you to take a stand, hypocritical listener, to be as subjective as the composer. As for the interpreter, it is up to him to transmit to you the devil's attacks; he will compromise

stablish himself as high priest of this
less murkily than you are inclined
ill become sufficiently, but subtly,
its grid—hypothetical diagram—
ire-like choice of the interpreter.
d this sound, you *may* accelerate,
ort, one has chosen henceforth to

... are getting back to? Constantly to a refusal
...oice. The first conception was purely mechanistic, automatic, fetishistic; the second is still fetishistic, but one is freed from choice not by numbers but by the interpreter. One transfers one's choice to the interpreter's. In this way one is protected, camouflaged; not very cleverly, for nonetheless arbitrariness, or rather a kind of tip-of-the-finger arbitrariness, imposes its presence. What a relief! The hour of choice is once again put off: a superficial subjectivity has been grafted onto an aggressive conception of initial objectivity. No! Chance is too shameful to be diabolical . . . .

We might note, between benign parentheses, that a certain kind of analytical procedure has taken the same blind alleys. A sort of smugly statistical report has replaced a more intelligent and more hard-hitting method of investigation. The brain is used like a photoelectric cell that picks out the various components according to their special features: thanks to a formulation of intervals or of figures, the *vice* is recorded as equaling the *versa*—which, it must be admitted, is a poor lesson. As for the composer's choice, it is slurred over with a lack of virtuosity that is painful to behold. How can analysis be limited to an ordinary inventory, to a rough cadastral survey? In spite of best intentions and most earnest attempts, I am unable to make out the precise reason for this fear to approach the true problem of composition. Perhaps this phenomenon also is due to a kind of fetishism of numeral selection—a position that is not only ambiguous but completely unsound when the work under investigation structurally refuses these procedures, which are, after all, excessively coarse and elementary.

Thus in addition to chance by inadvertence, we find a chance by automatism, whether this automatism tries to be pure or is accompanied by a notion of controlled bifurcation. However, since the obsession with what *may* happen takes the place of what *should* happen, it is not due only to the weakness of the compositional methods involved, nor due only to the desire to introduce the subjectivity of the interpreter or of the listener within the work and thus to create for these two a constant and obligatory instantaneous choice. It would be possible to give still other apparent reasons with quite as much justification. And first of all, as far as the structure of the work is concerned, there is the .... of a preestablished structure, the legitinate desire to construct a sort of labyrinth with several circuits; on the other hand, there is the wish to create a moving, constantly renewed complexity, specifically characteristic of played, *interpreted* music, as opposed to the fixed and not renewable complexity of machines. Certainly, in a musical universe from which all notion of symmetry tends to disappear, in which an idea of variable density assumes an increasingly primordial place on all levels of construction—from materials to structure—it is logical to look for a form which does not become *fixed,* an evolving form that will rebelliously refuse to permit its own repetition; in short, a relative formal virtuality. We are getting around to the determining factor of this research which, in my opinion, can concentrate on the necessity of destroying any immanent structure.

How has this need been able to become progressively explicit? For, classically, composition is the result of a constant choice. Haven't I said so enough myself? It means, within certain networks of probabilities, being led—from one solution to another—to refusing, to choosing. The composer's arbitrariness intervenes to render efficacious certain propositions of structures that will remain formless until, thanks to their elaboration, they acquire a stamp of experienced necessity. However, in the course of this elaboration there arises once again, and always, chance. Is such-and-such a possibility more "profitable" than another? Certainly, because you have thought it so at that point of your development. On the basis of my experience, it is impossible to foresee all the meanders and all the virtualities contained in the material you start out with. However full of genius one might be in this premonitory vision, in this rapid effort to estimate—to appraise—it seems to me, first of all, that the composer would be deprived of his most outstanding quality: surprise. It is easy to imagine the boredom of an omniscience and an omnipotence that would have nothing to reveal to you along the way. Composition ought to reserve at every moment surprises and ways of its own regardless of all the rationality that must be imposed in other respects in order to attain an unquestionable solidity. I thus once more come, by another route, to the irrational: so it is that, as a result of asking oneself questions, one gets back to this obsession which lurks even in the most rigorous ordinances. Despairingly one tries to dominate one's material by an arduous, sustained, vigilant effort, and despairingly chance persists, slips in through a thousand unstoppable loopholes. "And it's fine that way!" Nevertheless, wouldn't the composer's ultimate ruse be to *absorb* this chance? Why not tame these potentialities and force them to render an account, to account for themselves?

Introduce chance into composition? Isn't that madness or, at most, a vain endeavor? Madness, perhaps, but it will be a *useful madness*. In any case, to adopt chance through weakness, as the easy way, to turn oneself over to it, is a form of renunciation that could not be accepted without denying all the prerogatives and the hierarchies that a created work implies. In what respect then can composition and chance be reconciled?

Since musical development is a function of duration, of the physical time during which it unfolds, it permits the introduction of "chances" at several stages and at several levels of composition. When all is said and done, the resultant of this would be a sequence based on the greatest probability of chance-determined happenings within the limits of a certain duration that would also be indeterminate. That may seem absurd in the context of our Occidental music, but Hindu music, for example, by combining a kind of structural "formant" with instantaneous improvisation, arrives very easily at this kind of problem and provides an everyday solution for it. Obviously it also requires a completely different way of listening and exists in an open cycle, whereas we conceive of the formulated work as a closed cycle of possibilities.

Let us see, however, whether by surmounting certain contradictions it is not possible to absorb chance.

We begin at the most elementary level, the one at which one gives a certain freedom to the performer. Let's make no mistake: if used summarily, this will be no more than a kind of generalized rubato, somewhat more organized than before (I mean a rubato that can be applied to dynamics, to registers, and to tempo, of course). If the interpreter can modify the text as he likes, this modification must be implied by the text and not merely added afterwards. The musical text should contain inherently this "chance" of the interpreter. If, for example, in a certain succession of sounds, I insert a variable number of grace notes, it is perfectly evident that the tempo of these sounds will be made constantly changing by the intrusion of the grace notes, which provoke each time an interruption, or more exactly, a rupture of different tension. They can contribute to giving an impression of nonhomogeneous time. Similarly, in the case of a rapid succession of notes and chords that are of equal rhythmical length but that require very pronounced shiftings (registers either very close to one another or very far apart), very different densities (aggregates of from two to eleven sounds), and excessively differentiated attacks and dynamics, if I ask the performer to regulate his tempo according to the difficulty of performance, it is clear that this succession will not have a regular rhythmic pulsation, but that the rhythm will be physically tied to the mechanical differentiation that I require of him. Another example: I can ask the interpreter not to slow up or to accelerate, but to oscillate around a given tempo, within more or less strict limits. I can also make certain caesuras depend rather freely on the dynamic level but without defining a rigid limit to the *ad libitum*. In this way I introduce by means of the text a necessity of chance in the interpretation—a directed chance. A word of caution: these words rubato, *ad libitum* are used here only to facilitate expression, since the notions thus introduced for the first time in composition have nothing to do with the conceptions that these terms generally refer to—conceptions, that is, which are connected simply with flexibility of articulation (we may associate with them the fermata and the pause, of which usage has completely changed the meaning). I have taken here the case of a single performer, but it is easy to surmise the kaleidoscope offered to the imagination by several performers or several groups of performers. For then, one will be free to utilize an interchange between the two dimensions of the text, one rigorous, the other interpreted. In so doing, one enters a pragmatic realm that deserves examination, since the performance or conducting of such pieces of music presents completely unprecedented problems (notation has its role also in what is implicated here); but experience has already proved that scores conceived in this way are practicable. We will come back to this subject later, limiting ourselves for the moment to the "theoretical" aspect of the question.

However, even though implied by the musical text, this "chance," let us repeat, occurs at an elementary level. It already gives appreciable possibilities of aerating, of liberating, the interpretation; it seems to resolve the dilemma between strict interpretation and free interpretation. Perhaps now the performer needs more boldness than before to "fit in" with the composer's invention, but—without excessive optimism—good results from this more effective collaboration can be hoped for. However, let us remember how much this liberty needs to be directed, projected, for the "instantaneous" imagination is more subject to lapses than to illuminations. Consequently this liberty is exercised not, strictly speaking, on the invention itself, but on the pragmatism of the invention. I think everyone will admit the prudence of this position.

At the level on which the structures themselves are called into play, I believe that one can first *absorb* chance by establishing a certain automatism of relationship among various networks of probabilities drawn up beforehand. But, someone will remind me, you are in contradiction with your initial statement, in which you refused this automatism, this objectivity, as a fetishism of numbers. I naturally expect that this automatism should not take in all creative thought, but that it may play a role in such thought as a particularly efficacious means at such-and-such a given moment during the elaboration of a work. There is nothing like it to give an impression of nondirection, of weightlessness, to impose the sensation of an undifferentiated universe. However, depending on whether this automatism is more or less preponderant, one will have a more or less tempered solution of chance. The proliferation of these automatic structures will have to be watched over with care if one does not want a seemingly ordered anarchy to completely eat away the composition and so to deprive it of its privileges. Depending on the greater or lesser strictness assigned to the networks of probabilities, one will obtain a single encounter or multiple encounters at different degrees—that is, a single or a multiple chance. In practice, how will we translate that? Let us suppose that I choose series of durations and dynamics and that, assuming that the result of the encounter of these two series is fixed, I want to apply it to a series of pitches. If I give to the series of pitches definite registers, it is clear that there will be only one solution for a given note—that is to say, this note will be ineluctably fixed in its register (absolute frequency), in its dynamic, in its duration: the unique chance of encounter of these three organizations at this "point" of sound. But, supposing that we keep the same series of sounds without imposing a register upon it, and that this register is left to the improvisation of writing, we will immediately have a "line" of registers, if I may use the expression, the geometrical meeting place of all the "points" that satisfy the three other characteristics: relative, generic frequency; dynamics; duration. By assigning progressively the relativity of the registration to duration, then to dynamics, I will have obtained a determined "plan," then a determined "volume," in which my "point" of sound will find its justification. If I have adopted this geometrical convention, it is simply in order to have a term of comparison and not in order to refer to an exactly similar situation. For the different combinations of characteristics, there are therefore fields of encounter in which lies the chance of the definitively fixed musical event.

Such a manipulation of combinations requires a complete absence of choice in the execution, although choice intrudes more and more as probabilities multiply. In this way the following phenomenon arises: the less one chooses, the greater is the dependence of the unique chance on the pure hazard of the encounter of objects; the more one chooses, the greater is the dependence of the event on the coefficient of hazard implied by the composer's subjectivity. It is the varying degree of interchange between the terms of this antinomy that will arouse interest in a passage of the work so composed.

We have been careful to point out that the preceding case concerned the most elementary stage of automatism, purposely not oriented. If we want to integrate chance into the notion of structure itself in an oriented ensemble, we must call upon more subtle differentiations and introduce such notions as those of defined or undefined structure, amorphous or directional structure, divergent or convergent structure. It is undeniable that this development of chance in composition will create a universe decidedly more differentiated than before and will mark a more acute development of a renewed perception of form. In a conducted ensemble, these various structures ought to be obligatorily controlled by a general "phrasing," ought necessarily to have an initial and a final sign, ought to call accessorily upon kinds of platforms of bifurcation—all this in order to avoid a complete loss of the global sense of form as well as in order to steer clear of an improvisation with no other necessity than free choice. For, as we said earlier, the liberty—or the liberation—of the performer changes absolutely nothing about the notion of structure, since the problem is actually merely put off until a little later and since the solutions still remain to be found. I think that a well-founded objection can be made here: doesn't such a form carry with it an enormous danger of compartmentalization? Aren't we going to be guilty of one of the faults that have done the most harm to composition as it has been understood—the fault which consists of juxtaposing "sections," each with its own center? This argument is justifiable only in case one actually does not think of a general form but develops, if I may use the expression, step by step. In order to cover up this disappearance of composition, one ought to have recourse to a new notion of development that would be essentially discontinuous, but discontinuous in a predictable and foreseen way. And from this would follow the necessary introduction of the "formants" of a work and of the "phrasing" that is indispensable to the interrelation of structures of various kinds.

It would accordingly be possible in such a form to conceive junction points, platforms of bifurcation, kinds of mobile elements capable of adapting themselves (with certain modifications that would be written in as possibilities) to eligible fixed structures in an arbitrary way, but with the restriction that, in the "course" of the development, any given happening could occur only once. Finally, in order to oppose the horizontal and the vertical by means of an enlargement of this simple notion, certain structures would be juxtaposable or superposable, either completely or partially; that is to say, either beginning at a given junction point or until one is reached—with the positive or negative criterion that the necessity or the absence of superposition will impose upon the written text. We are thereby faced once more with the demands of writing: how indeed are the requirements of these structures going to manifest themselves in their actual realization? Obviously, they will be evident first of all in the timbres, which are the most easily perceptible phenomena; by referring to instrumental groups or, less categorically, to certain instrumental combinations, we will make outstandingly clear to the listener the intercrossing and multiplicity of the developments; this will be one of the most effective ways of making them come alive, of having them constantly reach our sense understanding. But if one does not want to have timbre as a principal basis— it may happen that a concern with monochromy is all-important—the tempo, either fixed or changing, will be made to intervene as the predominant characteristic; it is, in effect, the speed at which a structure unfolds (sometimes variable, sometimes less so) that contributes most notably toward characterizing it. I have just spoken, in sum, of two "enveloping" phenomena, namely tempo and timbre; the third, similarly "enveloping" phenomenon will be the kind of writing, by which I mean the external aspect of the writing itself in its horizontal, vertical, or oblique conception. Realized in this manner, and limited by these three external characteristics, a structure ought to correspond to the nomenclature that we developed earlier.

We have spoken of definite and indefinite structures, of divergent and convergent ones; these terms characterize two families that are dialectically opposed to each other. Returning to the comparison we made earlier in connection with the probabilities of a musical "point," we can extend it to the structure itself. One will move from the indefinite to the definite, from the amorphous to the directional, from the divergent to the convergent according to the greater or lesser degree of automatism one leaves to the factors of development, depending on the negations that one opposes, in greater or lesser number, to the limitless expansion of their possibilities. One thus moves from complete freedom to strictly limited choice, which is a classical opposition that has always distinguished severe style from free style. If I have chosen to use these different expressions, it is in order to underline the importance I attach not only to the internal constitution of a structure, but also to its possibilities of being linked to other structures, whether by isomorphism or polymorphism or from one unit of development to the next. It is undeniable that these expressions fit music only approximately and that, in the absence of more directly appropriate terms (it will be up to musicology of the future to discover them), we must make do with a vocabulary whose scientific elements run the risk of being misunderstood because their meaning will not be transposed. We must, however, accept this temporary risk in order to clarify notions that are still in their infancy. One sees, consequently, how the "formants" of composition can link together in families these different types of structures more intrinsically than the circumstantial "envelopants" of which I spoke earlier are able to; one also sees how a general notion of phrasing can foreshadow, in a way, the disposition and agogics of these structures in the composed work. Beginning with an initial, principial sign and ending with an exhaustive, conclusive sign, the composition manages to involve what we were looking for at the beginning of our investigation: a problematical "course," depending on time—a certain number of aleatory happenings inscribed in a mobile period of time—but having a logic of development, an over-all sense of direction—with the possibility of caesuras, either silent ones or platforms of sound—a course going from a beginning to an end. We have respected the "finished" aspect of the Occidental work, its closed cycle, but we have introduced the "chance" of the Oriental work, its open development.

However, what we have just described applies, in a way, to a homogeneous sound-space of timbres, of time, of intervals. If we attempt to achieve a total variability and relativity of the structure, we must use a space that is not homogeneous, particularly with regard to its time and its intervals. In its development, today's music proves that it calls increasingly upon notions that are variable in their very principle, obeying hierarchies in evolution. That is why we have already seen the series of twelve equal sounds replaced by series of sound-groups, always of unequal density; that is why we have seen metrics replaced by the series of durations and of rhythmic groups (rhythmic cells or combinations by superposition of several durations); that is why, finally, we have seen dynamics and timbre no longer be limited to their decorative and emotive qualities but acquire, in addition to these privileges, a functional importance that reinforces their powers and their dimensions. Thanks to electro-acoustical means, and even to various instrumental techniques, we can break the homogeneity of the sound-space in the changing distribution of its frequencies, either by creating various forms of temperament or by completely excluding temperament. In the same way, the continuity of the machine and the discontinuity resulting from the inner pulsation of the interpreter destroy at its very base the homogeneity of musical time. It is not our aim in this article to show how these nonhomogeneous spaces are arrived at; accordingly, we shall do no more than call attention to the fact in order to make apparent what repercussions it can have on the notion of structure; it imposes upon this notion in its principle a new "chance"—one that is certainly the most discrepant.

The danger of these investigations, if they are turned aside by weakness or inadvertence from their true goal, consists in the composer's running away from his own responsibility, in his shirking the choice inherent in any kind of creation. Even on a superior level, the *ossia* cannot be the last word of invention. But, on the other hand, the possibility of adapting to composition the notion of the series itself, by which I mean the possibility of endowing the structure with the more general notion of permutation—a permutation with limits that are strictly defined by the restriction of the powers imposed upon it by its self-determination—such a possibility is a completely justified, logical evolution since the same organizational principle rules both morphology and rhetoric.

From the practical point of view of performance, what do the un-usual dimensions of a work created in such an esthetic and poetical context require of the interpreter? Is it even possible to bring into ac-cord the work and the instrumentalist or the work and the conductor who is supposed to direct it? Assuredly, yes; there are already examples to prove so among those works that usher in this new form of musical being. If there is only one performer, there is no difficulty, unless it be that he must have more initiative than before, since this initiative, this collaboration, is required by the composer. A certain number of signs, different typographical characteristics will serve as sure guides to the interpreter in the choices that he will have to make. (Let us not forget that this choice is not necessarily a selection, but can be limited to a variable freedom of execution.)

When there are two instrumentalists, two pianos, for example, the problem remains practically the same, with the supplementary adop-tion of signals and guide marks in common. If, for example, a fixed tempo for one piano is superposed on a variable tempo for the other (an accelerando, for instance), it will be enough to indicate the meeting places—departure and arrival—of the two structures, points whose co-ordinates the composer will have calculated with the greater or lesser amount of precision he requires at that particular moment. It may even happen that, once the composer has chosen appropriate registers, the two time structures may be entirely independent, in which case he will merely indicate within what interval of time he wishes such sequences to be played. Simple familiarization with these guide marks and signals quickly effaces the impression one may have of being "abandoned" by one's partner when one is no longer linked to him by a strictly synchronous metric.

Finally, when one directs a piece of music conceived in this way, the conductor's role consists essentially in giving signals, which a convention clearly understood by his musicians will separate into specialized signals to indicate the departure from the principal tempo, the return to this tempo, or the periodical coincidence with it. If the musicians deviate individually from the general tempo, the conductor "centralizes" the indications, so to speak. But when—with an orchestra—a group of musicians is supposed to adopt a variable tempo, either a first-chair player or an assistant conductor will be called upon, and he will rely on the principal conductor for all fluctuations. These problems of group performance actually are not radically different from the difficulties encountered every day in the theater; their solution is relatively simple. The only obstacle to be overcome, from the very beginning, is seeing to it that the musicians feel *free* with regard to the conductor and not "abandoned" by him; it is essential, therefore, to make them aware of their individual tempo in relation to the individual tempo of each of the others. When this is accomplished, the divergences blend into a balanced whole.

It is certain that one cannot go "toward this supreme conjuncture with probability" with an unalienable sense of security. In this connection people will not fail to put us on trial once more for "dehumanization"; the high-flown ineptitudes that are passed around on this subject are inexhaustibly monotonous; they can all be reduced to a signally low conception of what is meant by "human." A lazy nostalgia, a predilection for *pots-pourris* (very *pourris*) that are sometimes called syntheses, such are the "heartfelt" longings of these vigilant disparagers. We can answer, on the most elementary level, that far from denying or annihilating him, we reopen the creative circuit to the interpreter, who for a number of years has been asked merely to play the text as "objectively" as possible. Why, what we wind up with is actually a glorification of the interpreter! And not at all an interpreter-robot of terrifying precision, but an interpreter who is involved in what he is doing and is free to make his own choices.

As for those who might be worried by this dynamite introduced into the heart of the work, by this chance that resists "composition"—and who would point out to us that human poetics and extra-human chance are inalienable, irreconcilable enemies incapable of providing any positive result by being amalgamated—we will quote for their benefit this paragraph from *Igitur:* "In short, in an act involving chance, it is always chance that accomplishes its own Idea by asserting or denying itself. Negation and affirmation come to nought in the face of its existence. It contains the Absurd—implies it, but in a latent state, and prevents it from existing: and this makes it possible for the Infinite to be." Perhaps it is reckless—and insolent—to embark upon this voyage, shrouded in uncertainty, but isn't it the only way to try to *fix the Infinite?* Such is the unavowed pretension of anyone who rejects pure and simple hedonism, limited craftsmanship, in a creative universe that is overwhelmed with its burden of humble frauds. Any dilettante will find himself torn to pieces by a responsibility that lies beyond these schemes, any toiler— frightful notion—will be reduced to nothing by the inanity, the vacuity of his labor. In the end, would this not be the only way to kill the *Artist?*

[Translated by David Noakes and Paul Jacobs]

MUSIC: A VIEW FROM DELFT

EDWARD T. CONE

A LTHOUGH this discussion is to be concerned primarily with music, it received its impetus from the puzzled delight long afforded me by the contemplation of Vermeer's *View of Delft* — puzzled because of my inability to account for my reaction to this apparently objective representation that, without obvious sentimental or personal associations, was nevertheless deeply moving. To have dismissed the problem would in no way have interfered with continued enjoyment; yet it seemed worth while to try to uncover the reasons for the picture's attraction, in the hope of revealing some principle of wider application to painting in general and to the other arts.

The method by which I arrived at a preliminary solution was to compare actual scenes with hypothetical Vermeer-views. What did my own eyes fail to catch that the painter's depiction would have revealed? Some kind of unity, perhaps; for on this much all traditional esthetics seems to be agreed. In the case of the *View of Delft* it is true that on whatever aspect one concentrates, one finds visual coherence: in its surface texture, in its unobtrusive composition, in its subtle harmony of color, in its pattern of light and shade. Whether the painter found these designs in the scene before him and emphasized them, or whether he imposed them upon a formless visual matrix, the high degree of relation they exhibit is the most obvious difference between the painted landscape and the actual one. But it is not the sole difference, for the casual observer misses not only the unity in the scene before him but its bewildering multiplicity as well. It is the endless complexity of every visual event that furnishes the painter with his apparently inexhaustible store of motifs, and the most complete view is the one that does greatest justice to the variety of these forms.

The Vermeer-view, then, embraces the complexities of the scene and relates them in an all-pervading unity. The artistic value of the representation is the result of the tension between these two poles. To enjoy the *View of Delft* because of its unity of design, or because of its complexity of motif, or even because of both, is to miss the point. Perception comes at the breath-catching moment of realization that the tension between the two has been brought into balance by the vision of the artist. The test of the balance is whether the unity seems to grow out of the complexity on the one hand, and to engender it on the other. The two aspects are not merely realized simultaneously; they are organically united. What is more, the unity is immediately perceptible within the medium of the art itself — it is primarily visual, not intellectual.

Further investigation led to the conclusion that the poles of unity and complexity are only the first and most important of numerous possible tensions, and that on a higher level the artist's job is to create a perceptible unity out of the complexity resulting from just this multiplicity of tensions. This complexity I call textural complexity, each of its components being a dimension of the texture. Such dimensions in a picture might consist of the following sets of poles: detail vs. whole, brushstroke vs. area, color vs. form, light, and line in turn. The completed picture must not only resolve each of these polar tensions but also combine the resolutions in such a way that they appear to be the multiple aspects of a single all-inclusive structure.

Crucial for painting is the tension between abstract and representational form, for the moment the element of representation enters a picture every motif must respond equally to the demands of the abstract design and of the depicted subject. It is not enough that the demands of a polar couple be satisfied simultaneously; they must be satisfied together organically, so that each member of the pair grows out of the other. Thus the two structures, abstract and representational, must be more than parallel. They must fuse by mutual analogy, so that they become two ways of looking at one single, basic structure — two points of view, either of which can be interpreted as an analogue of the other. It is consequently impossible to look at the *View of Delft* as either representation or design alone; each implies the other.

If the apparently multiple structures comprised in the complete work are united in this way, none can lead away from the others — that is, out of the picture. The adjustment is difficult and often fails; but the attempt of some painting to solve the problem by banishing the subject refuses to recognize one more implication of Vermeer's masterpiece: that for fullest enjoyment we want the medium of an art to be saturated — used to the fullest extent in every dimension. If this is so, non-objective painting must be ultimately less satisfying than painting that successfully exploits the tension between subject and design. For many observers, this proves in fact to be the case.

II

These principles — of polar tension, of fusion by mutual analogy, and of saturation — I now propose to apply to music. Two points must be stressed at the outset, both so obvious that they may otherwise be forgotten. The first is that the unity of the musical composition must be perceptible within the medium: it must be heard. The second point is that the apparently simple surface of some music may in fact conceal great richness. The unfortunate result of Gounod's attempt to add a melody to Bach's Prelude suggests that the latter, in spite of its superficial transparency, is in fact a highly saturated composition of considerable textural complexity.

Since music is a temporal art, certain possibilities are open to it that are unavailable to painting. Time, of course, yields the dimension of rhythm, which will be discussed in some detail later. It also makes possible a kind of suspended saturation: the development of an idea which on first presentation may seem of insufficient moment, but which through its treatment grows in interest, its true purport being revealed only gradually. Beethoven's *Diabelli Variations* are a triumphant example of a completely saturated form arising from an unpromising hypothesis.

Time also permits the development of the tension between the detail and the whole in a new and important way. In painting, the relevance of the detail to the entire composition is ideally immediately comprehensible. In music, the appearance of each new detail is an occasion for suspense: how will it be related to its context, and how will the context fit into the whole? One could write a history of music — at least of the last two hundred years — in terms of varying solutions (and dissolutions) of the problem arising from just this polar couple.

The detail-whole tension is of course not the only source of suspense, which is such an important characteristic of all time-arts that without some form of it the medium inevitably seems insufficiently saturated. Traditional tonality was fortunate in having at its command a built-in technique, so to speak, for producing and controlling suspense; and one of the fundamental tasks of the atonal idiom has been to find substitutes or analogues for its powerful effects.

Time, then, is the source not only of opportunities and advantages but of problems and responsibilities as well. Other difficulties, equally fundamental, arise from another characteristic of the musical medium: its abstractness. These have to do with the question of expressive content, and with the role of so-called extra-musical elements — verbal, programmatic, or purely emotional. Are these just extraneous adjuncts, at best useless and at worst dangerous? Are they optional embellishments? Or are they properly speaking not extra-musical at all but intrinsic to the art? Perhaps the argument from Delft can throw some light here.

I shall not try to decide whether or not music can express or communicate or embody emotions or moods or types of activity, nor shall I try to explain how such expression or communication or embodiment might be possible. I propose a simpler investigation. Assuming that music can express emotion (and you may substitute whatever verb and object you prefer), I shall try to determine a few of the consequences.

If such expression is possible, its presence will open another dimension much as the representational subject does in painting. But just as the mere presence of a depicted subject is far from being a guarantee of quality and may even be a detriment if clumsily handled, so with the expressive content in music. To say of a composition that it conveys sorrow or embodies agility or induces contemplation is to make a statement of only preliminary esthetic importance. The artistic value arises from the coalescence of the abstract form and the expressive design in such a way that each can be interpreted as a consequence of the other. Every event demanded by the purely musical pattern must correspond to an event demanded at that point by the psychical pattern. If the composition is successful, the two streams, musical and psychical, of the mingled flow are felt as analogically fused — in effect as one. Realization of the unity thus created produces an excitement like that occasioned by the moment of perception we experience before the Vermeer.

It follows that if such enrichment of the medium is possible, failure to take advantage of it is a violation of the principle of saturation. I think this is rarely a danger. If expression of this type is possible at all, in a medium apparently unrepresentational, it is probably because its vehicle is as deeply embedded within the medium as the meaning of words in a language. It would be as hard to write music without expressive pattern as to write literature independent of verbal connotations.

The question next arises whether the use of a specific extra-musical program would not offer similar, and even greater, enrichment. If so, then the principle of saturation would suggest that Liszt and Strauss were on the right track after all. But I shall try to show that the desirability of a program does not necessarily follow from the preceding argument, and that the use of one exposes a work to real danger.

Expression of the type so far expounded neither requires nor invites non-musical formulation. It is based on largely preconscious and subconscious attitudes that are uncovered only by the action of the music itself and hence defy every effort at verbalization. It is no wonder that most composers are unable or reluctant to give an account of this aspect of their work, since it depends on processes of which they are at most only partly aware. For convenience, I shall call expression of this kind, characteristic of what is usually called absolute music, inherent expression.

The program, on the other hand, by definition a non-musical formulation of content, suggests expression of quite a different kind — literal, specific, descriptive — the appropriateness of which cannot be deduced from the argument applied to the case of inherent expression. Assuming as before its possibility, we see that content of the second kind can hardly appear in a composition except as the result of deliberate effort on the part of the composer. Its nature and origin always encourage suspicions that it is wholly or partly adventitious — doubts that have no occasion to arise with respect to the inherent expression of absolute music. It is possible, of course, and frequent in the case of the best program-music, for the composer to ignore the more literal aspects of his subject and to use it purely as a suggestive source of musical thought. The results then fall into the first category and can be judged quite apart from their ostensible program.

If, however, the composer insists on employing a program in the fullest sense of the word, and if he actually needs such a stimulus to his musical imagination, what is the positive danger? Let us assume that a non-musical subject can be adequately communicated through music, by imitation, movement, and mood, and further, that a composition has grown naturally out of this subject: why should we not find in the music the same kind of added textural dimension as that afforded by a subject in painting? The comparison falls down at first examination. A painting does not move in time; the entire scene and the entire design are equally before our eyes as we look at it. The relationships of part to part and the analogical connection binding its various dimensions are constantly open to view. Music, as it moves through time, must make its formal relationships clear from moment to moment; and for most listeners it is task enough to assimilate these as they flow by. The program insists that the listener follow it as well, an independent verbal structure, and at the same time try to relate it to the musical form. What happens in fact is that the hearer concentrates on the music, in which case the program is superfluous; or he concentrates on the program, in which case he is taken out of the music (just as one is led out of a picture by bad story-telling); or he compromises and spends an uneasy time trying to direct his attention now here, now there, now somewhere in between.

There is good program-music, to be sure. If a program is simple enough to be grasped without effort and obvious enough to make its point in music without elaborate translation, or if the music is so completely formed that the program is unnecessary, then one can listen with enjoyment. Otherwise the program, far from enriching the general texture, contributes to the weakening and even the disintegration of the musical fabric.

III

An obvious objection to the foregoing argument will have occurred to the reader. How can song exist? Isn't this the supreme example of the attempt to unite two structures of dissimilar media? And doesn't opera become quite impossible? The questions are proper, but the answers may prove surprising.

The universality of song attests that neither musicians nor their audiences have found practical difficulties in this direction. Obviously we can and do hear words and music together as forming some sort of unity — a unity, moreover, that ideally includes the meaning as well as the sound of the words. On the other hand, it is instructive to remember the failure of the Romantic melodrama, which attempted in a thoroughgoing way to create a musical accompaniment expressively paralleling the text; it turned out to be only program music with the program read aloud. The unresolved tension between word and tone makes it impossible for the listener to attend to both — a difficulty that haunts even *Sprechstimme,* a much closer approach to true song. (The effectiveness of such rare exceptions as the melodramatic passages in *Fidelio* and *Der Freischütz* depends on careful musical and dramatic preparation.)

These difficulties indicate that it is not sufficient for the music to *accompany* the words, no matter how illustrative or expressive the accompaniment may be. Nor is it sufficient for it to *set* them — to approximate as closely as possible the pattern of the verbal rhythms; for in this case the music only emphasizes what is already evident to the sensitive reader. But both accompaniment and setting have their functions in the fulfillment of the proper task of the music: to *compose* the words — to surround and envelop them in such a way that both their sound and their meaning become part of the musical texture itself. The music assumes a form and mode of expression analogous to those of the poem, but to the poem as modified in turn by the music — the poem as sung rather than as read or recited. Some poets object that the result is actually a new poem — and with some reason. For the text not only shapes the music but in turn is shaped by it, in every feature susceptible of such control: its meter, its pace, its larger and smaller rhythms, its melodic rises and falls, its climaxes. Only by this interaction can the desired resolution be effected.

What is more, this unique relation of the musical and the modified poetic forms must be revealed by the primary role of the human voice, entrusted alike with the words of the poem and the controlling line of the music. Whatever the composer may wish to do besides in the way of accompaniment, of illustration, or background, is well and good; but if he forgets that the voice is the one element through which the unity of the song is manifested, he jeopardizes all — as even Wagner magnificently did. Too often his orchestral flow usurps the primary role to such an extent that the effect is only one step away from that of melodrama. The voice still sings, it is true, but only to convey the words; it has lost its musical function.

Another danger is the one into which many Baroque arias fall. They achieve a unity, but a purely musical one. The words are treated not as a text but as a pretext for the exploitation of the vocal instrument.

The successful song, as described above, is one more example of the principle of analogical fusion. Music and words appear to be, not parallel structures, but two aspects of a single organism. For this reason the text and setting of the best songs give the illusion of being "twin-born" even when not actually so.

Such masterpieces as these, rare though they may be, show triumphantly that words and music, properly combined, produce no conflict of attention in the listener. Nevertheless, discretion in choice of text and of musical idiom increases the chance of effectiveness. It is no accident that opera-composers have resorted to recitative of comparatively simple musical content in order to put over complicated expository passages and have built sumptuous musical edifices out of arias with comparatively easy words. I do not mean to imply that relative complexity of music and text must always be in inverse ratio, but that too much activity in both may lead to the fatal division of the listener's attention. Exceptions like Bach's highly developed choruses on important doctrinal clauses are only apparent. In the first place, he could depend on the familiarity of the text to his audience (an important consideration in most liturgical music); moreover, he treated the words relatively abstractly, building huge sections out of single clauses.

Oddly enough, it can be argued that opera needs less justification than any other type of vocal music, except possibly that associated with ritual. The action on the stage, if properly coordinated as functionally analogous to the combined form of music and text, can actually clarify the relations between these two and make them more immediately, since visually, perceptible — just as the dance can sometimes clarify rhythmic relationships by creating visual analogies for them. This may not often happen, but it is the ideal that operatic composition, both of libretto and of music, and operatic staging, direction, and performance, should always keep in mind.

As a short, suggestive example I shall take a familiar passage from Verdi, whose operatic superiority to Wagner is indicated in some measure by his simpler, more immediately apprehensible, and hence theatrically more suitable style. In fact, at first glance an aria like *La donna è mobile* may seem too simple, until it is remembered that in music, and especially in opera, a relatively unpromising idea may be in a state of suspended saturation, depending on future developments to make its import clear. Such is the case with this aria, whose virtue lies in the fact that it will be immediately grasped and constantly retained by the audience. Just as the figure of the Duke, gradually retiring from the visible scene, remains nevertheless constantly in the dramatic background, so his tune, now as the bassoon underlines the conspiracy against him, now as he tries to sing sleepily from his bedroom, produces an analogous musical structure. The effect could be clinched by clever staging that never lets the audience forget his presence as the focal point of the intrigue. The same kind of staging could emphasize the threefold irony of the last appearance of the same air: its carefree melody, the Duke's cynical words, and the calm after the storm — all in utter contrast to the actual situation. The simple-minded tune should break upon the audience with the full horror of Rigoletto's own realization. The material is there, in the libretto and in the score. Imaginative stage-direction could use it to produce an over-whelming effect.

It is thus not simply the combination of elements that gives opera its peculiar fascination; it is the fusion produced by the mutual analogy of words and music — a union further enriched and clarified by the visual action. It is not impossible that vocal music, by virtue of the added com-plication of the text, works in a more completely saturated and hence more satisfying medium than purely instrumental music does. If this is the case, it would seem to follow that opera, with the added third dimension of the stage, must offer the most intensely satisfying experience of all. For whatever reasons, many people have certainly thought so, and many evidently still do.

IV

It is now time to look at music from a more technical and hence less controversial point of view. What pattern, if any, can Vermeer's eye discern in the developments of the past two hundred years? What advice has Delft to offer us today?

The Golden Age of functional tonality, which I take to be a rough century including Bach and Handel, Mozart and Haydn, Beethoven and Schubert, witnessed a synthesis of all musical elements into forms as self-sufficient as any that music has ever known. The tension between detail and whole was here brought into equilibrium; musical suspense was under complete control; the shapes demanded by the respective needs of melody, harmony, and rhythm were integrated into a rich, multidimen-sional whole. Previous Golden Ages, which had produced the master-pieces of Gregorian chant and of Renaissance polyphony, had depended to a large extent on the shaping power of the word. The 18th century found all the form-giving factors it needed in music alone. When it used the word it did so as another dimension, analogous to the purely musical ones.

The ways in which this coordination of the compositional elements was achieved are well known. In view of what follows, however, I must recall one obvious but important point. It is impossible, except by analy-sis, to separate melody, harmony, and rhythm in the masterpieces of this period. Functional harmony has a life and laws of its own, but in the actual music it is constantly and indissolubly the support of the melody. Conversely the melody, or melodic line in a polyphonic texture, can be heard, not only for its own sake, but as an element of the harmonically controlled part-writing. Most subtle of all is the rhythmic organization, which even up to now has defied proper analysis. Rhythm, which after all exists only as a series of relations, is during this period so deeply embedded in the other elements through which it speaks that it seems to disappear whenever we try to search it out. But everywhere we look, whether at general proportions, at phrase-structure, at harmonic rhythm, or at rhythmic motifs, we find patterns interesting not only for their own sake but also, and especially, for the way in which they control, and are controlled by, the other elements. In no other respect is the mastery of the composers of the Golden Age displayed so clearly.

It was precisely with this most fundamental and at the same time most delicate of relationships that the dissolution began. The rhythmic breakdown was the first and one of the most unmistakable of the signs that the Golden Age was over. There were indications of what was to come even in Beethoven, whose employment of rhythmic motifs sometimes seems over-emphatic to those who prefer the exquisite balance of Mozart, and in Schubert, whose sense of proportion sometimes failed him in his recapitulations. Beethoven's usage heralded a development he would have deplored: the gradual dissociation of rhythm from the other components of the synthesis, a phenomenon that, while producing interesting and varied patterns in the small, nevertheless led to the ill-proportioned forms, the monotonous phrase-structure, the endless sequences, and the other excesses that blemish some of the best music of the later 19th century. Schumann deliberately played with the dissociation, even though he was a victim of it. Brahms strove heroically to take advantage of the resulting ambiguities (which constituted the positive contribution of the new rhythmic techniques) by bringing them into a new synthesis, emulating that of the previous century. But the course of the evolution could not be stayed. As great a master as Wagner failed to solve the rhythmic problem; it overwhelmed lesser ones like Bruckner.

The disintegration was proceeding in other ways as well. The Romantic conception of a "melody" was an important indication. For composers of this period, a melody was just that: independent of harmony, of accompaniment, of texture, even of rhythm (witness the thematic transformations some of them were so fond of). These other elements often seemed to be regarded as mere decorative adjuncts, and one melody could appear in many garbs. Contrast with this the Classical ideal, which was hardly one of a "melody" at all, but of a unique and characteristic combination in which melody, harmony, rhythm, and texture all played their parts. The rise of orchestration as an independent skill during the 19th century is further evidence of the same trend, the implication being that choice of instrumentation is simply an additional means of coloring a preconceived passage.

The breakdown of harmonic cohesion in favor of the proliferation of details, especially in Wagner and Strauss, has often been noted. At the same time, the harmonic integrity was being threatened in another way: by the overelaboration of function. Bruckner, particularly in his last works, stretched chordal implications further than the ear could follow them, since he failed to support them by adequate melodic and rhythmic analogies.

Now, it would be an oversimplification to call Impressionism, as represented by Debussy, an attempt to solve the rhythmic problem, and Expressionism, with Schoenberg, an attempt to solve the harmonic one; but I believe the values of the generalization in the present context outweigh its dangers. Debussy cut the tenuous thread still holding the musical elements together, so that rhythm and melody could develop independently of harmony. What this really meant was that they developed at the expense of harmony, which became static and coloristic, almost an aspect of the newly important dimension of timbre. In turn, melody and rhythm suffered their own impoverishment. The former, deprived of functional support, found its line broken into fragmentary motifs; and even these are often less memorable for their contours than for their rhythmic patterns. Rhythm, for its part, could no longer express itself in strong harmonic movement and thus lost one of its most powerful embodiments.

The same traits of static harmony, rhythmic independence, and fragmentary melody characterize some 20th-century music not usually classified as Impressionistic, including, for example, much of Stravinsky and Bartók. In spite of successes that number some not inconsiderable masterpieces, the style must inevitably suffer in comparison with that of functional tonality. The forcefulness of its integration, particularly on the level of the detail-whole tension, is questionable; its saturation with respect to the harmonic dimension is low.

Schoenberg's interest in solving the harmonic problem represented by the continuing decadence of traditional tonality led to his discovery and systematic use of serialism, particularly in its twelve-tone form. As opposed to the Impressionistic method, Schoenberg's is a thoroughgoing attempt at reintegration; as a result it is by far the more vital of the two today. But it brought with it its own difficulties, two of which are especially relevant to this discussion. The first question is one raised by atonality in general, whether serial or not: does this style exploit the medium as thoroughly, with as great richness and complexity, as functional tonality? In a word, is its saturation as complete? A negative answer, as in the case of Impressionism, would by no means invalidate the style or the music written in it; but it would point up its limitations. The second question is related more specifically to the twelve-tone method itself. Has it adequately solved the rhythmic problem? Has it found a way to build rhythmic structures analogous to those of its other dimensions?

The answers to the first question are as varied as the composers who produce them. Schoenberg soon discovered the value of row-transpositions, not simply to add variety but to fulfill a form-giving function much as modulation did in older music. These transpositions, in connection with the hexachordal make-up of his rows, produce the effect in his later works of a kind of super-tonality, perceptible even when not precisely definable.

Berg was much more explicit in his tonal references, which seem to some critics trivial and obvious. It is true that the tonal functions to which he adverts are simple and in themselves not very interesting. What he was after, I think, was a new kind of tension produced by the poles of tonality and atonality appearing simultaneously or successively in the same composition. It is the precarious balance between them that gives much of Berg's work its peculiar intensity and individual flavor.

The music of Webern, the most thorough of the three in its rejection of traditional references, is harmonically the simplest and texturally the most transparent. Two points should be noted, however. Webern was primarily a song-writer. The added dimension of the voice, to which he was unusually sensitive, may not only compensate for the thinness of the purely musical component but at times even require it. In the second place, Webern's transparency enabled him to emphasize coloristic, polyphonic, and rhythmic aspects that were more important to him than the harmonic. The apparent simplicity conceals beneath it a web of subtle relationships, the tensions between which are held in delicate balance. Some listeners find the web too fragile, its substance too slight. None can question its exquisite workmanship.

In the best of this music, then, the medium is used with something that corresponds to or at least substitutes for the richness of tonality. Indeed, this is the surest criterion of quality in twelve-tone compositions. The rhythmic situation is more problematic and is still a source of deep concern to serious composers.

The tonal references of Berg and the quasi-harmonic system of Schoenberg go hand in hand with considerable reliance on traditional rhythmic procedures. The results are well integrated in their own terms, and the unity produced is both audible and esthetically satisfying. But many dodecaphonists now believe that these older masters failed to realize the full potentialities of the system, which should be made to yield its own rhythmic types. Complete saturation of the twelve-tone medium, they feel, implies a rhythmic structure somehow derived from the principles that govern the tone-row itself. Webern, in this respect as in others, came nearer to the radical ideal. So far as I have been able to discover, he did not serialize his rhythm, but he did often try to order it in a pattern parallel to that of the pitches. Thus the palindrome, in which a stated passage immediately retrogresses in both pitch and time-value, was a favorite device. At the same time he must have realized two points: the impossibility of a true rhythmic retrograde involving attacks (something becoming dubiously available only now by electronic means); and the fundamental psychological fact that whatever arbitrary direction may be assigned to events in space or on paper, we can experience them in only one direction — forward. It is for these reasons, I think, that he was always careful to project his abstract designs against a strict, steady meter. Performance is difficult, since it must try to do justice to the almost irreconcilable demands of the rhythms and the meter; but when it is successful it reveals that Webern's rhythmic sense, for all its responsiveness to the demands of the new style, was firmly rooted in the past. The patterns that appear rigid on paper sound free and flexible precisely because they are supported by the composer's mastery of the traditional methods of articulation.

Today these apparent compromises fail to satisfy the demands of the radicals. More and more attempts are being made to serialize not only time-values but every type of relationship: dynamics, modes of attack, tempos, proportions. Superficially, it might seem that the result would be a completely saturated structure of analogies in many dimensions. The crucial question remains: Do they coalesce in an aurally perceptible unity? In an attempt to demonstrate that they do not, I pass over such techniques as the serialization of dynamics and attacks — any application of which can, I believe, be shown to be arbitrary — in order to concentrate on the exemplary problem of the durational row, whether applied to simple note-values or to longer sections.

The great stumbling-block in the way of the integration of a pitch-row with a durational one is that no common measure exists. There can be none even by analogy, since we perceive time and pitch in markedly different ways. We hear time-segments as durations, and we measure one against another, more or less proportionally. Pitches we hear as discrete points, ordered but not quantified. Numerical values assigned them by frequency are useful in physics but not in music; we simply do not hear tones in this way. Even if we accept some kind of proportional measure (such as Krenek's based on the comparison of interval-sizes) as perceptible in the domain of pitch, we cannot compare it with durational measure without first transforming each into arithmetical terms. The connection between the two remains indirect and intellectual, not perceptual; it is based, not on mutual analogy, but on the relation of each dimension to an abstract third one.

Similar objections hold against the claim that no common measure is necessary, that the principle of serialization itself is sufficient to unite its own divergent exemplifications. By whatever criterion the time-sequence is chosen, the combination of tone-rows and time-rows produces no synthesis but rather the unfolding of two parallel strands, each logically ordered within itself but lacking the cogent connection with the other necessary for a unitary aural impression. The relationship between the two types of series is not audible — only inferable from an abstract, extra-musical premise. If the desired connection is in fact heard, the success depends on factors derived from outside the system — just as in the music of the three early masters.

There are other difficulties as well. How would one apply the fundamental operations of the serial system to the time-row? Retrogression is easy, but what of inversion and transposition? Babbitt's suggestion that numerical complementation is analogous to inversion is brilliant, but as a practical technique it suffers from the kind of abstraction pointed out above. We do not actually hear complementation and inversion as similar operations; we come to this conclusion only after associating each with an arithmetical equivalent. But art is not a branch of mathematics, and quantities equal to the same quantity are not necessarily equal to each other. The same argument applies to the various analogies that have been suggested to effect temporal "transposition."

The trend towards abstraction is a dominant one today, and an unhealthy one for art. The devices criticized here, introduced in the hope of achieving a perfect unity within the twelve-tone system, have resulted in producing a unity, it is true — but outside the medium, in the realm of arithmetic. They take us out of the music as directly as any program ever did. In some of the serial compositions written today the application of the tone-row itself has become so abstract and far-fetched that it is no longer felt as a form-building force. In this case, the listener perceives nothing but chaos, or else he is forced to find some new kind of order. If the former, then the composition is only nominally music. If the latter, then of what value is the supposed serial order?

By the foregoing I have not meant to imply that some kind of rhythmic structure unique and proper to the system cannot be found, but I insist that it will not be discovered by the doctrinaire application of rigid principles. Rhythm, the most fundamental of musical dimensions, is the most vital and has never submitted for long to the fetters of formulation and schematization. If the new principle finally emerges, it will be in and through the music itself. It may even turn out that the classical twelve-tone composers were on the right track after all, and that the answer lies in the evolution of traditional procedures rather than in a revolution against them. If no solution is found, the serial method will nevertheless remain a noble attempt to establish another Golden Age.

BEYOND ANALYSIS*

EDWARD T. CONE

E X A M P L E S 1–3 present the beginnings of three hypothetical compositions. If they sound both oddly familiar and familiarly odd, that is because they were derived by the simple application of a mirror to three well-known sources: Schoenberg's *Klavierstück,* Op. 33a, and the first and third movements of Webern's *Variationen für Klavier,* Op. 27. Hence if the reader wishes to complete these constructions, he will find it a straightforward and even mechanical task.

Ex. 1

Ex. 2

Ex. 3

* This paper was presented in slightly different form as a lecture at the Summer Institute of Compositional Studies of the American Society of University Composers at the Berkshire Music Center, August 1967.

The possibility of such derived compositions was suggested to me by a famous passage from Schoenberg's essay "Composition with Twelve Tones":

The unity of musical space demands an absolute and unitary perception. In this space, . . . there is no absolute down, no right or left, forward or backward. Every musical configuration, every movement of tones has to be comprehended primarily as a mutual relation of sounds, of oscillatory vibrations, appearing at different places and times. To the imaginative and creative faculty, relations in the material sphere are as independent from directions or planes as material objects are, in their sphere, to our perceptive faculties.[1]

No doubt I have taken this passage more literally than its author intended. So far as I know, Schoenberg never tried to demonstrate that the strict mirror inversion of a twelve-tone composition must be as valid as the original—but this might indeed be one conclusion that could be drawn from the quoted passage. It is also—and this is my real starting-point—a conclusion that might be drawn from reading much, and perhaps most, accepted twelve-tone analysis today.

My research into this question has been by no means exhaustive; furthermore, although I feel confident that the analytic essays I have studied constitute a representative sample, I have no way of proving this. The only fair way of presenting my case, then, is to list the actual examples I have used and the results I have obtained.

To begin with, the master's analyses of his own works in the essay just cited would apply equally well if the compositions in question were replaced by mirror inversions of themselves. One need only make the obvious adjustments: substitute for the original form of the set its inversion, for any transposition its complement, and so on, and the analysis can easily be made to read accurately. Only the references to instrumentation (which appear by way of description rather than analysis) might cease to be relevant.

One may immediately counter that what Schoenberg was presenting was not analysis but an explanation of a method—and a very primitive explanation at that. One could not expect him to have developed the sophisticated and powerful tools of analysis at our disposal today. Very well, then, look at as varied a compilation as the following: Milton Babbitt's three classic statements, "Some Aspects of Twelve-Tone Composition,"[2] "Set Structure as a Compositional Determinant,"[3] and "Twelve-Tone Invariants as Compositional Determinants";[4] Ernst

[1] Arnold Schoenberg: *Style and Idea*, New York, Philosophical Library, 1950, p. 113.

[2] *The Score*, No. 12 (June 1955), pp. 53–61.

[3] Below, p. 129ff.

[4] *Problems of Modern Music*, ed. Paul Henry Lang, New York, W. W. Norton, 1960, pp. 108–21.

Krenek's analysis of his own *Lamentatio* and *Sestina* in "Extents and Limits of Serial Technique";[5] the entire second issue of *Die Reihe,* devoted to Webern; and, despite their promising titles, George Rochberg's "The Harmonic Tendency of the Hexachord"[6] and his "Webern's Search for Harmonic Identity."[7] In none of the foregoing would the line of argument have to be changed if the entire body of twelve-tone composition were magically transformed into its exact inversion, for in every case the only pitch relationships discussed are those that remain invariant under inversion. Even such extended monographs as Joseph Rufer's *Composition with Twelve Tones*[8] and George Perle's *Serial Composition and Atonality*[9] exhibit only a few unsystematic exceptions to this general principle. One further example that is especially indicative is Allen Forte's analysis of the Schoenberg Fantasy Op. 47 in his *Contemporary Tone-Structures,*[10] for it is the only analysis in the book that foregoes some sort of Schenker-like linear reduction. In demonstrating the continuity of the Fantasy it relies entirely on connections between row-statements, all of which would work equally well for the mirror inversion of the composition.

As might be expected, PERSPECTIVES OF NEW MUSIC offers an unusually rich harvest of apposite examples. These include David Lewin's "A Theory of Segmental Association in Twelve-Tone Music";[11] John M. Perkin's "Dallapiccola's Art of Canon";[12] Babbitt's "Remarks on the Recent Stravinsky";[13] Perle's "An Approach to Simultaneity in Twelve-Tone Music";[14] Peter Westergaard's "Toward a Twelve-Tone Polyphony";[15] and about a half-dozen of the "Younger Composers" series.

Especially interesting is another essay of Babbitt's, "Twelve-Tone Rhythmic Structure and the Electronic Medium,"[16] which develops a method of deriving a rhythmic row from the intervals of the basic set. Perhaps here one can find a criterion for distinguishing the original composition from its inversion. But no: since the direction we choose for counting notes or for calculating intervals is a matter of pure convention, an inverted set can always be made to yield the same rhythmic row as its original (i.e., by counting intervals *down* rather than up from the origin).

[5] *Ibid.,* pp. 72–94.
[6] *J.M.T.,* Vol. III, No. 2 (Nov. 1959), 208–30.
[7] *Ibid.,* Vol. VI, No. 1 (Spring 1962), 109–22.
[8] Translated by Humphrey Searle, New York, The Macmillan Co., 1954.
[9] Berkeley, University of California Press, 1962.
[10] New York, Teachers College, Columbia University, 1955, pp. 110–27.
[11] Below, pp. 180–207.
[12] Vol. 1, No. 2 (Spring 1963), pp. 95–106.
[13] Vol. 2, No. 2 (Spring-Summer 1964), pp. 35–55.
[14] Vol. 3, No. 1 (Fall-Winter 1964), pp. 91–101.
[15] Below, pp. 238–260.
[16] Below, pp. 148–179.

Allen Forte's "Context and Continuity in an Atonal Work"[17] shows, by its treatment of Schoenberg's Op. 19, that my suggested transformation need not be limited to twelve-tone works. From this essay (as well as from appropriate sections of Perle's book) one might go much further and conclude that, barring purely instrumental difficulties, a new composition can always be constructed to fit any purely contextual analysis merely by inverting the original—regardless of its style and technique.

(It should perhaps be pointed out here that the aforementioned instrumental obstacles to literal inversion are not so formidable as one might think. Much twelve-tone music is conceived in a texture that, even when not strictly polyphonic, nevertheless depends on an equalization of voices and registers. When the analyses refer to instrumentation they usually do so to point out identities and contrasts that can easily be maintained under inversion.)

So far I have said nothing about the possibility of another kind of systematic transformation, namely, complete retrogression, which, if accepted, would in turn imply the availability of retrograde-inversion as well. Although Schoenberg insists that, just as there is theoretically no "absolute down," there is no absolute "forward or backward," there are nevertheless occasions (as often when a row is divided among two or more voices) when an exact reversal would fail to produce a correct set-form. The reversion of a twelve-tone piece, then, cannot always be depended on to produce another "correct" twelve-tone piece. On the other hand, there are certainly many examples that can be reversed with impunity, especially if one is not doctrinaire and allows the reversal of approximate attack-points as an alternative method to the reversal of time-values. And slight modifications of the rules governing note-counting (such as the option of counting a note on its *last* appearance in a given context) would open the door to universal retrogression.

To be sure, the distinction between forward and backward ought to be made from a wider point of view than that of pure note-counting. Schoenberg himself, later in the above-quoted essay, implies that, regardless of theory, practice may require such a distinction. His statement that "One could perhaps tolerate a slight digression from this order [of the basic set] . . . in the later part of a work, when the set had already become familiar to the ear,"[18] suggests that a composer must, sometimes at least, take into account the order in which musical events take place. But this rule is vague and by no means self-evident; besides, there are many compositions to which it does not apply, since they never depart from the original set except in canonical ways. And when these methodical departures are used, Schoenberg's rule is frequently disre-

17 Vol. 1, No. 2 (Spring 1963), pp. 72–82.
18 *Op.cit.,* p. 117.

garded. We have his own example, in the Fantasy Op. 49, of a composition that begins by developing a single hexachord, stating the definitive set only when the piece is well under way. And Milton Babbitt's Composition for Four Instruments reserves its definitive statement for the end, after a systematic treatment of derived sets.

One may nevertheless feel intuitively that something is wrong: that retrogression in music, whatever its technique, should have as little general validity as in literature or in cinema. And certainly compositions planned according to traditional rhetoric—e.g. introduction, statement, development, climax, restatement, peroration—hardly admit of intelligible reversal. Yet it is just these elements of form in the music of those composers, such as Schoenberg and Berg, who relied on older models, that a later generation has found old-fashioned and is trying to purge from its own music. Accordingly, it is just these elements that are ignored in many analyses today.

If we search the above-cited essays, we find very little help in deciding just why those compositions lacking a text move in the direction that they do, or—a related question—why they end just when they do. The analyses, with few exceptions, demonstrate connections—how one section is related to another—rather than progressions—how one section follows from another. Such relationships as repetition, similarity, contrast, common-tone linkage, and the like, are as independent of temporal as of pitch direction. Similarly, discussions of harmony concern themselves with the derivation of simultaneities, but hardly with the justification of the motion from one to another; criteria for melodic construction are never mentioned. Thus, for purely instrumental compositions lacking passages where the exigencies of strict note-counting determine the direction of events, forward and backward indeed seem to be indistinguishable. Webern's fondness for the palindrome, which celebrates musical reversibility, may be an indication that his own thought was moving in this direction.

(In this paper I have not considered the systematic transformations effected by equating the chromatic scale with the circle of fifths. I leave to others the exercise of determining to what extent the cited analyses would remain applicable to versions so derived.)

So far, none of the transformations I have discussed has affected the internal structure of the compositions in question. Now, however, I should like to suggest the possibility of operations of this kind. One of the points that emerges from a recent colloquy among Babbitt, Perle, and Lewin on the Schoenberg Violin Concerto[19] is that, although it may be imprecise to treat transposition as analogous to tonal modulation (as Perle at

[19] Lewin, *op.cit.* Perle, "Babbitt, Lewin, and Schoenberg: A Critique," PERSPECTIVES OF NEW MUSIC, Vol. 2, No. 1 (Fall-Winter 1963), pp. 120–27; followed by Babbitt's reply, pp. 127–32.

one point seems to try to do), transpositions can nevertheless create the effect of a more or less wide departure from an originally stated quasi-harmonic area—not just by differences in register, but also and especially by common-tone relationships among segments of two or more forms of the set. The number of such common tones, e.g. between the first hexachord of the original statement and that of a given transposition, might be a measure of the "harmonic" distance of the transposition; and measures of this kind might then form a basis for "harmonic" progression through a piece. To return now to a composition to which I have already done violence, and which I intend to manhandle still further, let us see how this concept applies to Schoenberg's Op. 33a, and how it can be used to compose an alternative development to Schoenberg's—an alternative that, according to the accepted principles, should be an adequate substitute for the original. Here are the set-forms Schoenberg uses (with P and I reading left to right, R and RI right to left):

$P_0:$	Bb	F	C	B	A	F#	C#	D#	G	Ab	D	E	$:R_0$
$I_0:$	Eb	Ab	Db	D	E	G	C	Bb	Gb	F	B	A	$:RI_0$
$P_2:$	C	G	D	C#	B	G#	D#	F	A	Bb	E	F#	$:R_2$
$I_2:$	F	Bb	Eb	E	F#	A	D	C	Ab	G	C#	B	$:RI_2$
$P_7:$	F	C	G	F#	E	C#	G#	A#	D	Eb	A	B	$:R_7$
$I_7:$	Bb	Eb	Ab	A	B	D	G	F	Db	C	F#	E	$:RI_7$

First trichords arranged in fifths:

$$
\begin{array}{ccccccccc}
 & I_0 & & .I_2 & & P_7 & & & \\
Db & Ab & Eb & Bb & F & C & G & D \\
 & & I_7 & & P_0 & & P_2 & \\
\end{array}
$$

Common tones in first hexachords of P_0 and I_2: Bb F A F#
Common tones between end of development and beginning of recapitulation: C F Bb Eb Ab

Of the above forms, the exposition employs only the T_0; the development uses the T_2 and T_7; the recapitulation returns to the original forms.

Now, it can be shown that, in making his first transposition (T_2), the composer has exploited two relationships, both indicated in the above chart: the common tones of the first hexachords of P_0 and I_2, and the series of fifths implied by the first trichords of P_0 and I_0 and explicitly stated in m. 25. These fifths, extended, then help to make the connection between T_2 and T_7. But in this piece every statement of a P-form (or R) is complemented by its combinatorial I-form (or RI). The same common-tone and fifth relationships, then, could equally well have been exploited by the composer in the reverse direction by using T_{-2} (i.e. T_{10}), followed by T_{-7} (i.e. T_5). Thus:

P_{10}:	A♭	E♭	B♭	A	G	E	B	C♯	F	G♭	C	D	:	R_{10}
I_{10}:	D♭	G♭	C♭	C	D	F	B♭	A♭	E	D♯	A	G	:	RI_{10}
P_5:	E♭	B♭	F	E	D	B	F♯	G♯	C	D♭	G	A	:	R_5
I_5:	A♭	D♭	G♭	G	A	C	F	E♭	B	B♭	E	D	:	RI_5

First trichords arranged in fifths:

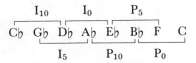

Common tones in first hexachords of I_0 and P_{10}: A♭ E♭ G E

Common tones between end of development and beginning of recapitulation: F B♭ E♭ A♭ D♭

I have written out a hypothetical new development section along these lines (Ex. 4).

Schoenberg's development initially exploits the E♭-B♭-F fifths; mine, the A♭-E♭-B♭. For his common-tones between R_0 and I_2, I have substituted those between RI_0 and P_{10}. The rest of my development can easily be followed by comparison with the original. At the recapitulation, Schoenberg makes a connection from the last tetrachords of R_7 and RI_7 to the first of P_0 and I_0. My version, leading from R_5 and RI_5, preserves the same number of common tones between the tetrachords of the development and those of the recapitulation—five; four of them, including the important connectives B♭ and E♭ (the first notes of the recapitulation) are the same as in the original. (In fact, of the eight tones constituting the end of my development, all but one are the same as those of the original.)

Before going further, I must insist that my attempt in none of these rewritings has been to improve on, or even to equal, the original. I am merely trying to show that the analytical methods used by the essays cited offer no criteria for deciding in each case between the two versions.

Ex. 4

It is now time for a brief look at those analyses that do try to offer criteria for distinguishing up from down, forward from backward. My admittedly incomplete survey disclosed several worth noting for their efforts in this regard. Claudio Spies's discussion of Stravinsky's *Abraham and Isaac,*[20] like Edward Laufer's account of Sessions' *Montezuma,*[21] can call on the demands of text-setting and on other associations between music and words; but deprived of these, Spies's analysis of the "Huxley" Variations[22] has to fall back on such concepts as those of antecedent and consequent phrases—usefully evocative, perhaps, but undefined in this context. In the same spirit, René Leibowitz, in his *Qu'est-ce la Musique de Douze Sons,*[23] makes vague analogies between Webern's phrase-construction and Beethoven's. His *Introduction à la Musique de Douze Sons,*[24] in its long analysis of Schoenberg's Variations for Orchestra Op. 31, points out the traditional models the composer used to give shape and temporal

[20] PNM, Vol. 3, No. 2 (Spring-Summer 1965), pp. 104–26.

[21] PNM, Vol. 4, No. 1 (Fall-Winter 1965), pp. 95–108.

[22] *Ibid.,* pp. 62–74.

[23] Editions Dynamo, Liège, Pierre Aelberts, 1948.

[24] Paris, L'Arche, 1949.

direction to his large-scale designs but evokes no further criteria of the kind we are seeking—save the quotation of the BACH motif. Even the discussions of orchestration emphasize symmetries, parallelisms, similarities, and contrasts that, as I have already suggested, can easily be retained under inversion.

Peter Westergaard gives us a glimmer of hope in his attempt to justify the meter of the second movement of Webern's Piano Variations Op. 27.[25] He suggests that here the invariable appearance of the lower of each pair of three-note chords at the beginning of the measures in which they appear emphasizes the two-four meter. But even if one decides that Boulez is wrong in maintaining that Webern's meters are purely conventional and not meant to be observed in performance,[26] one must point out that the placement of low chords in the other two movements gives us no indication whatsoever of their meters. One would also question whether the regular appearance of the *higher* of each pair of chords on strong beats might not equally well establish the meter. In fact, this movement, the inversion of which is such a trivial operation that it can almost be performed at sight, offers a simple and complete demonstration of the problem I am raising. (It should be noted that Westergaard, in his mention of "the Haydnesque wit" of the two-quarter rest just before the end, does give us one reason for preferring the original direction of this movement to its reversal. But one might wonder why, if such a gesture so clearly—and so wittily—marks the end, the entire section is then repeated. And might not the same gesture wittily serve as an introduction?)

Of the remaining critiques that I have considered, most of those that make a structural distinction between soprano and bass—to put the problem of total inversion in its simplest form—and concern themselves with progression—to do the same with reversal—do so by means of linear and harmonic outlines vaguely derived from Schenker's methods. Attempts of this kind may be seen in two articles on Sessions: one by Andrew Imbrie[27] and the other by Edward Laufer.[28] Richard Swift also moves in this direction in his account of J. K. Randall's *Demonstrations*.[29] But what right has one to call on such devices in this context? In tonal music, the motion of the bass can be derived from some expansion[30] of the tonic chord; that of the soprano, by passing-motion within the scale. But what does either tonic or passing-note mean when there are no previously or permanently defined chords, and no functionally operative

[25] "Webern and 'Total Organization,'" PNM, Vol. 1, No. 2 (Spring 1963), pp. 107–20.

[26] "Propositions"; *Polyphonie* 2me cahier, 1948, p. 67.

[27] "Roger Sessions: In Honor of His Sixty-Fifth Birthday," PNM, Vol. 1, No. 1 (Fall 1962), pp. 117–47.

[28] *Op.cit.*

[29] PNM, Vol. 2, No. 2 (Spring-Summer 1964), pp. 77–86.

[30] I.e., by the elaboration of the interval between root and fifth.

scales? Can this music really be approached through attitudes and habits derived from listening to tonal music? And would a tentative and qualified assent to that question commit us to an acceptance of the tonal analogies Spies finds in the late Stravinsky,[31] or to approval of Martin Boykan's still bolder tonal approach to the same composer[32]— not to speak of Hindemith's rigid application of his own tonal principles in his well-known analysis (or mis-analysis) of a passage from our old friend Op. 33a?[33] Or should we put all such interpretations in the same category as the explanation of the French word-sequence *Pas de lieu Rhône que nous* as making sense in spoken English?

Again, should even the presence of clear triadic references be taken at tonal face-value? Leibowitz recognizes the possibility of their creating a "tonalité *vague,* incertaine," especially in the works of Berg, although ultimately it is the "logique du maniement sériel" that must provide justification for all that happens.[34] Rufer, on the other hand, seems to believe that such tonal impressions are more illusory than real, and at any rate are useless for our purposes:

> Thus triads of tonal structure can appear too, as, for instance, the "Ode to Napoleon" shows. But these, like *all* chord-structures in twelve-note music, are of purely local importance and do not produce harmonic progressions which have the effect of creating form, as happens in tonal music; for the relationship to the key-note is missing.[35]

Who is right?

The fact that one can raise such questions shows that we have arrived at a crucial point in the history of Western music. Up until now there has been no ambiguity between up and down—at least not since the fourth was distinguished in effect from the fifth; there has been no question of choice between forward and backward since the appearance of the melodic cadence—and, later and a fortiori, the harmonic cadence; there has been no transpositional relationship that could not be explained by reference to some sort of tonic. But these aspects of composition, hitherto accepted as basic, are apparently unaccounted for by twelve-tone theory.

If one accepts this conclusion, one can adopt one of three attitudes toward it. One can welcome it wholeheartedly, agreeing that there really is no basis for choice among my hypothetical versions beyond the con-

---

[31] "Some Notes on Stravinsky's Requiem Settings," PNM, Vol. 4, No. 2 (Spring-Summer 1967), pp. 98–123.

[32] " 'Neoclassicism' and Late Stravinsky," PNM, Vol. 1, No. 2 (Spring 1963), pp. 155–69.

[33] *The Craft of Musical Composition,* Book I, New York, Associated Music Publishers, Inc., 1937, pp. 217–19.

[34] *Introduction,* pp. 282–85.

[35] *Op.cit.,* p. 126.

venience of accepting what is already given and the comfort of familiarity. But that only throws the problem back where it really belongs in the first place: on the shoulders of the composer. How did he make his decisions in these matters?

This leads us to a second point of view: that twelve-tone theory is as yet incomplete, and that the superiority of one version of a composition over another depends on purely formal factors as yet unanalyzed but nevertheless eventually analyzable, analogous to the laws of linear and harmonic progression in tonal music, possibly similar to those but not necessarily so. A composition is successful insofar as its composer has made his implied choices among conceivable alternatives in accordance with his intuitive, or, better, his partly rational understanding of these presumed laws.

Finally, one can accept the primacy of the composer's concrete choices but insist that, far from being made in obedience to laws known or unknown, they are so fundamental to the composer's conception of his work as to belong, so to speak, among its basic assumptions. They are determined by what may be called *absolute decisions,* i.e. decisions for which no adequate analytical reasons can ever be adduced.

If many of us at first glance opt for the second point of view, it is because the success of theorists of tonality, notably Schenker and his followers, has given us hope that all the secrets of contemporary composition await analogous types of explication. But a more sophisticated generation of theorists—as exemplified by Milton Babbitt and Michael Kassler —has been pointing out what a flimsy systematic basis even Schenker's splendid construction rests on.[36] In trying to establish tonal theory more firmly, they dismiss Schenker's appeals to Nature, the Human Spirit, and the Overtone Series, in favor of a strictly logical system derived from a limited number of axioms and rules of inference. For these axioms they offer—naturally—no proof whatsoever. But if we accept this approach, we must admit the possibility of equally consistent systems that we might call anti-tonal. By regular and easily definable modifications of the axioms and rules of inference such systems could lead to compositions that are the total inversions, retrogressions, or inverted retrogressions, of conventional tonal compositions. Other transformations too, are possible. Deprived of all natural bases, what appeals could the conventional system make against such rivals save those of convenience, tradition, custom, and familiarity? (It is instructive here to note that in

---

[36] See Milton Babbitt, "The Structure and Function of Musical Theory," above, pp. 10–21; Michael Kassler, "A Trinity of Essays," a dissertation for the Ph.D. in the Department of Music, Princeton University, 1967. The essay dealing with the twelve-tone system was published in PNM, Vol. 5, No. 2 (Spring–Summer 1967), pp. 1–80, as "Toward a Theory That Is the Twelve-Note-Class System."

the earlier case we could perform the hypothetical operations on individual works, for the operations themselves constitute "rules of inference" of the system. Since this is not true of tonal music, the operations must be applied to the system as a whole, not to individual works—a possibility adumbrated in the case of inversion by proponents of harmonic dualism from Zarlino to Riemann.)

We can perhaps recognize here one motive that has driven so many theorists to find some kind of support in the existence of the overtone series, and we can sympathize with them even though we cannot follow them. They seem to consider the role of the series as somehow analogous to that of gravity in architecture: a raw fact of physics that must be taken into account in creating viable structures. But the analogy can be turned against them: every building is a success insofar as it defeats gravity. Moreover, the gothic vault and the cantilever attest the futility of arguing that good design is necessarily based on the *visual* exploitation of physical principles. True, the overtone series does indeed make a distinction between up and down within the individual tone, since overtones are, after all, above the fundamental. Furthermore, one must take account of the series in the physical construction and practical use of instruments. Neither of these facts, however, justifies the claim that the *auditive* structure of music, whether tonal or not, necessarily depends on the composition of the series. In fact, only today, through electronic means, is it becoming possible to integrate, in a systematic and thoroughgoing way, overtone spectra, whether natural or artificial, into musical structures.[37] Ironically, the same media now offer for the first time the theoretical possibility of inverting the audible spectra. Such complete tone-color inversion would at last deprive the individual tone itself of the possibility of distinguishing up from down!

If now, in spite of the discouraging example of the tonal system, we still insist on seeking some basis for making distinctions that we still feel to be somehow essential, let us turn to the third alternative: that there is, and can be no analytical ground for concrete musical choices, i.e. no ground within the internal structure of the music itself; yet that these choices are crucial in determining musical values, i.e. salient characteristics that afford a basis for distinction, comparison, and judgment. (Critical listeners, as well as composers, must also make such choices, although in a slightly different sense; for all judgments are based on implicit comparisons between actual and possible compositions, and hence on a choice among concrete values. Indeed, it was from this point of view that we initially approached the problem.) To put the position succinctly:

[37] See, for example, J. K. Randall: "Three Lectures to Scientists," below, pp. 116–26 and 208–13. The third of these, "Operations on Waveforms," deals with this possibility.

concrete musical values depend on absolute decisions. Remember that by absolute I do not mean arbitrary: there may be, as we shall see, good reasons for making one choice and not another. By absolute I mean independent of purely analytical considerations and unsusceptible of purely analytical justification.

Let me try to clarify this point by referring to another art, this time painting. Suppose an artist is painting a monochromatic picture, or simply making a drawing. Every formal element of the pictorial structure will then depend on line and light-value, not on color-relationships. But how does the painter decide what color to use? He might rule out certain colors as incapable of sustaining his design—yellow might be too light, for instance; but he would still have a wide range of choice. If the decision is not a purely capricious one, it must be based on reasons; but these reasons cannot be analytical, since the internal structure of the picture will be the same in any case. The reasons must therefore be external to the structure. The picture may be intended for a room with a given color-scheme. The artist may feel that a warm or a cool color might be more appropriate to the subject of the picture. He may even feel that one color has a vague expressive value consonant with the subject. Or he may simply revel in the sensuous quality of one color.

Let us take another example, one somewhat analogous to the problem with which our discussion began. How does an artist (or an observer) decide which way a picture should hang—which way is right-side up? Good design seems often to be independent of whether or not it is inverted —an assumption supported by the habit, common among painters, of testing their compositions by viewing them upside-down, as well as by the frequency of mistakes in the hanging of abstractions. (We seem to measure balance with reference to a vertical axis, possibly because of our own physiological orientation, so that ninety-degree rotation is seldom a live option—although Carl Pickhardt has experimented with free-form abstractions that can be hung at *any* angle.) In the case of a representational picture the answer to our question is obvious—unless the artist is Chagall (or, apparently, sometimes Matisse, whose *Le Bateau* hung upside-down in the Museum of Modern Art in New York City from Oct. 18 to Dec. 4, 1961).[38] But we arrive at this answer by a reference outside the picture—to the depicted subject. Indeed, from the point of view of pure design, the orientation of a picture must often be based on an absolute decision—one made with reference to representational rather than to structural values. Apparent arguments from design will in such cases merely conceal external references. For example, to the claim that a landscape must hang as it does because the lighter area looks better at

[38] Norris and Ross McWhirter, *Guinness Book of World Records,* Rev. and enlarged edition, New York, Bantam Books, 1966, p. 157.

the top, one can counter that the only justification for this preference is that this is the way landscapes look in nature, and one can point to many abstractions in which the lighter areas are below. How, in fact, does one determine the orientation of an abstraction? How does the artist himself make that decision? In the absence of any clear indication from the design, the decision must be absolute. The reasons on which it is based will be external to the pictorial structure, whether the artist says simply, "This is the way I like it," or more specifically, "The expressive effect of the picture would be harmed if it were inverted."

We have arrived here at an important point. Expressive values in any art—if they exist at all—depend on concrete values. They cannot arise from analytical values alone. How could they? Unless one wishes to explain what it could possibly mean for a work of art to "express itself," then one must agree that expression, by its very definition, implies a relationship between the work of art and something else; while analytical values are derivable purely from internal structure. This is in no way meant to suggest that structure has nothing to do with expression. Just as communication in a verbal language depends on both semantics and syntax, so artistic expression must involve both concrete and analytical values. Without the former, the structure could convey no message; without the latter, the message would be limited to the equivalent of primitive substantives and exclamations. Thus the expressive power of an abstract canvas cannot stem from its design alone; it must depend in part on some covert representational or other associative element (as, for example, the illusion of "mass" or "movement").

The foregoing suggests that those who wish to make special claims for the role of the overtone series in tonal music, or for what can be much more easily defended, the primacy of the fifth, a more fruitful analogy than that of gravity in architecture might be that of representation in painting. For whereas gravity is a law of nature that controls all construction even though it may be apparently refuted to the eye, representation is merely a reference to nature that can be utilized or not according to the purposes of the artist. Similarly, even if one holds that the supremacy of the fifth in tonal harmony derives from a natural law, one must admit that a great deal of music ignores it; hence it must be a law in a different sense of the word than the law of gravity. Yet it could still be a law to this extent: that in all music that exploits the fifth in a tonal sense, the special relation of fifth to fundamental, whether due to definite though ill-defined roots in physical and anatomical nature, or simply to the growing force of conventional habit over several centuries, inevitably determines the orientation of the music, i.e. its direction both in pitch and in time—just as representation determines the orientation of a picture.

Such a view of tonality is by no means inconsistent with the recent attempts to explain the system axiomatically. It merely insists that such explanations can never adequately deal with the problem of orientation. If tonal music carries with it its built-in orientation, then it is built in absolutely, not analytically. It rests, not on the internal consistency of the system, but on some connection between the axioms and rules of inference on the one hand, and the external world on the other—whether that world is represented by acoustics, psychology, physiology, or history. The orientation is, so to speak, semantic rather than syntactic.

One who accepts the analogy implied in the last sentence may be willing to go further and admit the relevance of tonal orientation to the problem of musical expression. If the effect of the fifth in tonal music is, to some extent at least, independent of context and external to pure design, then elements of musical form inferable from the role of the fifth (e.g. tonal cadences) could serve as vehicles of some of the associative elements necessary to expression (e.g. the association of a perfect cadence with fulfillment or satisfaction). It is tempting to say of such instances that the structure alone is the vehicle of the expression; and from this error it becomes easy to generalize to the extent of basing all musical expression on pure syntax. That is because tonal music marries the semantic and syntactic aspects so closely that it is difficult to conceive of the semantic element in isolation. One should really speak here, not of syntactic and semantic, or of analytic and concrete, but of *fused* values; for in the best tonal music the two aspects of tonality are indeed indissoluble. But recent music has suggested new possibilities. Just as representational implications (such as those of mass and motion) can impart some meaning to a pictorial abstraction, so tonal references can function in non-tonal music, not so much syntactically as associatively, bringing with them implications of the orientational and expressive values inhering in tonal contexts. At the same time these references, arising as they do from syntactical origins in tonal music, must, if they are to be successfully employed, satisfy whatever syntactical expectations of this nature they arouse. Such references may vary from, say, a bald statement of consonant triads to a generalized adaptation of melodic-harmonic relationships and phrase-structure.

Thus music whose syntax is primarily twelve-tone may nevertheless legitimately call upon implicit tonal functions to clarify its concrete values—so long as the functions, once summoned, are permitted, so to speak, to fulfill their tonal responsibilities. A complete explication of this music must then take these tonal allusions into account—whether they are overt, as is often the case with Berg, or concealed, as in much of Schoenberg. (Note, for example, in Op. 33a, the V-I effect created by the bass connection B♭-E♭ from the development into the recapitulation—an effect signally, and perhaps disastrously, lacking in my version.)

Today composers can choose for themselves whether or not to utilize tonal references. For centuries, of course, the individual composer had no such option. The decision was already made for him, just as the decision as to the use of representation was already made for the painter. Nations and historical periods, as well as individuals, choose concrete values through absolute decisions; hence we can speak of national and historical as well as individual styles. That is what style is: the totality of the concrete values characterizing a given body of work as a whole. The stylistic decision of a group may seem to be so completely determined by evolution, environment, or culture, that it should not properly be called a decision at all; yet it functions in the same way as an individual decision, for it results in one mode of action that rules out all alternative modes. Perhaps because of their deterministic origin, these decisions are even more binding on the individual than his personal choices, which may vary from work to work. Thus if tonality carries with it certain associations, then these associations are bound to leave their mark on all music of the tonal period just as inevitably as the presence of the realistically depicted human figure is bound to affect the content of painting from the Renaissance up to the end of the nineteenth century.

Tonal functions are, to be sure, not the only source of associative values. Once one admits the relevance of these values at all, one finds them involved in almost every area of concrete musical choice. And once we leave the specific problems of tonality, we find that many concrete values have been equally at the disposal of composers in many styles, using diverse techniques. But all these values presuppose absolute decisions; so, although the tonal composer may never have had to wonder whether or not his composition was running in the right direction, even he, like his present-day successor, was constantly confronted by choices that could never be made on analytical grounds alone. How did he determine tempo? The internal structure of most compositions imposes certain limits within which a tempo must be sought, but these limits are often very broad indeed. We can all think of compositions that would still make perfect musical sense if taken at a tempo twice as fast or twice as slow as that indicated; why then should the indicated tempo have precedence? Because the composer chose it? But why did he choose it?

Register is another example. How would the structure of the Chopin C minor Prelude, or of his Funeral March, suffer if the piece were written a fifth higher—or even an octave higher? Yet such transpositions would manifestly alter the effect of the pieces, and hardly for the better. (Roger Sessions reports that he once succeeded in turning Scriabin's

"Black Mass" Sonata [No. 9] into a White Mass by playing it an octave higher, and in turning the "White Mass" [No. 10] into a Black Mass by reversing the process.)

Even instrumentation depends to a large extent on absolute decisions. This is especially easy to demonstrate with regard to monochromatic media, where the problems of interrelationships among colors hardly arise. Beethoven, for practical purposes, was willing to transcribe his *Grosse Fuge* for piano four-hands. Brahms did the same for his two string sextets. They are fun to play that way—but it is hard to get anyone to listen. Why? What crucial analytical values, present in the string version, are lost in the transcriptions?

Decisions in these matters must be made by all composers, regardless of style and technique. Each one of them determines certain concrete values that, moreover, are associative values; and whether we like it or not, these associations are bound to inhere in the music itself. Tempo is inevitably measured by unconscious comparisons with rates of human action; register relates itself to our concepts of height, weight, and mass; tone-color brings with it obvious connotations of all kinds, from our tendency to identify melody with the human voice to resemblances of the sort that so delighted the little Stravinsky in the "dubious" noises produced by the red-haired peasant.[39] Many other areas in which associative values are unavoidably implied will come to mind: absolute dynamics, melodic direction, rhythmic and metric patterns. Again, whether the associations are in some sense "natural" or whether based on generations of conditioning, they cannot be escaped by anyone musically trained in the Western tradition.

To be sure, choices in these areas are influenced by structure—but they control structure as well. Insofar as they characterize even the primitive gestures of the composer's initial ideas, and hence precede the musical design itself, they are independent and necessarily defy analysis. The design must take shape in accordance with their directions.

If one accepts the possibility and the relevance of musical expression, one may indeed feel that one's decisions here are governed, consciously or unconsciously, by the expressive potentialities of the associations inherent in one's concrete choices. Or one may insist that the decisions are, in every sense of the word, absolute. What I suspect, but am unable to prove, is that any concrete choice made on the basis of pure personal preference functions in the same way as one made with expressive intent and that the two may indeed be equivalent. To put the case at its most trivial: Why is my composition superior to its inversion? Because its melody descends. Why should the melody descend rather than ascend? Because I like it that way! But why do I like it that way? Because I want it

39 Igor Stravinsky, *An Autobiography,* New York, Simon and Schuster, 1936, pp. 3–4.

to have the effect that can be produced by descent but not by ascent. Or—because I want it to express whatever it is that descent can express and ascent cannot express.

It should now be obvious that what I have been calling concrete choices are in many cases not choices at all, in the sense of representing the exercise of a live option. The absolute decisions of a composer—for *this* melody, in *this* tempo, in *this* register, for *this* instrument—are seldom the result of the conscious dismissal of other alternatives, even though any voluntary action implies the rejection of every other action possible on that occasion. The composer decides what piece he is going to write, not all the pieces he is not going to write; what I have been calling choices are really the assumptions basic to his concept of that piece. Yet there are certain occasions, especially frequent in connection with the development of previously stated ideas, that do seem to offer several workable alternatives. As I tried to show by means of a change in the development of Op. 33a, it is often difficult to advance analytical reasons to justify one's choice at such a point; we may perhaps now be willing to admit the example as evidence that the domain of a composer's absolute decisions embraces even the internal structure of a twelve-tone piece. As a final task, I shall try to show the same principle at work in tonal composition.

For obvious reasons, it would rarely be possible to invert successfully the harmonic direction of a tonal development as I tried to do with Schoenberg's. But one field of choice presents itself with a high degree of regularity: the opportunity of changing mode. Once the convention of the tierce de Picardie was overthrown, it became a matter of the composer's choice whether a piece in minor ended in major or minor; later on, in the nineteenth century, it became increasingly common for works in major to end in minor. In many cases it seems impossible to find adequate analytical reasons for the ending actually adopted. Think over Schubert's *Moment Musical* No. 3 in F minor. Can you adduce any analytical evidence for the inevitability of its conclusion? Could you not rewrite the coda so that it ended convincingly in minor? Compare the C♯ minor *Moment Musical* No. 4 with Chopin's Etude in E minor Op. 25 No. 3 and his Nocturne in C minor Op. 48 No. 1. All three of them move to the tonic major in the middle section, so that all have, so to speak, a motive for ending in major. Only the Etude does so; the Nocturne remains in minor; while the *Moment Musical,* after a short reference to the major section, returns to minor. And what of Chopin's Nocturne in B major Op. 32 No. 1? Is there any necessary reason for its conclusion? (And just what is this conclusion, by the way? Some editions end in minor, some in major. Historical evidence seems to favor one over the other. Would you be willing, on analytical grounds, to decide which?)

If you deny that these romantic examples are in the front rank of tonal structures, then work on Beethoven's String Quartet in F minor Op. 95. You can perhaps justify certain aspects of the coda by analysis, but that is not the same as proving its inevitability. Can you, on internal evidence, show that just this coda, in this tempo, above all in major, is the only possible ending for this quartet?

Whether Schubert, Chopin, and Beethoven—or, to return to our original problem, Schoenberg and Webern—made their decisions on expressive grounds or whether they wrote their compositions the way they did simply because they liked them that way, my point is the same: their reasons are beyond analysis. And if we as critical listeners conclude that the composers were right, it should not disturb us to find that our own reasons are often beyond analysis, and that, when we try to explain the superiority of a composition over any alternative version, sometimes all we can say is, "It sounds better."

A great deal of current writing on music seems to imply that nothing about composition, or nothing important about composition, is beyond analysis. But surely the single most important thing anyone can say about any composition is beyond analysis: namely, "I like it." It is especially disturbing to find that many young composers, who presumably write about the music of others the way they think about their own, are either insensitive to non-analytical values or—as I think more likely—afraid to admit their importance. As a result they often seem to be writing, not about actual compositions, but about abstractions derived from compositions. Now, I recognize the great debt we all owe to increasingly rigorous methods of analysis, and I am fully awake to the dangers of impressionistic criticism; yet I find myself completely on the side of the young composer—a rather well-known one—who, when asked why he wrote as he did, replied, "I like the tunes."

ON THE PROTO-THEORY OF
MUSICAL STRUCTURE

RICHARD M. MARTIN

JUST AS music history is a species of history, so no doubt is music theory a species of theory. Hence music theory should have some structure in common with other theories. The question is, then, what is this structure? And of what species of theory is music theory?

To specify a theory in logically acceptable terms is usually no easy matter. Every theory involves an underlying logic, and the many alternative logics clamor here for attention. Even after the underlying logic has been agreed upon to be of such and such a kind, we then must worry about (i) the special domain of objects allowed as values for variables and (ii) the basic classes (or domains or sorts) into which these objects may be grouped as well as the basic relations whereby they may be related. Item (i) has to do with the choice of an *ontology* for the theory and (ii) with the choice of suitable non-logical *predicate* or *relational constants* as primitive or undefined. Only after (i) and (ii) have been well settled is it of any interest to start the search for axioms. In the process of getting a theory, the gaining of axioms comes at the very end.[1] Let us begin then at the beginning with (i) and (ii), the ontology and the primitive predicates. This much might be called "the *proto*-theory of music."

We should first note that proto-theory need not involve the complexities exhibited by many scientific or philosophical theories. For example, music theory need not, it seems, involve *modal* logic, or *three-valued* logic. In modal logic, it will be recalled, notions of *necessity* and *possibility* play fundamental roles, and in three-valued logic a "value" intermediary between the truth-values *truth* and *falsehood* is admitted. It is very doubtful that such notions need play any role in music theory. Nor for that matter need music theory assume such complicated mathematical axioms as the axiom of choice, or, say, the continuum hypothesis. In fact it is not clear that music theory need even

[1] For additional comments see the author's *Belief, Existence, and Meaning* (New York: New York University Press, 1969). On being values for variables, see W. V. Quine, *Word and Object* (New York and London: The Technology Press of the Massachusetts Institute of Technology and John Wiley and Sons, 1960), esp. pp. 242ff.

involve a second-order or higher logic.[2] Presumably lower logic, the familiar elementary logic of first order, may be made to suffice. Let us follow, here and wherever possible, the Ockhamite principle that *frustra fit per plura quod potest fieri per pauciora*.

Actually three frameworks for music theory will be sketched in this paper: first, one presupposing a second- or third-order logic, then a first-order version of essentially the same, and finally a first-order version of a theory based on *events*.

In first-order logic, it will be recalled, we have the various truth-functional connectives 'and,' 'or,' 'if—then,' 'if and only if,' and 'not' as well as the quantifiers 'for all x,' 'for some x,' and identity. The variables range only over the *individuals* in the ontology of the theory at hand. In second-order logic, we have, in addition, variables and quantifiers over classes of individuals and relations between or among individuals, and in third-order logic, still additional variables and quantifiers over classes of and relations between these latter. The resources of third-order logic are thus very much more powerful than those of the former. It will become clear in a moment just why a third-order logic is needed for the first formulation.

The distinction between *sign-designs* and *sign-events* is a familiar one in logical syntax. A sign-design is an abstract shape or pattern, outside of space and time. A sign-event, on the other hand, is a phenomenal occurrence within both space and time as well as (presumably) within some human experience.[3] In music theory, we have two analogous distinctions to make. We must distinguish the *note-shape*, or class of notes, common to all texts or editions of a given composition, from the *note-event*, a certain ink-mark on a certain page of a certain text. Likewise we must consider what these are supposed to stand for. We may speak here of *tone-* or *pitch-shapes* or *-classes* as over and against *tone-* or *pitch-events*.[4] We may ask, then, whether music theory should be concerned with pitch-classes or pitch-events—for which we take would entail an enormous difference in the resulting theory. (The theory of note-shapes and/or note-events constitutes presumably the

---

[2] On second-order logic, see especially Alonzo Church, *Introduction to Mathematical Logic*, Volume I (Princeton: Princeton University Press, 1956), Chapter V. See, however, Michael Kassler, "Toward a Theory That Is the Twelve-Note-Class System," PERSPECTIVES OF NEW MUSIC, Spring-Summer 1967, pp. 1–80, which involves a still more powerful set theory.

[3] See R. Carnap, *The Logical Syntax of Language* (London: Routledge and Kegan Paul, 1937), esp. pp. 15f., and the author's *Truth and Denotation* (Chicago: University of Chicago Press, 1958), esp. pp. 64ff.

[4] This terminology is adapted from Milton Babbitt's "Twelve-Tone Rhythmic Structure and the Electronic Medium," below, pp. 148–179.

theory of musical notation. For the present, however, no more will be said about these.)

Logical syntax and semantics have been developed to date primarily in terms of sign-shapes rather than sign-events. Therefore, it would probably be simpler likewise to base music theory, at first at least, upon pitch-classes rather than upon pitch-events. Later, however, an alternative will be suggested in terms of the latter.

The ontology of the theory of musical structure includes then an at most finite number of distinct pitch-classes, regarded as individuals. The latter are just the pitch-classes of the chromatic scale, ranging from the lowest to the highest. For some purposes, this domain might have to be enlarged, e.g., if we consider electronic music, or music based on a quarter-tone scale, or the like. In any case, the total number being finite, each pitch-class can be given a proper name, 'C' for middle C, 'C♯,' 'D,' etc. No doubt a *null* pitch-class is also to be admitted to handle rests, cesuras, and so on.

We must now bring in time. The fundamental truth here is, no doubt: time marches on and so do musical compositions. But the marching is not of an especially complicated sort: merely one or more pitch-classes succeeded by one or more (perhaps the same) pitch-class or -classes. The late Leopold Godowsky is supposed to have remarked that the art of piano-playing is really very simple: merely the right note at the right time in the right way. In the sheer description of musical structure this is all that is needed, basic structure being a matter of pitch-classes combined with times in certain ways.

The characterization of time needed for the theory of musical structure is, it would seem, best given by the so-called *epochal* or *pulse* theory.[5] Time flows on in little pulses, the shortest of which would be determined by the limits of human discrimination. They would be the minimal durations required for the production of musical sound. Longer durations are then merely sums or fusions of such pulses.[6] There is no need to assume these pulses further divisible, for they are the ultimate atoms of musical time just as pitch-classes are the ultimate atoms of musical sound — "ultimate," i.e., for present purposes. These pulses we assume to be serially ordered by a relation of *temporally preceding*. The relation is thus assumed to be irreflexive, transi-

[5] See especially J. H. Woodger, *The Axiomatic Method in Biology* (Cambridge: Cambridge University Press, 1937) and *The Technique of Theory Construction* (*International Encyclopedia of Unified Science,* Chicago: University of Chicago Press, 1939). Also Milton Babbitt, below, p. 151ff. and of course "Some Aspects of Twelve-Tone Composition," *The Score and I.M.A. Magazine,* Vol. 12 (1955), pp. 53–61 and "Set Structure as a Compositional Determinant," below, pp. 129–147.

[6] On sums or fusions, see especially H. S. Leonard and N. Goodman, "The Calculus of Individuals and Its Uses," *The Journal of Symbolic Logic,* Vol. 5 (1940), pp. 45–55.

tive, and connected, with such other properties as are needed. All music is then "serial" with respect to the underlying ordering of time.

It is assumed, of course, that pitch-classes and times are quite distinct kinds of entities. Our ontology is thus increased by regarding times as additional individuals. Having now two kinds of individuals available, how then do we get them together? Consider the *cardinal couple* of middle C with a certain time t

$$\langle C, t \rangle.^7$$

Such couples of pitch-classes with times may be regarded in the present formulation as the ultimate constituents of music, not pitch-classes alone nor times alone but cardinal couples of the two. Cardinal couples are classes and thus variables and quantifiers over them are needed in the underlying logic, which must then be of at least second order.

How do we go on to chordal combinations? Two ways suggest themselves. One is to admit an operation of pitch-class summation. Given any two pitch-classes x and y, there is another pitch-class $(x + y)$ as their *sum*. Suitable axioms, presumably of a Boolean kind, concerning pitch-class summation must then be laid down. By means of such an operation, however, we might be thought to overpopulate the musical realm, for we then in effect admit all combinations, many more elements than are perhaps needed. In practice we never have more than a rather small finite number, and hence, it might be asked, why should we admit more in theory? Again an Ockhamite principle can guide us: *Pluralitas non est ponenda sine necessitate.*

A second method suggests itself as follows. Regard the dyad consisting of $\langle x, t \rangle$ and $\langle y, t \rangle$ merely as the class whose only members are these two cardinal couples. The major triad consisting of middle C with E with G at time t then becomes the class whose only members are the cardinal couples $\langle C, t \rangle$, $\langle E, t \rangle$, and $\langle G, t \rangle$. Here there is no overpopulation intrinsic to the theory, the various cardinal couples and classes being available in the underlying logic. In this second method, a third-order logic is needed to provide for variables and quantifiers over chordal combinations.

We have talked here of *real* classes of *real* cardinal couples. But there has been recent renewed interest in *virtual* classes, occasioned in part by Quine's recent book on set theory.[8] Virtual classes differ from

---

[7] On cardinal couples, see *Principia Mathematica*, *54.

[8] On virtual classes, see W. V. Quine, *Set Theory and Its Logic*, Revised Edition (Cambridge: The Belknap Press of Harvard University Press, 1969), pp. 15ff., and my *Belief, Existence, and Meaning*, Chapter VI.

real ones in not being values for variables. With only slight readjustment we may reconstrue the foregoing in terms of *virtual* cardinal couples, and hence of *virtual* classes of virtual cardinal couples. Combinations of pitch-classes, whether simultaneous or sequent, thus become virtual classes of virtual cardinal couples. A musical composition itself then likewise may be regarded as such a virtual class. The order in which the component couples are taken is immaterial, for the temporal order of pitch-classes is determined always by the time-members of the couples. If this suggestion is sound, we have a description of the "ontological status" of the musical composition, within proto-theory, as merely a virtual class of virtual couples of the kind described.

An alternative suggests itself in terms of *event-logic*. This latter, including a logical theory of tenses, in one form or another has been under intensive recent investigation. The leading idea, which harks back to some extent to Reichenbach,[9] is to admit events and events only as values for variables. Suitable event-predicates are introduced, including expressions for relations providing for a temporal ordering of events.[10] No other kinds of variables need be admitted. In place of $\langle C, t \rangle$ above, we now admit expressions of the form

$$\text{`}Ce\text{'}$$

to express that e is a middle-C event. Such an event may be said, for example, to be before or simultaneous with (or whatever) some middle-E event e'. Such events can be of long or short duration. A numerical measure of them may be introduced in terms of which the theory of rhythm may be developed. In this way the proto-theory of musical structure becomes wholly absorbed in event-logic, if to the latter are added predicates such as 'C,' and so on.

If the foregoing provides an adequate vocabulary for the purposes at hand, we may summarize the proto-theory of music as follows. The first two methods suggested employ a first- or second-order logic with identity and two sorts of variables, one ranging over a finite number of elements, the tone- or pitch-classes, the other over time-stretches. The second method utilizes virtual classes in place of real ones. The axioms needed for time provide a suitable ordering, with a time-measure. If an operation of summation for pitch-classes is needed, suitable quasi-Boolean axioms must be given. It is not clear that such an operation *must* be introduced, however, its effect being achieved by

[9] *Elements of Symbolic Logic* (New York: The Macmillan Co., 1948), Chapter VII.

[10] See the author's "On Events and the Calculus of Individuals," *Akten des XIV. Internationalen Kongresses für Philosophie* (Vienna: Verlag Herder, 1969), Vol. III, 143–157, and *Logic, Language, and Metaphysics* (New York: New York University Press, forthcoming).

virtual classes and relations. In the third method, only one style of variables is used, event-variables, the effect of time being achieved by the temporal ordering of events. In any of these methods, the further development of theory is merely a matter of introducing definitions of the various notions of harmony, counterpoint, and thorough-bass, and so on and drawing out their logical consequences.

These theories provide for only basic musical structure. Matters of dynamics, timbre, phrasing, and the like remain to be considered. The presumption is that these can be handled suitably by additional primitive predicates.

THE QUESTION OF ORDER
IN NEW MUSIC

HENRI POUSSEUR

SERIAL MUSIC is often thought of as the fruit of excessive speculation and the result of an exclusive mustering of the powers of reason. Everything that occurs within it is constructed according to preestablished quantities and justified by the rules of a purely combinatorial logic. Except for the rules and quantities themselves, nothing would seem to have been left within the realm of free invention, to gratuitous inspiration or to a more subjective intuition. In short, a pitiless regimentation would appear to rule over this music, controlling the course of events even in their most intimate details.

But if one goes beyond a simple analysis of such music and beyond a dissection of its notations, if one relies primarily on concrete hearing—a hearing which might even be concentrated enough to put all one's receptive faculties into play—it often happens that one perceives just the contrary of such regimentation. Precisely where the most abstract constructions have been applied, it is not seldom that one has the impression of finding oneself in the presence of consequences of an aleatory free play.

If (to cite a particularly relevant example) we listen to the third piece in the first book of *Structures* for two pianos by Pierre Boulez— music composed in 1951 according to norms which fix the place of each element in the ensemble precisely, and in all respects—we can hear a kind of massing together of sounds into statistical groups of varied densities; many of the metrical relations intended by the composer remain cut off from our hearing and are therefore practically absent with respect to our perception. If the charm of the music is undeniable nonetheless, that is less the result of a perfectly clear and transparent "geometry" than of the more mysterious charm to be found in our awareness of many distributive forms found in nature: the unhurried dispersion of passing clouds, the twinkle of pebbles in the bed of a mountain stream, or the breaking of surf against a rocky coast.

A close examination of some examples may enable us to better understand the paradoxical relationship between the intention and the result (one might say, between the end and the means). Two particularly demonstrable examples should help us. Both fragments, taken from the first part of the same work, involve a bare exposition of the same series of twelve tones in two different "forms" which, theoretically at least, are mutually symmetric. The second example is the exact retrograde of the first with respect to chromatic material (by note-names), and both begin on G. However, the notes of the two are continually distributed over the entire keyboard range; and their beginnings and ends consist of notes in the extreme top and bottom registers. For this reason it is difficult to pick out any perceptible relationship between the two (whether of identity or of immediately recognizable transformation), even though the distribution of notes may include some exact register-inversions. What is perceptible is a statistical analogy between the two which is based upon similarity in the material and in its manner of over-all distribution. An important factor of this perception is the rhythmic structure of the two: for, even though the twelve notes are provided in both cases with the same twelve durational values,[1] these are permutated in a manner so complex that the ear can discern no striking similarity (or diversity) in the figuration of the two passages.

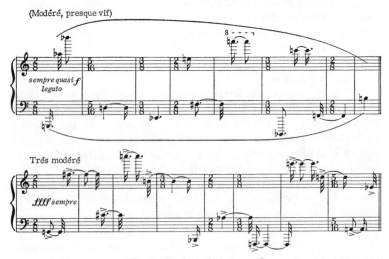

Ex. 1. Boulez: *Structures I*

Our difficulty in making a precise comparison between the two figures when we listen to them is caused, among other things, by the

[1] With one exception, irreducible to the system.

fact that each one is organized in the most irregular, least periodic fashion possible. Both passages might be likened to what are called "Brownian movements," i.e., movements lacking (from the observer's viewpoint) in all individual signification and therefore offering a high degree of resistance to unified over-all apprehension and to distinct memorization.

Thus the rigorous serial procedures which determine all the detail do not seem to have a positive function. Far from establishing perceptible symmetries and periodicities, regularity in similarity and in differentiation—in other words, an effective and recognizable ordering of diverse figures—they seem instead to *hinder* all repetition and all symmetry: or to put it another way (insofar as order and symmetry may be assimilated one with the other), all true *order*. The effect of statistical disposition (differentiation of dynamics, tempo, and attack as in the two fragments of Ex. 1, or differentiation in density between the two and other moments of the piece) upon the "over-all form" is to guarantee a *permanent renewal*, and an absolute degree of unpredictability, at this higher structural level.

Articles written by Boulez at the time of *Structures*, as well as some by other musicians, the present author among them, confirm the impression described above and reinforce our suspicion: one cannot impute the fact that one fails to perceive the serial relationships at work within a piece of music to either a lack of culture or to insufficient familiarity. The divergence between serial procedures and the perceptible result is sought after and exists effectively. Boulez affirms his intention of manifesting the essential irreversibility of time; this is clearly a negation of all periodicity and of all repetition, no matter how varied.

A search into the reasons for this divergence of an end and the means to achieve it is needed. Above all, we must look for the real reason for choosing precisely such an *end*, and also: to what extent this drive toward absolute asymmetry, toward an indetermination as radical as possible, has affected the earlier as well as the more recent serial music.

To do this it seems to me necessary to make a critical examination of our traditional conception of order and to expose the elements from our past which have conditioned this conception. Some examples from tonal music, such as it was in Europe during the eighteenth and nineteenth centuries, suggest themselves readily.

Consider the *Goldberg Variations* of J. S. Bach: the principal ingredients of "classic" order come immediately to mind, and we are able to survey the historical movement which is illuminated so brilliantly by this work, one of the most perfect expressions it was ever to attain. A comparison of the sections of the work—the first variation, for instance—with the examples of recent music discussed above throws light on certain important points. We are immediately struck by an extreme symmetry, principally on the rhythmic-metric level.

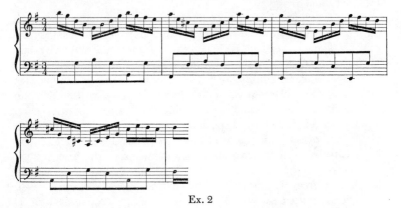

Ex. 2

At the lowest stage we find the smallest units, the sixteenth-notes, which perform the function of time-building material, below which no metronomic subdivision is possible and upon which the greater durational values are superimposed in clear and simple proportions. Next come the smallest multiples, the eighth-note and the quarter-note. The latter represents "time," or the beat of the measure, since the major melodic figurations as well as certain harmonic progressions coincide with its articulation; while the eighth-notes merely represent rhythmic subdivision in the interior of harmonic fields or of melodic motion.

The harmonic fields themselves are articulated at still a higher level: that of the measures, which always consist of three equal beats. Four measures are invariably grouped into small periods, unified as much through motivic structure as through harmonic motion (see Ex. 3). There are four such periods in each of the two sections which comprise one variation, and these sections are themselves repeated so that we hear four sections.

This symmetrical disposition is entirely objective in nature. Indeed, it can have value only insofar as our hearing appropriates it as a psychological system of reference; because we are capable of identifying it with our own experienced time. (It might otherwise be indicated with the aid of "exterior" means: clocks, metronomes, etc.) Such classic symmetry functions as an autonomous order, whose nature is verified by our experience of our surroundings and does not depend directly upon our *participation*. However, we claimed above that such symmetry relied upon harmonic phenomena. In examining these more closely, we find other order-creating relationships which strengthen and enliven this primary metric order. Most important, we find another sort of symmetry which should help us in our understanding of the nature of classic order.

As indicated above, the beginning of each measure is marked by a change in harmony. The four chords of a period comprise a unified harmonic progression; the third is the one with the greatest degree of tension; it "aspires" with the most energy toward a resolution which is provided by the appearance of the fourth harmonic field.

Ex. 3. The harmonic scheme common to the Aria and the thirty variations. The bass lines of the even-numbered measures are transpositions of one another, as are those of mm. 3 and 7.

The chords which end the different periods and bring them to a more or less complete state of repose themselves form a progression of a higher structural order. To the question posed by the end of the first period, the end of the second period answers; the end of the fourth responds to the question posed by the end of the third, and so on. . . . Ultimately, the total structure of the variation is disposed symmetrically with respect to "degree progression": that which is affirmed at the end of the second period (in the middle of the first section, here the supremacy of the tonic) is challenged or balanced at the end of the same section (also the end of the fourth period, with its energetic affirmation of the dominant). In the second section, on the other hand, the question (or contestation) comes first, opposite in order to that of the preceding pair (affirmation of the relative minor, which is organically closer to the subdominant); and it is answered in such a way that a complete resolution of the exposed contradictions and conflicts results. Thus each variation remains closed and self-sufficient within itself, thanks to a clear, perfectly balanced cyclical movement whose function is to centralize the over-all flow of events and to subordinate it to the preestablished tonal order.

Moreover, this order is itself nothing other than a metaphor of the interior order of the listener: indeed, more than a metaphor, for the listener is the subject wherein this order is realized and affirmed. For the questions and answers, the stresses and resolutions so far discussed exist nowhere other than in perception. This symmetry is of a purely psychic nature: it is a state in which I affirm myself the center of the world (perceived by me); in which everything which occurs in this world is referred to me and categorized according to my references and criteria (criteria of appropriation, for example). This is indeed the universe of great constructive individualism such as we find it in the work of Descartes and Pascal, Leibnitz and Newton; which dominates literature as well as painting or architecture in the classic era; such as is also expressed in the scientific, political, and economic systems of the time.

We are in the presence of a moment of high and fruitful equilibrium between the two conceptions whose often strained relationship had dominated and determined the dialectical evolution of the entire humanist period. On the one hand is the idea of a world which is entirely predetermined, such as we find it in Aristotelianism and which forms the basis for the theology and theocracy of the Middle Ages. On the other is the idea of a fundamental individual liberty, an idea implied by Christian teachings but which remained at a rudimentary level during the whole of the feudal period. This idea found its first opportunity to grow during the expansion of urban societies during the thirteenth century. It did not at first possess, if one might put it this way, the radical aspect of an absolute subjectivism which it was to acquire later; it was, above all, the affirmation and defense of a multitude of individuals against a more and more sclerotic hierarchy. The idea found its musical expression (and its terrain of musical experience) in primitive polyphony, which came into conflict, in some respects, with modal homophony and its ideal of submission. (It is of course not the purpose here to dispute the positive virtues of the latter.) We know further that this aspiration toward an autonomy of separate voices was subjected, from the fifteenth century on, to the increasingly severe controls imposed by their resulting harmony. Thus a pluralistic and personalistic conception grew into a representation of *absolute ego* which was to be most exactly realized in economic liberalism and in enlightened monarchy—institutions which rested, as we know, upon the capitalist bourgeoisie. Such was the age of orthodox tonality. The *Goldberg*

Variations are among its most perfect expressions; in them we find a marvelous balance between the affirmation of a universal harmony and the assigning of a supreme role to the individual subject. The richness of this display must nevertheless be partly attributed to the fact that polyphony—expression of the plurality of human experience as cherished and preserved by Protestant ethic and practice—was still in a vigorous state at the time of the work's composition.

Once polyphony is pushed outside the area of invention, such richness must be considerably reduced, and something will be needed to take its place. In the music of the epoch of *Sturm und Drang*—incongruously called the Viennese "Classic Period"—as well as in the music of the early nineteenth century, the accent falls with an ever-increasing stress upon states of tension, upon crises, upon moments calling the prevailing order into question. The psychological impulses of aspiration, supplication, and impatience (which had, indeed, played an important role in the work of Bach, but which there were nevertheless integrated into a more complex environment) now become the absolute center of interest. Naturally such a development could only distort the previously sovereign role of universal harmony. The numerous excursions outside the perfect order which one is obliged to make in order to affirm the authority of the latter have the effect of greatly increasing our realization that the world (first of all, the interior world of the affections) is neither simple nor transparent, that it includes many things that are difficult and even hostile. In romantic subjectivism, the individual no longer vibrates in unison with a universe which he wholly dominates; he feels more and more strongly that he has been thrown into an alien world. This feeling leads directly to the Twilight of the Gods (i.e., to the loss of all faith in any possible harmony). Post-romantic expressionism, a major part of whose expression is musical, speaks no longer of anything but a tottering universe, but rather of a world in a state of perpetual chaos.

When we listen to the music of Schoenberg, it becomes apparent immediately that the symmetries found within it—especially if one compares them with those of a Bach—are the fruits of a harsh irony, or, at the most, of bitter nostalgia. They are proof enough that its composer is still dreaming of what he considers a "golden age" (though it may have been gilt) while at the same time he is well aware that it has long since vanished into the past.

The radical error of classical thought, here developed to an absurd degree, was to believe that one might make time stand still: that one might appropriate things and their immediate appearance in a definitive manner. In effect, this denies the reality of their (and our) ephemeral nature. The consequence of the error was such that one found oneself cast into an impetuous torrent, impossible to hold back, within which one had no reference points to grasp. Time, ill-understood, revenged itself; the instantaneous present was never more than the irrevocable consequence of the past and the feverish pursuit of the future; nothing retained intrinsic value.

Schoenbergian expressionism attempted once again to solidify objects (to "objectify" musical events) by imposing the symmetry of classical art upon them; but it was unable to prevent the nontonal relationships which it developed so logically from refusing to be subordinated to a centralized consciousness. It is this which creates the extreme laceration of Schoenberg's music and so powerfully reflects analogous contemporary realities outside the world of music.

It was possible to solve the great difficulties confronting our musical language only by avoiding such hopeless contradictions. Anton Webern took the first decisive steps along this path. He refused to oppose the flow of time with attempts at consolidation: he recognized the autonomy of time—unpredictable and irrevocable—and knew that one can communicate with things only in the distance of their transitivity, in their innate alternation between presence and absence. Paradoxically, he thereby invested the present moment with an unvarying power of astonishment. The phrase of Rilke which he set to music in his Two Songs, Opus 8, might be engraved above the whole of his work:

Weil ich niemals dich anhielt, halt ich dich fest.

To verify the difference, it is enough to make an auditive comparison of the Third Quartet of Schoenberg with the Bagatelles, Opus 9, of Webern (composed several decades before the former). The Bagatelles are a music of pure instantaneousness, of undiluted acceptance (and thus of particularly intense recognition), of the appearance and disappearance of objects; and the music brings a very fresh (because unfamiliar) note into our Occidental cultural atmosphere: one finds no correspondences to it other than in certain of the thought of the ancient world and in the art of the Far East.

Technically, the character of the work is a result of methods quite directly opposed to those of the classic system. In the latter, as mentioned above, extreme symmetry and the greatest degree of periodicity prevailed. Evoking a docile response in psychic tendencies involving a minimum of exertion, these regularities produced an abstract spatial-temporal framework, a grid whose existence seemed to antedate the objects appearing in its interior and thus to create the illusion of an absolutely existing objective order. In the work of Webern, the eventual existence of a preestablished order is nowhere denied, but the question is simply passed over in silence: until the appearance of events, time and space remain wholly indeterminate. Revealing themselves only during their momentary appearances and having reference, according to the form thus defined, to nothing outside these moments, they return after completion to the depths of an absolute virtuality. *Silence*, surely ineffable but also incomparably certain, is here the source from whose generative power all perceptible forms spring forth, and to the shelter of which they are always ultimately returned.

Asymmetry seems then to be the principle most generally prevalent, and if short periodic sequences appear here and there, they need be attributed merely to the fact that successive events manifest a similar structure within themselves (a duration, for instance) and that their repeated appearances automatically create a repetitive result. But as soon as they have passed by, their regularity ceases to have an effect upon what follows. Aside from such elementary symmetries (such as simple repeated notes), an absolute minimum of symmetry is to be found in the works of this period, and we find a carefully arranged discontinuity in all the analyzable aspects of the musical edifice.

Discontinuity, moreover, is the distinctive characteristic to which Webern remained faithful throughout his evolution. In his later works it is even more apparent in certain respects, especially on the elementary level. On the other hand, we find an increasing use of symmetry in his late works at the higher levels of organization, among larger figures, and it seems legitimate to attribute this to Webern's desire to compose works of longer duration.

The young musicians who felt the necessity of pursuing Webern's research after his death believed nevertheless that one of their first tasks must be to remove what they considered the remains of an out-of-date rhetoric. This was the period when efforts were made to construct a "total serial organization," of which Boulez' *Structures* is one of the earliest and most remarkable examples. The series employed by Webern had permitted him to achieve a high degree of emancipation from the definitively rejected classic order; they had permitted him to establish a new space possessing great flexibility as well as miraculous consistency. These series, applied to other levels and to different aspects of composition, were now intended to guarantee the final elimination of the last remaining contradictions.

The examples from Boulez' *Structures* reproduced above may have already given us an idea of these early results. We may now be better able to understand the causes underlying their specific quality—the elusive poetry inherent within them. We may also more easily explain the momentary contradiction in method which they represent: a contradiction which comes about through the attempt to realize an integral aperiodicity with the aid of material borrowed from periodic musical order—i.e., metric notation and a serial system born of thematic techniques. One may succeed with these means, to be sure, but only by applying them in so complicated a fashion that their effects are inverted; and their use leads to a result which is exactly their opposite: a sort of nonmeasurable asymmetry implying their own imperceptibility.

For Boulez, *Structures* represented a sort of "absolute zero" in his research, a trial by fire (or ice) to which he resolved to submit his imagination and his craftsmanship, "in order," as he has recently explained it, "to see which elements would resist." (He had, in fact, intended to entitle the work "At the Limit of Fertile Land" after an engraving by Paul Klee.) This one experiment was enough for him. He learned enough from it to move on to a less strictly negative path and to carry his intentions further in the manner considered below. Other musicians, meanwhile, continued the strictly antithetical attempt to remove contradictions in their search for an integral asymmetry.

Attempts were made, for example, to generalize the conclusions reached regarding statistical groupings, by introducing aleatory principles, either at the compositional stage (by leaving certain decisions to chance) or at the moment of execution (the results of free play among several musicians being determined only approximately in advance). An effort was also made, chiefly in electronic music, to bring asymmetry into the musical material itself, as far as the interior structure of sound and the wave formants which define its character. My own short work, *Scambi*, realized in 1957 at the Studio of the RIA in Milan, is an example of this tendency: nothing to hear but noises, i.e., sound phenomena whose attributes, especially pitch, are only vaguely defined, one differing from another only in "color," in relative brightness or dullness, in its more or less prolonged modulation, or in its role within different grouping combinations.

In all these antithetical procedures, one was confronted by a new difficulty not unrelated to various earlier ones encountered by Western music, and one which perhaps was destined to bear fruit.

On the one hand, it was possible to carry the search for indetermination to its ultimate limit, a goal to which one may logically reduce all tendencies toward integral asymmetry. But in doing this, one approaches a point of formal impotence. Indeed, indetermination is nothing other than a lack of determination, that is, of all characterization having the power to distinguish one thing from another and to determine it specifically. It is really nothing other than indifferentiation, for if one erases every trace of definable characterization nothing remains but a neutral emptiness. In fact, the various "informal" procedures so far discussed all realize this indetermination and indifferentiation in a more or less decisive manner, at many levels and in respect to many different viewpoints. Even though the sound materials of Boulez' *Structures* are well defined in their various aspects (pitch, attack, etc.), the continual use of all possibilities, including the most contrasting juxtapositions (of registers, for example) creates a rapidly exhausting capacity of renewal, a rudimentary variation potential, a truly structural silence, at least in respect to these characteristics. The same remarks might be applied in a different way to the electronic piece mentioned above: if we mix enough of these timbre-dots together, we quickly arrive at a state of advanced entropy, in which all of the possible mixtures are practically the same. The final result is one of those colored surfaces which present nothing more than the vaguest degree of articulation: either the details distribute themselves according to a sort of approximate, statistical repetitive pattern or there are imperceptible modulations, ill-defined and continual. Recent "all over painting" gives us many eloquent examples of such background patterns created for their own sakes.

As mentioned above, phenomena of this type may possess great charm. Indeed, they bring us as close as possible to that ineffable silence which we recognized, with Webern, to be the general and absolute basis of experience. But they cannot succeed in transporting us unless they maintain a minimum of differentiation! If one tries to surpass their degree of indifference, if one tries to approach silence in a more immediate fashion, one falls inevitably into a total and unbearable monotony, into an incurable insignificance (and of this there is no lack of examples). Here the contradiction implicit in this unilateral tendency is revealed: just as classic ideology endeavored to impose something clearly defined as its fundamental order, its absolute reference (a rhythmic pulsation, a tonal hierarchy, a recognizable thematic material, for instance), here one attempts to reach the absolute (which one has nevertheless characterized as being indefinable) with the aid of means of determination. It is as though one wishes to embody silence. All in all, the two goals are not so different: and like all antitheses, this one commits an error which is symmetrical to the one within the thesis from which it issues.

The other alternative solution consists of integrating determining elements, not despite oneself, but in a conscious and voluntary manner—to retain, not the negative conception of asymmetry (which is inclined to lead to a state of total neutrality and thus, ultimately, to the opposite of true asymmetry), but rather the idea of differentiation, of discontinuity among elements which themselves must remain perfectly perceptible. In order to do this it is essential to set up defining forces, elements of limitation and order dealing with symmetry, no matter how hidden it might remain, no matter how obscured by differentiating factors.

Examples of this procedure, though on a rudimentary level, are in fact to be found in the works discussed above. In *Structures*, Boulez limits himself to certain well-defined note values; he makes effective use of methods of grouping of pointillist elements through criteria of characterization and homogeneity, such as those, mentioned above, involving dynamic, attack, and polyphonic density. In my *Scambi*, it may be that the varied distribution of noise types over rather long time periods is sufficient to create a high enough degree of over-all variation. A closer look at this distribution reveals nothing other than a certain proportion of periodicity. For the variation of any one given aspect will have its effect in two complementary directions: positive and negative (high and low, slow and fast, etc.), and clearly this may be considered a type of undulatory (periodic) motion. No matter how great a degree of variation accompanies and characterizes each "waveform," there should remain enough in common among "waves" to allow us to distinguish and compare one with another.

A second look at the use of apparent (often complex and flexible) symmetry in the late work of Webern reveals it to be, not the remains of an obsolete classical system, but an attempt to regulate the proportion of regularity which must exist within any irregularity.

Webern too had gone through a sort of "crisis of indetermination." In the works of his early period one finds a clear tendency toward silence and tenuous elocution which is related as much to the predominance of low dynamics as to the extreme brevity of the pieces. His pieces for cello and piano, Opus 11, represent the extreme point in this tendency; but they may also be considered a pivotal work at the threshold of something new and stronger. In these pieces, Webern begins to be quiet about silence: he no longer strives to embody it. Insofar as this is evidence of his new confidence, it is through the positioning of well-defined and clearly perceptible units, articulating themselves by means of reciprocal effect, each one limiting and defining the nature of its fellows.[2] Thus an available space is established among the units, an emptiness within which they may reign calmly in all their abundance.

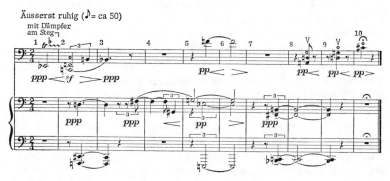

Ex. 4. Webern: Op. 11, No. 3 (the piece consists of a single line)

Symmetry and asymmetry, determination and indetermination, equality and inequality, are thus more than simply contradictory principles excluding each other in an absolute manner; rather, they are complementary properties, each conditioning the other and mutually dependent. An excess in one sense or the other leads to the same pathological disorder. Only a correct proportion, a balanced tension (which may be realized in an infinitely varied manner) can engender a free order, vital and significant, representing multiplicity and communication, individuality and recognition.

What we might call modern anarchy is certainly justified in its extreme opposition to classic exclusivity, to the usurping bourgeois hierarchy: the exorbitant accent placed on the "I" by the latter led to a form of unbearable disorder. We are well aware of how much the concepts of objective order and symmetry have contributed to this; and we also know how far our social relations as well as our most secret feelings are from being completely purified of it. Thus

[2] Here one might quote some fine definitions in "L'Art Poétique" of Claudel, dated 1904, the year Webern began to work with Schoenberg: "Each note of the scale calls for and implies the others. None claims to satisfy the sensibility. Each exists on the condition of not sounding as the others, and on the equally imperative condition that the others will call it forth in its place." And further, speaking in the voice of one of the members of an interval: "This object is not what I constitute; it does not exhaust existence; the simple fact of my existence prevents it from integrating the sum and I enrich it by adding myself to the number of things which it is not; I am invested with the right to deny it totality; and I find in it the point from which this right is refused to me."

"anarchy" has a long, hard task of "cleansing" ahead of it: among languages for instance—music among them—it must remain an important ingredient of our poetic attitude. But it would be in error, and would mistake its true objective, if it denied the necessity of all order, of all discipline (that is to say, of all *signification*). Even the experiences of our tradition may be useful to us, if we separate them from their mistaken ideological context and confront them continually with a complementary principle of openness and of relativity. This is exactly what Webern does in his late works. His way of using the serial system, of dialectically elevating thematic methods by transcending without abandoning them, remains a precious indication of the path which we must follow.

One more example might serve to convince us. The series used in Opus 24 is made up not only of the twelve notes of the chromatic scale, but of four different forms of the same little three-note figure: the original figure (a), its retrograde (b), the inversion of the retrograde (c), and the retrograde of this inversion (d).

Ex. 5

This internal symmetry permits a disposition of correspondences which are perceptible toward the "exterior." It is possible, for instance, for there to be an "orthodox" transformation of the series (a transposition of the retrograde inversion) in which the same four groups will appear in the same order: only their constituents will appear in inverse order (Ex. 6). In another form, a transposition of the retrograde, the internal structure of the four groups remains unaltered: only their disposition is transformed in a most regular manner: they are exchanged, two by two, and we now have B-A, D-C (Ex. 7). In still another form, the half-series, otherwise unaltered, are the units which exchange positions: C-D or A-B (Ex. 8). And if we consider the retrogrades of each of the four forms already presented, we find examples of partial combinations of these transformations, groupable in twos: exchange of sounds and exchange of groups (Ex. 9); exchange of sounds and exchange of halves (Ex. 10); exchange of groups and of halves (Ex. 11). Paradoxically, the transformation which is least similar to the original, from this point of view, is the retrograde, since all three transformation types are to be found added together within it (Ex. 12).

Ex. 6

Ex. 7

Ex. 8

Ex. 9

Ex. 10

Ex. 11

Ex. 12

Provided that audition of the work permits an effective compari-son of its pitches (a condition fulfilled by Webern in his composition of other aspects, by a momentary placing of the same notes in the same registers, for instance), these combinations, which do not exhaust all of the possible permutations of the series, will attract the whole of our attention to themselves. We will perceive a structure com-posed of four well-defined groups endowed with a very great freedom, a relative, reciprocal indeterminacy, i.e., a structure within which—without the over-all coherence of the work being put in danger— there is a true mobility.

The series of twelve tones (or, more precisely, the series of specific intervals so defined) which remains unaltered throughout these trans-formations, is not at all perceptible as such. It no longer possesses the thematic rigidity of the series of Schoenberg, but assumes instead the more secret function of guaranteeing harmonic homogeneity on the one hand (by avoiding all relationships and groupings which would endanger the distributive equilibrium—an equilibrium which is directly opposed to that of tonality because its specific harmonic weight is equally distributed at all points), and of maintaining the conditions of mobility as defined above on the other.

Ex. 13. The next to last measures of the first movement of Webern's Op. 24, in which the three "forms" appearing in Exs. 8, 11, and 12 are used, a semi-tone lower, from which one quickly sees the relations existing among the transformations; from each one to the next there is never anything but a *simple* transposition, from *one* point of view, whether it is an exchange of notes within the groups or an exchange of groups in pairs.

Webern never denies either the existence of a regulating or of a regulated element; but, compared with classic order, the relationship of the two seems to be exactly inverted. In the latter, the ordering element was also the one most clearly defined; it moved in the foreground and strove to subordinate all other determinations exterior to itself. Here, on the contrary, the determiner retires behind the determined and leaves the latter with an autonomy which is perhaps the most positive aspect of its transitory character. It is, then, not *indetermined*, but rather *indeterminable*, for the simple reason that it is too rich and too pregnant to be categorized by a single definition or characterization. It is thus literally *overdetermined* and possesses the virtues of a formative symmetry as well as those liberating ones which were attributed above to asymmetry.

Thus the term "original form," applies to a series by Webern, is misleading except for demonstrative purposes. Actually, none of the possible presentations of the series may be considered more original than others; and the series, once presented, includes the group of all its metamorphoses.

With this in mind, the aleatory character encountered in the "mobile forms" of recent compositions may be considered from a different viewpoint. What in Webern was expressed at the level of compositional technique is now developed in the domain of inter-

pretive practice. The written work, the final degree of abstraction
before the concrete musical act, may no longer be identified with any
one of its particular realizations; it is the nontemporal area where a
certain number of possibilities are assembled. In a work, for example,
such as my *Caractères*, composed in 1961, clearly recognizable
"formants" exchange their respective positions in response to the free
will of the pianist but also within certain well-defined limits imposed
by the physical nature of the score. It is always the same thing and
it is always different: it should seem to continue to live in the interval
from one performance to another and should give the interpreter the
possibility of living freely too, that is, creatively. This is made
evident also at the level of the notation itself, whose distinct media-
tion depends less upon a rigidly quantitative metric system than on
an appeal to, and a confidence in, the concrete, vital, and inventive
understanding of the performer.

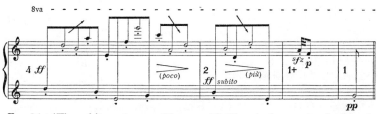

Ex. 14. (The white notes are "dampened." The rhythm, quite flexible, is
easily comprehended through the graphic distribution)

If pieces of this sort are to be as communicative as possible, and
if their interior liberty is not to lead to a lack of signification or necessity, their variable elements (which must, of course, be indeterminate
to a certain extent) must also display a definition, a characterization,
a *sense* of sufficient development. The "technique of groups" already
presented, though on a modest scale, in Boulez' *Structures*, is useful
in achieving this. It has the great advantage of preserving the negative moments which were a feature of primitive serial technique,
moments the necessity of which is far from having lessened. Thanks
to this technique, we have learned how to remain faithful to these
moments and at the same time to better exercise a constant control
over the "formants" employed within a work and to situate them in
a more distinct fashion. The principal landmarks in this direction are,
besides the later works of Boulez,[3] the large compositions by Stock-

---

[3] *Le Marteau sans Maître*, for example, composed by Boulez in 1953—shortly after
Structures. In this work, although the negative aspects of what in this article is
called "musical anarchy" are still present to a considerable degree, the first resolute

hausen, such as *Gesang der Jünglinge* and *Zeitmasse*, *Gruppen* and *Kontakte*, and also the works of Berio and of some others. Certain features to be found within these works appear as reprises (re-coveries) of possibilities which had been momentarily excluded from the musical vocabulary: relatively regular rhythms, for example, and well-defined harmonic superpositions (to mention simple, elementary aspects). If these possibilities are no longer presented as "order imposing," but rather as "features whose order is imposed along with others"—something which of course necessitates a whole series of precautionary measures, the invention of which constitutes one of the requirements of new musical craftsmanship—there is no longer a reason for continuing to exclude them. I would even hazard the prediction that evolution in the near future will be in a direction such that all types of musical expression known up to the present will be made usable again (along with other, entirely unknown types relating to other domains of our auditive experience). The only condition which it would seem necessary to respect is that no one of these elements be allowed to predominate over the others; in other words, that the Webernian principle of reciprocal relativity, of what earlier in this article was called equilibrium of distribution, or "multi-polarity," will continue to be in effect where momentarily significant relationships are articulated. Serial methods, when properly dis-posed and "generalized" in an entirely fresh manner, surely remain the best means for achieving this effect. The most probable and legitimate natural consequence of such a widening of expression would be the ability of new music to reach vaster auditive capacity; and the possibility of its finally achieving the major muta-tion in collective sensibility which it carries within it in embryonic form. And it seems useless to insist that such a system, once realized, would fail to purge itself of all contradiction, or that it could not be considered a representation of absolute progress with respect to preceding systems. At the least, it would seem to me capable of attaining a relative equilibrium and stylistic stability. In addition to its internal "harmonic" virtues (virtues of juxtaposition of a great number of elements hitherto considered irreconcilable), and partly

---

steps are taken toward a "synthesis" which promises to be quite the opposite of a compromise. One can detect this at the purely technical level, in the use (always quite brief) of rather simply periodic rhythms; or in a manner which is more significant because it is more complex, in the use of a more voluntary and clearly drawn figura-tion (although still invested with a sufficient "obscurity"). One can find it also at the more poetic level. An example is Boulez' acceptance of the possibility of leading his music in the direction of certain decidedly traditional expressive currents belong-ing for the most part to various non-European cultures (although here it is concerned with apparently secondary questions such as instrumentation).

because of them, it would respond to a whole series of varied, urgent, and timely needs.

We have surely learned once and for all that our action can never encompass the universe and its fundamental nature; but we also remain convinced that in its best moments our action is capable of receiving the world's message, and that this is accomplished above all through powers of ordering, clarifying, and establishing relationships which are within the domain of *form*. The latter is not called on to explain the whole of reality once and for all, but to make as vast a space as possible inhabitable for us—the largest of which we are capable. It is not enough for us to alter the "exterior" world in order to accomplish this, but also—above all, perhaps—*ourselves*, our attitude, and our "resonance" (like a violin's, a filter's, an antenna's).

The measures to take are both external and internal, individual and collective; no doubt they are, above all, arrangements on the linguistic level, where, as Michel Butor has recently demonstrated, music has an important role to play.[4] Though mindful of our inability to reach the absolute through our own efforts, we may at least hope that it will reach us (is not each moment of plenitude, each *present*, a sign of this?): and our effort toward receptivity, the precise technical implications of which we now understand more fully, is the active motive force of our hope.

[Translated by David Behrman]

[4] "Les oeuvres d'art imaginaires chez Proust," *Répertoire* (Paris, 1964), II, 258-60 and *passim*.

TWO LECTURES TO SCIENTISTS

J. K. RANDALL

I

Theories of Musical Structure as a Source for Problems in Psycho-acoustical Research

[Read to the Acoustical Society of America, Boston, 6/3/66.]

LET US explore for a moment some paradoxical consequences of the view that a piece of music—whatever else it may or may not be besides —can be viewed as an anthology of sound-events each of which can be psycho-acoustically investigated on its own; and that the scientific investigation of the perception of such sound-events has nothing in particular to do with the artistic capacities of the investigator. Even at the risk of having to disinter it first, I would like to cast doubt upon this view—not because I suspect that psycho-acousticians are too prone to graze in the pastures of art, but because I suspect that their own work suffers a severe malnutrition resulting from their not being too fussy about what they eat when they do graze there.

A psycho-acoustical investigation of a sound-event (or sequence or combination of sound-events) is normally carried out utilizing not only the usual variety of washed and unwashed auditors, but also a variety of sound-event contexts in which the test-event is imbedded. For example, a typical event in a perception test will be designed to elicit from an auditor a statement that two sounds are roughly the same in some clearly (or not-so-clearly) defined respect or that, in this respect, one is more this or that than the other. Now since the scientist is well aware that responses to any one event may depend in part upon the exact context provided by the sequence of events which constitutes the test as a whole, he is properly concerned to build any central event into a variety of contexts; and hence he is properly concerned to develop some contexts for this event which, in his judgment, might tend to suggest one response and others which might tend to suggest another, perhaps even an opposite, response. It would seem then that a scientist framing a perception test is required not merely to know a great deal about the interactions of the various perceivable aspects (durational, intervallic, etc.) of sound-sequences upon one another in influencing whatever may be "perceived" about some individual element or elements within those sequences; he is required also to exercise no little skill in inventing sequences which will possess the double virtue of introducing a relevant variety of influences without at the same time introducing influences whose operation the scientist may be unaware of. (With luck, of course, his evaluation of responses to his test might lead him to discover these unintended influences. But luck is apt to be fickle: it seems at least equally probable that, were the responses nicely uniform, the case would be prematurely closed.)

At the risk of sounding faintly socratic, I would like to ask by what name we traditionally refer to someone who exercises no little skill in inventing sound-sequences which reflect the kinds of knowledge and possess the kinds of virtue just described. At the least, we call him a composer; and we call his inventions compositions. Yet it is essential to the scientist's alleged artistic non-involvement that he modestly insist upon a radical distinction in kind between the humble perception test and the lofty realm of musical composition, a distinction which is alleged to thrive upon the fact that perception tests traditionally (and intentionally) lack artistic merit. But mere lack of artistic merit is insufficient. The "clean" psycho-acoustician's claim of artistic non-involvement rests additionally upon our ability to view his "artistically" worthless sequences of sound-events as *non*compositions rather than as *bad* compositions: for if his noncompositions carry with them that power to elicit misguided responses to individual component elements in anything like the degree to which *bad* compositions so notoriously do (as any composition teacher who has on occasion been frustrated in his attempt to identify "the trouble" with some dismal undergraduate concatenation of notes can testify), then it would be more germane—indeed, it would be essential—to the scientist's purposes simply to classify his traditionally artistically worthless sound-sequences as *bad* compositions, admit that his artistic non-involvement is a myth, and proceed to improve his compositional technique. It seems to follow that the "clean" psycho-acoustician must stake his professional life upon his (or someone's) providing a satisfactory answer to this double-barreled question: What *is* a *non*composition? And wherein lies its safeguard against our shredding its scientific insulation by mistakenly or unwittingly listening to it as if it were simply a bad composition? I can't answer this question. But more importantly, I can't imagine how it *could* be answered by anyone who was not invoking rather elaborate techniques of specifically contextual (i.e., specifically musical) analysis: how else could we be sure that our "noncompositions" really *lacked* some all-too-suggestive qualities of (good *or* bad) compositions than by thoroughly investigating at least the qualities of compositions? And since *any* technique of organizing sound—however inadequate when unsupported by other techniques—is likely to enter into full-fledged musical composition from time to time and to be extensively explored there and to become willy-nilly a technique of *musical* organization, how can the "clean" psycho-acoustician eventually construct "clean" sound-sequences (i.e., noncompositions) without mastering the compositional technique of utilizing only those techniques of musical organization which serve his nonmusical purposes while eschewing all those which might get in their way? that is, without becoming not merely a composer, but a spartanly disciplined composer to boot?

Thus we have arrived at the following dilemma: Either the distinction between noncompositions and bad compositions is tenuous, in which case there is no such thing as "clean" psycho-acoustics; or there is indeed such a distinction, in which case the psycho-acoustician must master whatever compositional techniques are appropriate to the production of noncompositions, and hence in which case there is no such thing as "clean" psycho-acoustics.

If my reasoning has been more or less correct thus far, then I hope it is clear that I do not wish to say to psycho-acousticians: Quit grazing in my pasture. On the contrary, I want to say something like this: Inasmuch as you must graze in my pasture whether you mean to or not, please examine the terrain at least well enough to be confident that you are munching on what grows there rather than on what no one has bothered to remove yet. Now just how well is well enough?

In working with electronic sounds—especially with unfamiliar ones— it is a matter of everyday musical experience that compositional possibilities (that is, relevant musical contexts) for some sound may emerge only gradually: concomitantly, my very awareness of certain properties of the sound may emerge only gradually, and it is precisely my proceeding to exploit the sound in a variety of musical contexts that brings these properties to the fore. The essential point of this musical experience for psycho-acoustics is this: only after a certain amount of compositional exploitation is anyone in a very good position to know what to test.

Now perhaps it seems to the psycho-acoustician that there are a sufficient number of purely routine questions which must be asked about any sound-event, and which require virtually no special musical insight to formulate. But I think it perfectly realistic to say that the more adept someone becomes at specifically musical analysis, the more he justifiably tends to doubt the utility, and sometimes even the meaningfulness, of those allegedly "routine" questions.

Let me illustrate by invoking a very familiar musical example about which I will ask a couple of very elementary and routine psycho-acoustical questions. Notice as we proceed how heavily what we "do" hear comes to depend upon what we can hear if we try, and upon what we think we ought to hear in pursuit of whatever we think constitutes a coherent musical structure.

Look now at Chopin's Prelude No. 10 in E flat, mm. 9–16. The second half of this passage exhibits relations traditionally called enharmonic equivalences. In this case at least three major-minor scales are simultaneously, though perhaps over different time-spans in different registers at different structural layers, relevant for intervallic measurements: the major-minor scales whose tonics are, respectively, E flat, G, and B flat. (That this succession of local tonic notes spells out the tonic triad of the piece as a whole is something that a trained musician would notice on first hearing.) Pitch-classes 6 and 7 (counting here all C's, B sharps, and D double-flats, or whatever, as pitch-class zero; up through all B's, C flats, or whatever, as pitch-class eleven) are both contained in all three of the scales I mentioned. Only in the G scale, however, is the *scalar* interval from 6 to 7 *nonzero*. In this scale the pitch classes 6 and 7 are distinct, consecutive scale-steps—which is to say that they delimit an interval of *one* scalar unit. In the E flat or B flat scale, by contrast, 6 and 7 are simply alternative versions of the same scale-step—which is to say that they delimit an interval of *zero* scalar units even though they delimit, as always, a chromatic interval of one unit.

Now let me ask my very elementary and routine psycho-acoustical question about a particular place in this passage: Are the intervals G over C and G flat over C flat identical in size?

One defensible answer would be the following: At the most local level, yes. At the two-measure level, no: the C flat-G flat functions as C flat-F sharp and therefore is chromatically the same in size but scalarly different. In relation to the impending tonicization of B flat: perhaps. In general: the musical coherence of the passage subsists in part on the various functions of the dyad C flat-G flat, each of which induces a different scalar measurement. But presumably my elementary and routine psycho-acoustical question envisioned nothing more challenging to the auditor than unadorned chromatic measurement.

In other words, we have brought to light a sense in which my elementary and routine psycho-acoustical question—which merely asked for a comparison of the sizes of two intervals—contained a hidden assumption that any trained musician knows to be false in the context of the music we all know best: namely, the assumption that an auditor will at least refrain from measuring a single interval along incompatible scales simultaneously. It turns out that the structure of tonal music has been inducing just such precise simultaneous aural measurements along incompatible scales for at least two and one-half centuries. And our grasp of this structure would become shaky indeed were we henceforth to decline, in the context of classical tonality, to perform these prodigies of precise aural measurement which trained musicians perform on first hearing with about the degree of effort they expend telling a violin from a cello. (It follows that further musical analysis would be required to evaluate an assertion that the re-attack of G flat over C flat represents a change from a scalar 6th to a scalar 4th; and I would be happy to counterassert, on the basis of musical analysis performed on some other occasion, that such an assertion overdoes a good thing.)

Please notice the implications of this Chopin example (written well over a century ago) for an even more elementary and routine psycho-acoustical question such as this: "Are the following two pitches the same or different?"

In the context of the music we all know best, a succession of G flat—F sharp is both an identity of pitch and an inferable scalar descent. Furthermore, a violinist, for example, in playing a succession G flat—F sharp might actually play two noticeably different pitches in order to articulate the local function of each: and yet the harmonic context would undoubtedly require that we interpret these two distinct pitches as representatives of the same pitch. To make matters even worse, the violinist might legitimately play the F sharp slightly higher than the G flat; so that an inferable scalar descent might actually and legitimately be played as an ascent in pitch.

My example raises by implication two rather more general points which seem to me of fundamental importance to psycho-acoustical research: First: Any trained musician *could* hear that Chopin passage in the terms I have indicated whether or not he endorsed my description. Second: Any trained musician *could* edit out from his hearing of that passage at least some of those described characteristics which seemed to him irrelevant or detrimental to his own conception of the significant musical structure of the passage.

Thus far I have spelled out some familiar musical structural conditions under which a clear perception of unmitigated intervallic identity, or of a higher and a lower pitch, might be not just irrelevant but downright misleading. Very similar conditions can be spelled out—and yet only with the aid of specifically musical analysis—for such allegedly bread-and-butter concepts as octave-equivalence, consonance and dissonance, the definition of roots and tonics, etc.; and can serve to make even more palpable the dangers of discounting the possibility (discussed by a recent contributor to PERSPECTIVES) that "perceiving" music is (and ought to be) a process of inventing structures out of aural impressions derived not merely from "perceived sound" but from sound perceived in what-ever way best appeases our desire to invent structures. Nor should we discount the possibility that perceiving just plain sound, musical or otherwise, is similarly permeated by our desire to invent meaningful structures—a possibility which I imagine some psychologists would claim amounts to a virtual certainty.

My reason for believing that psycho-acoustical research should keep in touch with current concerns in composition is partly that musical composition continues to play the central role in defining the current frontiers of the aurally perceptible (and in shaping the modes in which we aurally perceive); and partly that the evolution of new musical systems is sometimes a prerequisite to our understanding old ones—and especially to our understanding that some old musical system was just a musical system rather than the perennial embodiment of the laws of perception. And unquestionably, the flowering of the so-called 12-tone system in our era has given us a new perspective on the system of classical tonality. The realization that such traditional musical concepts as the relative consonance and dissonance of intervals are irrelevant to the analysis of 12-tone music has led composers and musical analysts to re-examine the function of these concepts in their traditional context. What we have sought to define is some ahistorical sense in which these concepts may be said both to cohere and to cohere in such a way as to shed light on the layer-structure peculiar to music in the tonal system.

Even more surprising, perhaps, is the realization that the notion of timbre may be not too much more than one of those leftovers from a dead musical system. In electronic music, where spectra, envelopes, vibratos, and tremolos may be structured over a whole composition with the degree of subtlety and efficacy to which we have become accustomed in the domain of pitch, we must learn to stop hearing vibrato, for example, as a vaguely subliminal way of lushing-up a tone; that is, we must learn to stop mixing together a set of potentially independent musical dimensions into a monolithic dimension within which we can continue to get off easy by discriminating among "mellow timbres," "nasal timbres," and other similar bushel-basket catches. In the presence of music so structured, the perception of "timbre" must be viewed not as a difficult psycho-acoustical problem, but as a sloppy habit.[1]

The psycho-acoustician of the future who insists on asking questions about "timbre" in electronic music may be in the same awkward position as the legendary psycho-acoustician who tested perceptions of various "pitchvolurations" in music for conventional instruments—pitch-voluration being that monolithic bushel-basket dimension (of questionable utility) whose independent component variables are pitch, loudness,

---

[1] Cf. nos. 2 & 3 of these lectures for less cursory treatments of "timbre" and its alleged components.

and duration. I do, of course, hope that this legendary psycho-acoustician may have learned something he should have known to begin with: namely, that musical concepts uncritically accepted as perceptual dimensions generate loaded psycho-acoustical questions, no matter how many independent, component variables his view of some dimension may have left room for; and that loaded questions invite careless or recalcitrant answers. As a general rule, it seems to me that tests administered to the musically semi-literate by their peers (or tests which might just as well have been) yield results only for those disciplines which might take an interest, for example, in my impressions of what goes on inside a cyclotron; namely, the disciplines of sociology and folk humor.

Once again, let me make it clear that I am not advising scientists to quit meddling with music: on the contrary, it is perfectly clear that the benevolent interest and imaginative work of scientists has opened up vast new territories for composers to explore. But I think it no accident that such work has been done largely by scientists who, as a matter of policy, have collaborated closely with composers and have even taken the risk of committing composition themselves, thereby constantly testing their own familiarity with the musical problems to which they are devoting their professional talents. It seems to me that any psycho-acoustician who forges ahead blithely out of touch with current concerns in musical analysis and musical composition is putting himself in an excellent position to produce silly science, silly music, or silly both.

II
"New Sounds" vs. Musical Articulation

[Read to the Audio Engineers Society, New York City, 10/12/66.]

I have contracted to make some derogatory remarks about the search for allegedly "new" sounds—and I shall try not to disappoint. However, in order to avoid any misunderstanding, I would like first to make some derogatory remarks about the search for allegedly "old" ones; and I would like to approach this essential phase of my discussion indirectly— by first describing a malfeasance commonly practised in the analysis of a musical domain somewhat less thorny than the domain of timbre, and then proceeding to illustrate a sense in which similar analyses of the domain of timbre may be similarly malfeasant.

My stalking-horse is in the domain of rhythm.

Suppose we were to analyse the various renditions of three-eighth-note figures in a single performance of Beethoven's Fifth Symphony. And suppose that our analysis were directed toward the resolution of three questions:

No. 1: Are the three eighths within single figures usually rendered as three equal durations?

No. 2: What are the frequency and amounts of deviation from equal duration?

No. 3: Do some patterns of deviation emerge?

(I am resisting the inclusion of an obvious fourth question about uniformity of tempo among the various figures more in the interests of brevity than of adequacy.)

Now suppose that the following were a passable summary of our eventual empirical results:

The three eighths within single figures are but infrequently rendered as three equal durations; the amounts of deviation are usually tiny, although here and there they are quite large; and while certain patterns, especially in the form of gross limitations on kinds of succession and concurrence, do emerge, these patterns are not sufficiently detailed to dispel a somewhat random aura.

(Please notice, as my argument unfolds, that its drift would *not* clearly be affected were some much fancier-looking empirical results substituted for my very simple-looking ones.)

Next, let us further suppose that analyses of a large number of performances of a large number of familiar pieces yield results of a sufficiently striking similarity to our results for Beethoven's Fifth Symphony to lead us to believe that those first results cannot seriously be interpreted as revealing things peculiar to just Beethoven's Fifth.

And finally, let us suppose that we have arrived at the verge of electronic simulation: our first venture will be to electronically simulate not some specific already-existing performance of Beethoven's Fifth, but just a performance of it which we intend to be a musically acceptable one—that is, an excellent one; after that, the world.

Let me ask two questions which I have been heading toward from the outset.

First: In electronically rendering the very large number of three-eighth figures in Beethoven's Fifth, would it not be a musically sensible extrapolation from our hypothetical sets of empirical data to distribute somewhat randomly selected small amounts of deviation from equal duration somewhat randomly over most of the eighth notes, while at the same time enforcing those gross limitations suggested by our data?

Second and more generally: Would it not be sensible to do this in any electronic sound-generation in which we intend to produce conventionally "musical"-sounding renditions of equal note-value figures?

Notwithstanding the seemingly rhetorical quality of at least the first of these two questions, I think that both questions must be answered: No, these are not musically sensible extrapolations. Or rather: Insofar as they are sensible extrapolations from our hypothetical empirical results, they help expose the musical triviality of our initial three questions. While such questions cannot fairly be said to represent the nadir of musical analysis, they can fairly be said to represent the nadir of cognitive musical analysis. For the moment, let me indicate a major source of their musical inadequacy this way: Quite intricate and elaborate musical analysis is required to disrcriminate between those tiny deviations which are just deviations and those tiny and not-so-tiny deviations which are part and parcel of the projection of an entire musical structure and which are therefore intimately involved in, and qualified by, a complex developing musical context. Those rubatos don't just occur in x percent of the population: they probably belong right where they are—for instance, right there where that middle-register line joins that upper-register line from a more background layer —and could easily suffer reduction to nonconsequence (or worse) if redistributed.

Let us recapitulate, but this time in the domain—or domains—of timbre:

Suppose we were to analyse the various renditions, by the violin, of the note A above middle C at a rather soft dynamic in a single performance of, say, the Kreutzer Sonata. And suppose that our analysis were directed toward the resolution of an analogous three questions:

No. 1: Are the speed and width of vibrato constant within single notes?

No. 2: What are the frequency and amounts of deviation from an average speed and width?

No. 3: Do some patterns of deviation emerge?

(On the model of the rhythmic example, I am resisting the inclusion of a fourth question about uniformity of tempo among vibrato-speeds on different notes.)

And now suppose that, having obtained our empirical results, we extend our investigation to cover many different pitches at various dynamics in a large number of familiar pieces; and we become convinced that our first results revealed nothing peculiar to just the Kreutzer Sonata or even to just violin performances.

And again we arrive at the verge of electronic simulation, armed with our hypothetical sets of empirical results and with my two questions:

First: In rendering vibratos in an acceptable electronic performance of the Kreutzer Sonata, would it not be a musically sensible extrapolation from our hypothetical sets of empirical data to construct a vibrato-population reflective of these sets of data in the way that we proposed to construct an eighth-note population reflective of those other sets of data?

Second and more generally: Would it not be sensible to do this in any electronic sound-generation where we intend to produce conventionally "musical"-sounding tone-quality?

If something in the structure of my argument leads you to suppose that I am about to answer these two questions in the same old way and for the same old reason, you are right. I also agree with you in supposing that the same form of argument would lead us to deny much musical relevance to similar approaches to problems of acceptably simulating acceptable spectra with acceptable transients, intermodulations, and so on.

On this basis, it is incumbent upon me to insist that the researcher who advocates as self-evident truth the claim that you can't simulate a violin melody until you can simulate a violin tone is, conceptually if not procedurally, putting the cart before the horse: that violin tone, in any specifically musical use, is at least *no less* than a local open-ended agglomeration of musical developments in progress whose degree of timbral acceptability and whose very timbral identity are, in part, determined by the particular developmental context which that melody provides.

It follows that the only evaluations of timbre we ought to indulge in are contextual ones. No less an authority than Jimmy Durante used to stop the band in the middle of a phrase and call on the trumpet player to repeat his most recent note over and over again—Durante exclaiming the while, "I wanna hear *that note;* that's a *good note!*" Since I have always supposed that Durante's description of that note was intended as a gag, I am sometimes mildly puzzled that no one laughs when a psycho-acoustical researcher renders the same gag by substituting "good sound" or "inherently interesting timbre" for "good note." But whatever the explanation may be for this collective failure in our senses of humor, I think we should in any case once and for all abandon the metaphysics of "inherently interesting timbres"—especially for laughs—and proceed with the cultivation of, at the worst, more complicated mistakes. If I claim that some timbre—say a raucous electronic buzz or a nicely shaped pear from the stage of the opera house—is a "good" (or "satisfactory," or "interesting," or "sophisticated") timbre, I should mean no more than that this timbre is an integral part of an actual or imaginable musical composition which I would consider to be a "good" composition. And if I deny virtue to that timbre, I should mean no more than that I can imagine no decent composition incorporating it—and if the history of music is any guide, such a judgment would prove to be no more than a tribute to the low quality of my compositional imagination.

A corollary of this contextual view is the obligation to suspect that an inadequacy of some timbre in some particular context is itself a function of the whole context, and hence a structural compositional inadequacy rather than a deficiency inherent in that timbre.

I hope what I wish to say about the search for allegedly "new" sounds is, by this time, predictably brief and anti-climactic:

If "new" sounds are the inferable or extrapolable other side of the coin from "old" sounds—and if the characteristics of the "old" ones are in the process of being discovered on the basis of research whose very questions powerfully suggest antecedently inadequate musical analysis of the old contexts—then the coin itself, both sides, must be a slug.

COMPOSITIONAL THEORY

SET STRUCTURE AS A
COMPOSITIONAL DETERMINANT

MILTON BABBITT

I PROPOSE, in this article, further to explain and expand certain observations made in a previous article[1] and to extend the investigation of the principles of set formation and transformation which was begun in another article.[2] In this latter paper I was concerned primarily with those set properties—pitch class and intervallic, order preserving and merely combinational—and those relationships between and among forms of the set which are preserved under the operations of the system, and which—in general—are independent of the singular structure of a specific set. Here, to the end of discovering certain compositional consequences of set structure, the concern will be with those attributes of set structure which maintain under the systematic operations only by virtue of the particular nature of a set, or of the class of sets of which it is an instance, together with a particular choice of operations.

Much of the discussion will be motivated by and centered about the initial measures (Example 1) of the third movement of the Schoenberg Fourth Quartet, the object of the observations mentioned above, not only—or even primarily—for the purpose of analyzing this excerpt, but in order to infer similar and further extensions of the properties and methods it exhibits. Many of these properties are what I have termed "combinational," to the extent that they are associated with collections of pitch classes within the set distinguished by pitch or intervallic content alone, and not necessarily by ordering, so that under the operations of the system, this collection remains fixed with regard to such content but not necessarily—or usually—in terms of internal ordering or order placement of the collection within the set.

The, by now, most familiar property of this kind embodied in the set of the Fourth Quartet is that of hexachordal combinatoriality, or, more precisely, hexachordal inversional combinatoriality, as a result of which any one of the two disjunct hexachords of any of the, at most, 48 set forms can be associated with the order corresponding hexachord of one or more inversions of that set form transposed by an interval or intervals deter-

[1] *Some Aspects of Twelve-Tone Composition,* in *The Score,* XII (1955). Henceforth abbreviated: SA.

[2] *Twelve-Tone Invariants as Compositional Determinants,* in *The Musical Quarterly,* XLVI (1960). Henceforth abbreviated: TT.

Example 1

mined by the pitch class ordering of the pitch classes within the hexachord, so that each such pair of hexachords contains all twelve pitch classes. This is equivalent to stating that a set is so constructed that the content of one of its hexachords is an inversion of the pitch classes of its other hexachord, ordering considerations aside. Although I do not wish to devote considerable space to the question of inversional combinatoriality or its generalizations, since I have done so previously—albeit informally—in SA, I feel obliged to review certain aspects, for the purpose of introducing necessary concepts, and because of the definitive and consequential role this property plays in the excerpt under discussion.

The hexachordal inversional property can be expressed:

$H_0 + T_t IH_0 = A$, for some t   (1.1) where H signifies "hexachord,"

and the subscript to H denotes the order number associated with the first element of this hexachord (thus, for simplicity, an ordering of the H is assumed, but the property is independent of the particular ordering); I signifies the inversion operator (permutation), and T the transposition operator, with subscript t denoting the transposition number, which—for this type of combinatoriality—can assume any odd integral value (See TT, p. 254, and below); where the T operator is omitted, it is understood that $t = 0$. The $+$ sign is used in the sense of set union, and $\cdot$ in the sense of set intersection. The members of the "sets" (hexachord, in this case) are pitch classes; A signifies "aggregate," which—for the moment— may be taken to mean any collection of 12 different pitch classes. It must be recalled that the I and T operators do not commute (or, alternatively, commute only to within complementation mod. 12), and—therefore—the indicated order of operations is significant, and is to be read from right to left; the R and I, R and T, and T operators do commute.

Given a t that satisfies (1.1), then from that stated property, the following follow immediately, any one of which could serve equally well as the definition of this type of combinatoriality: $H_0 \cdot T_t IH_0 = \varnothing$ (the empty set); $H_0 + T_t RIH_6 = A$; $H_0 \cdot T_t RIH_6 = \varnothing$; $H_0 \cdot T_t IH_6 = H_0 + T_t IH_6$, etc., etc. by virtue of the rules of formation and transformation of the system itself. (It is necessary to remember that any twelve-tone set possesses the combinatorial attribute that S_{0--n} (the first n order numbers of a set) $+$ $RS_{(n+1)--11=A.})$

Given a set S which possesses only I combinatoriality, there are four (and only four, it will be seen) forms of the set combinatorially related to this S in the sense of (1.1), including S itself. These forms, represented by the operators or associated permutations which effect them (since S is the identity element it is not stated when combined with another operator) can be presented conveniently in a group table:

S	$T_t I$	R	$T_t RI$
$T_t I$	S	$T_t RI$	R
R	$T_t RI$	S	$T_t I$
$T_t RI$	R	$T_t I$	S

The combinatorially so-related forms thus constitute a "four group" isomorphic to the group of the totality of set forms, mod. transposition. (It must be understood that T_t, for instance, is not an element of the above displayed group; if it were, this array would not represent a group. T_tI is a single permutation of the group, merely notated in terms of its constituent permutations.)

It is seen, then, that this combinatorial property partitions the, normally, 48 set forms into 12 disjunct collections of set forms; although considered independently (by allowing t in T_tS to equal 0) each of these collections is a "four group," within the group of all forms of a set, only the collection containing S is a sub-group, since S is the identity. Since I have introduced and shall introduce discussions of group structure only to present succinctly the relations among an assemblage of forms, I shall not pursue this discussion further. (The reader with a knowledge of elementary finite group theory will recognize at once the necessary invocation of cosets and imprimitive systems.) Compositionally, criteria of such combinatorial relatedness will provide only four such "functionally related" forms, and other criteria must be introduced to provide for the presentation of other forms, or other such collections of forms, as we shall observe in Example 1.

It is easy to derive, with the most rudimentary formalism, the necessary and sufficient condition for a set's possession of IH combinatoriality. I shall do so, not for purposes of enumeration, since the twelve so distinguished independent source sets ("source sets" in the sense of not signifying a particular ordering within the hexachords, or of the hexachords) are easily constructible, but in order to expose the structure of this class of sets, and to be able to proceed to other, thus seen to be analogous, combinatorial types.

Let "a" be the pitch class number (henceforth abbreviated p.c.n.) of any element of an H, then—by definition of T, I, and this combinatorial property—there must be a p.c.n. "b" in the complementary hexachord of H such that $12 - a + t = b$ (mod. 12) where $+$ denotes, of course, ordinary addition; so that, therefore:

$$a + b = t \text{ (mod. 12)} \qquad (2.1)$$

(Incidentally, this demonstrates also the fact—derivable in many different ways—that t cannot be even (see above), since there would then be an "a" (and an "a" + 6) such that $a = b$, contradicting the initial assumption that a + b are in disjunct hexachords). For later purposes, any two collections of p.cs. (not only hexachords) satisfying (2.1) will be termed "inversionally similar." The t in (2.1), therefore, is the transposition number under which I combinatoriality is effected; however, its value is obviously determined by the p.c.n. assigned to a specific "a" (or "b") in any S. If this is not thoroughly understood, designatory ambiguity will result. For example, in the Schoenberg Fourth Quartet, S shall be taken as that set a compositional representation of which is stated at the very beginning of Example 1. Then, if as is customary, the first p.c. of this set is assigned p.c.n. $= 0$, then the value of t is 5; but, if the whole quartet is under discussion, and—accordingly—the first p.c. of the set presented in the first violin at the work's opening is assigned p.c.n. $= 0$, then the value of t for the now, in the third movement, $T_{10}S$ is 1. In other words, one is accustomed to think of a transposition number as defined by the interval determined by $(S_{0,a})$ and $T_tI_{(0,a+t)}$, but this t is derivable only from these two p.cs. and $S_{i,a+6}$ and $T_tI_{i,a+6+t}$ (see TT, p. 254), whereas t in (2.1) is the sum of the p.c.nos. $S_{i,a}$ and $T_tI_{i,b}$ where "i" assumes any order number value. Only in this latter sense can one speak of "the" transposed inversion of a S or H which is combinatorially related to the S or H for the general case, as opposed to the transposition of T_0I or the transposition of two elements of S. Therefore, it is suggested that a given H be ordered in "normal form," wherein the interval determined by the first p.c. − last p.c. is greater than any interval determined by successive p.cs. in H. (The further specification for "normal form" when there is no such unique interval need not concern us here.)

For the Fourth Quartet, the normal form of H_0 of the above designated S is, in ordered p.c.nos. with the first $= 0$: 0, 1, 4, 5, 6, 8; the combinatorially related IH is: 3, 2, 11, 10, 9, 7; t, in both senses, is 3. The compositional orderings of the two H's are: 0, 11, 7, 8, 3, 1 and 5, 6, 10, 9, 2, 4; here t, in both senses $= 5$. It must be observed that the symmetry relation between operations of the system makes it impossible to differentiate systematically between t and $12 − t$ in I related sets.

Much, far too much, importance has been attached to Schoenberg's choice of $t = 5$ (in the usual sense) for many of his orderings (the Wind Quintet, the Variations for Orchestra Op. 31, and *Moses und Aron* are significant exceptions). To be sure, since it has been shown that the t value is dependent upon ordering, it may be assumed that the use of this particular t determined the choice of the first p.c. But the other two inversionally related sets of the combinatorial group are, in no way, less important, and for their initial p.c.nos. to define the interval 5 (or 7) would require merely that, if $S_{0,0}$ be the first member of S, then the last element would be $S_{11,1}$ or $S_{11,6}$ or $S_{11,7}$; but Schoenberg does not make this further choice often enough to be considered significant (Op. 33a is an instance). In the Fourth Quartet, the t so determined is 1 (or 11); in Op. 31, where the t determined by what would be designated usually as S and its combinatorially related IS is 9 (or 3), that determined by the other two sets is 5 (or 7), but in *Moses und Aron*, 5 (or 7) is not determined by either pair of I related sets.

A slight extension of (2.1) results from assuming that for each "a," there are two values of b (and, thus, of t) such that:

$$a + b_1 = t_1$$
$$a + b_2 = t_2 \tag{2.2}$$

which requires that b_1 and b_2 define the interval 6, from which it further follows that

$$H_0 + T_t H_0 = H_0 \tag{1.2}$$

for t = 6. Thus, in addition to the trivial case: $H_0 + RH_0 = A$, it follows that $H_0 + T_6 RH_0 = A$, and thus the property shall be termed RH combinatorially. There is one, and only one, IH combinatorial source set of the second order (that is, satisfying (2.2) satisfying additionally only (1.2). In one of its two normal forms (identical to within transposition by t = 6) one of its hexachords is: 0, 1, 3, 6, 7, 9. Observe that (1.2) manifests itself in the property that the p.c.nos. of the first trichord are congruent mod. 6 to those of the second trichord. The only other source set satisfying (2.2) is all-combinatorial of the second order, and— similarly—the one source set that satisfies (2.1) for three values of b and t, and the one that satisfies it for six values are the third order and fourth order all-combinatorial sets, respectively (See SA, p. 57–8).

(2.1) also suggests a "dual," in which "a" and "b" designate p.c.nos. in the same hexachord of S ("a" and "b," therefore, may be the same number). a + b = t (mod. 12), in this sense, will be numbered (3.1). It follows that b = 12 − a + t, and:

$$H_0 + (or \cdot)\ T_t IH_0 = H_0 \tag{3.2}$$

or, equivalently, in a statement analogous to that of (1.1):

$$H_0 + T_t RIH_0 = A \tag{1.3}$$

so that such hexachords are termed RI combinatorial, and only collections of p.c. nos. satisfying (3.1) will be called "inversionally symmetrical," since such a collection can be mapped into itself under application of I and the appropriate t. Although (1.1) and (1.3), and—above all—(2.1) and (3.1) indicate significant similarities between the structure of IH combinatorial and RIH combinatorial sets, the seven source sets of the latter type differ from those of the former in an immediately manifest respect. (2.1) defines a relation between complementary H's such that one can be considered as derived from the other by the application of a twelve-tone operation: I, but (3.1) defines a property of a single hexachord, so that the complementary H's of an S which possess only this H combinatorial property cannot be so derived from one another. Further, it can be shown that S cannot satisfy (3.1) multiply, so that for each "a" there are two or more "b's" (and t's) without also satisfying (1.1) and (1.2), and cannot satisfy (1.2) without also satisfying (1.1). The group associated with set forms related in the sense of (1.3) is, again, the "four group."

The remaining possible type of H combinatoriality is termed "prime" combinatoriality, and can be expressed:

$$H_0 + T_t H_0 = A \qquad (1.4)$$

an equivalent form: $H_6 + T_t H_0 = H$ reveals immediately that the disjunct H's of such an S are transpositions of one another. In the notation of (2.1):

$$a + t = b; \quad t = b - a \qquad (4.1)$$

Since $b - a$ is, by definition, the interval determined by the p.cs. "b" and "a," t here designates the transposition relation between the two H's, and—therefore—the interval which must be excluded internally from each H; since $a - b = 12 - t$, the complementary transposition number of t, if (4.1) is satisfied for only one t, then t must equal 6, the only interval which is its own complement. There is only one source set satisfying (4.1) and no other H combinatorial condition; any S which satisfies (4.1) for more than one b also satisfies (1.1), (2.1), and (3.1); any S which satisfies (4.1) and (1.1) also satisfies (3.1); any S which satisfies (4.1) and (3.1) also satisfies (1.1); any S which satisfies (4.1) and (2.1) satisfies (1.1) and (3.1) multiply. The "four group" associated with the S satisfying (1.4) is:

S	T_t	R	$T_t R$
$T_t S$	S	$T_t R$	R
R	$T_t R$	S	T_t
$T_t R$	R	T_t	S

The final extension of H combinatoriality is the all-combinatorial set: three source sets of first order satisfying (1.1), (1.3), and (1.4), but (1.2) only trivially, for $t = 0$, and represented by a group of order 8; three source sets which satisfy (1.1), (1.3), and (1.4), and (1.2) doubly, trebly, and sextuply, respectively; the second order set is represented by a group of order 16, the third order set by one of order 24, and the fourth order set by one of order 48. These six source sets are stated in SA (p. 57).

Another direction of generalization of the concept of combinatoriality is suggested by regarding H combinatoriality as a partitioning of an aggregate into two parts of six elements each; in the usual partitional notation, all the combinatorial relations thus far discussed are represented partitionally thus: (6^2). Similarly, a class of combinatorial sets can be associated with each of the 77 partitions of the number 12, ranging from the case where the aggregate is, in fact, a set, a single set form, represented: (12), to that which involves the maximum number of set forms: (1^{12}). The "justification" for this extension need be no more than that an aggregate is thereby assured, in the light of the actual and possible use of the aggregate as a unit of compositional progression containing segments of set forms functionally related through the requirements of aggregate structure. There are singular properties attending the set classes associated with each partition and the classes of these classes. I cannot deal with this enormously extensive subject here; I do wish to point out, however, that even so apparently trivial an unequal partition as (11 1), where the two parts represent, say, RI related sets, is nontrivial when incorporated into the structure of a set which possesses (1.3) combinatoriality for the same t. The condition that S_{1-11} (the final eleven p. cs. of S) $+ T_tIS_0 = A$ for the same value of t for which $H_6 + T_tIH_0 = A$ is fulfilled is simply not possible in a first order or third order all-combinatorial set.

The extension from H combinatoriality (6^2) to the remaining equal partitions: (2^6), (3^4), (4^3), (12), (1^{12}), and to the remaining two part partitions: $(1\ 11)$, $(2\ 10)$, $(3\ 9)$, $(4\ 8)$, $(5\ 7)$ incorporate immediate generalizations of the fundamental intervallic property of complementary hexachords, the property that the total intervallic content of two hexachords (that is, the 15 intervals of an H, specified most conveniently in the form of the six possible intervals—since complementary intervals are equivalent—with their associated multiplicities) is the same, if and only if the H's are complementary. This property, which is true of any pair of hexachords insures that every H will define an intervallic collection uniquely associated with itself and its complement. Therefore, the 36 intervals not present in either hexachord are formed by the 6×6 pairings of the members of the two complementary hexachords. This characteristic of singular harmonic definition suggests one important reason for Schoenberg's compositional concern with hexachords as combinational units. But this property is but a special case of the more general property associated with any partition of a set into two parts: if S is partitioned (m n)—m is assumed, by the usual notational convention, to be larger than n—then, it can be shown that, if the multiplicity of any interval i is k in the n-part segment, then it is $(m - n) + k$ in the m-part segment. The hexachordal property is merely the special case where $m = n$, and—therefore—$m - n = 0.$[3]

An investigation of tetrachordal (4^3), trichordal (3^4), dyadic (2^6), or unitary (1^{12}) combinatoriality even as summary as the preceding of H combinatoriality would exceed the appropriate limits of the present article. Rather, I shall present merely an instance of a set embodying such extensions. It is that of my Composition for Twelve Instruments (1948); although the set possesses properties of a complex combinatorial nature, making

[3]A discussion of this property for both two-part partitions and partitions with an equal number of parts can be found in the papers by David Lewin, *Journal of Music Theory*, III/2, 298–391, and IV/1, 98–101.

it susceptible to use in forming aggregates with more than two unequal parts—(8 2 1²), for instance—I shall indicate merely its equal-part partitional characteristics for one group of operators. The twelve forms are stated linearly, timbrally in the work; the designation of S is arbitrary.

S:	0,	1,	4,	9,	5,	8,	3,	10,	2,	11,	6,	7.
T_4:	4,	5,	8,	1,	9,	0,	7,	2,	6,	3,	10,	11.
T_8:	8,	9,	0,	5,	1,	4,	11,	6,	10,	7,	2,	3.
T_1I:	1,	0,	9,	4,	8,	5,	10,	3,	11,	2,	7,	6.
T_5I:	5,	4,	1,	8,	0,	9,	2,	7,	3,	6,	11,	10.
T_9I:	9,	8,	5,	0,	4,	1,	6,	11,	7,	10,	3,	2.
R:	7,	6,	11,	2,	10,	3,	8,	5,	9,	4,	1,	0.
T_4R:	11,	10,	3,	6,	2,	7,	0,	9,	1,	8,	5,	4.
T_8R:	3,	2,	7,	10,	6,	11,	4,	1,	5,	0,	9,	8.
T_1RI:	6,	7,	2,	11,	3,	10,	5,	8,	4,	9,	0,	1.
T_5RI:	10,	11,	6,	3,	7,	2,	9,	0,	8,	1,	4,	5.
T_9RI:	2,	3,	10,	7,	11,	6,	1,	4,	0,	5,	8,	9.

A: $\left\{ \begin{array}{l} \uparrow 9,\ 8,\ 5,\ 0,\ 4,\ 1, \uparrow \\ \downarrow 7,\ 6,\ 11,\ 2,\ 10,\ 3, \downarrow \end{array} \right.$ (bracketed across T_9I and R rows)

These twelve forms (a sub-group of half the order of the total group associated with combinatorially related sets of the third order of H combinatoriality), display (12), (6^2), (3^4), (2^6), and (1^{12}) combinatoriality. For example: H_0S or T_4H_0 or T_8H_0 or T^1IH_0 or T_5IH_0 or T_9IH_0 + anyone of the six remaining H_0's in the table = A; similarly, with trichords: $S_{0--2} + T_9IS_{0--2} + R_{0--2}$ or T_4R_{0--2} or $T_8R_{0--2} + T_9RI_{0--2}$ or T_5RI_{0--2} = A, etc., etc. So, too, with dyads, and with single pitch classes. This latter case is not, as might be assumed hastily, a trivial attribute of any set, for the above table is not a set matrix, containing all set forms, or all the transpositions of any transformation. For all p. cs. of the same order number to produce an A for every order no. for a collection of set forms producing (6^2), (3^4), and (2^6) combinatoriality requires the imposition of stringent conditions upon the structure of S itself.

It will be observed that every possible equal-part partition (and its conjugate) is present except (4^3), the conjugate of (3^4), because every trichord of a third-order H contains at least one interval of 4 (or 8). However, (4^3) combinatoriality is present; not, of course, for every disjunct tetrachord, but among tetrachords containing the four central elements of every set form (this tetrachord is a first-order all combinatorial tetrachord): S_{4--7} or T_1I_{4--7} or R_{4--7} or $T_1RI_{4--7} + T_4S_{4--7}$ or T_5I_{4--7} or T_4R_{4--7} or $T_5RI_{4--7} + T_8S_{4--7}$ or T_9I_{4--7} or T_8R_{4--7} or T_9RI_{4--7} = A.

The large number of aggregates which can be formed as the result of set structure such as this, and the still very much larger number of possible compositional orderings of the p.cs. within each A indicate the extent of available and necessary choice, for all that the systematic ordering within the set segments—determined by the set structure—is "pre-defined" and preserved. The magnitude of the number of compositional statements of aggregates associated merely with a given H combinatorial pair can be inferred from the fact that there are 32 compositions of a single H. Therefore, the importance of this facet of twelve-tone composition, the spatial and temporal disposition of an aggregate and the relation of the structures of successively presented aggregates, can be appreciated as, at least, that of "middleground" harmonic structure, situated hierarchically between the "foreground" structure of simultaneities and their relations, and the larger areas including and subsuming aggregates as their constituents.

Still further—and, in a sense, different—extensions of partitioning are suggested, and have been employed, by extending the notion of an aggregate to include the registral specification of p.c. members so that all partitions less than and equal to those of the number 48 are available; by this approach, instrumental "doubling" and registral rhythm—for example—fall within the domain of combinatoriality, in this extended interpretation.

Again, the 2^{11} compositions of the number 12 all must be examined when the order of parts of a partition of an A is significant, as it is when the parts are—say—assigned linearly to classes of timbres, registers, dynamics, etc. Indeed, any compositional statement of an S or A necessarily is partitioned registrally, instrumentally, dynamically, and temporally.

Although one of the primary compositional applications of combinatoriality has been that of aggregate formation, the progression in twelve-tone units other than a form of S, the extension of the principle to produce "weighted aggregates" (a collection of twelve pitches in which the twelfth pitch does not appear until after, at least, one pitch class has been represented, at least, twice, with each of these representations supplied by segments of different set forms) or—the same concept differently described—"incomplete aggregates" (a maximal segment, with no pitch class repetitions of the kind just described, of a weighted aggregate) results immediately from the further properties of the intervallic structure of a subset, which structure completely determines the extent of intersection between such a subset and another of its forms.

The set of the Fourth Quartet possesses combinational characteristics in addition to, and independent of, those of H combinatoriality. Consider the p.c.nos. of the disjunct tetrachords. The first: 0, 11, 7, 8 is inversionally symmetrical, since $0 + 7 = 11 + 8$ (see 3.1); the second: 3, 1, 2, 10 and the third: 6, 5, 4, 9 are inversionally similar, since $3 + 4 = 1 + 6 = 2 + 5 = 10 + 9 = 7$ (see 2.1). So, under $T_7I : S_{0--3} \rightarrow T_7I_{0--3}$, $S_{4--7} \rightarrow T_7I_{8--11}$, $S_{8--11} \rightarrow T_7I_{4--7}$.

Further, consider the disjunct trichords: the first: 0, 11, 7 and the fourth: 5, 4, 9 are inversionally similar: $0 + 4 = 11 + 5 = 7 + 9 = 4$; the second: 8, 3, 1 and the third: 2, 10, 6 are each inversionally symmetrical under $t = 4$. So, under T_4I: $S_{0--2} \rightarrow T_4I_{9--11}$, $S_{9--11} \rightarrow T_4I_{0--2}$, $S_{3--5} \rightarrow T_4I_{3--5}$, $S_{6--8} \rightarrow T_4I_{6--8}$. Therefore, one sixth of the 48 set forms preserve H, or tetrachordal, or trichordal content.

So little attention has been directed toward the combinational structure of Schoenberg's sets beyond H structure that the examination of another instance seems appropriate. The set is that of the String Trio (It is not here germane to argue whether or not this is the set of the Trio, or whether or not there is such a set. This set and its other forms occur frequently enough, explicitly, to justify its examination): 0, 8, 1, 7, 2, 11, 9, 6, 4, 5, 3, 10. The t under which (1.1) holds is 5, but it is the tetrachordal structure which is of particular interest. The tetrachord 8, 1, 7, 2 is an ordering of the second-order, all-combinatorial tetrachord, and inversionally symmetrical for two values of t: $t = 3$, and $t = 9$. But as we have seen, such a collection must satisfy also (1.2), so that under $t = 6$ this tetrachord maps into itself. Consider now the forms of S which hold the pitch content of this tetrachord invariant:

S:	0	(8	1	7	2)	11	9	[6	4	5	3]	10
T_6S:	[6]	(2	7	1	8)	[5]	[3]	0	10	11	9	[4]
T_3IS:	[3]	(7	2	8	1)	[4]	[5]	9	11	10	0	[6]
T_9IS:	9	(1	8	2	7)	10	0	[3	5	4	6]	11

In terms of the primary consideration of H structure the tetrachordal structure of this S is clear and striking. The initial and final p.cs. of each H of S (here underlined) are an ordering of a first-order, all-combinatorial tetrachord, and the p.c. remainder of the second H of S (bracketed) is another ordering of the same source tetrachord. Therefore, these four set operations map the latter tetrachord into itself in those forms in which the former tetrachord maps into itself, and into the former tetrachord in those forms in which the former maps into the latter. Also, the tetrachord S_{1--4} is presented ("vertically") by the four p.cs. with order nos. 1, or 2, or 3, or 4. Similarly, the tetrachord consisting of p.cs. with order nos. 5, or 8, or 9, or 11 is a transposition of the same tetrachord as S_{1--4}. The remaining four "vertical" tetrachords are identical within themselves, and are representations of the third-order, all-combinatorial tetrachord. These four set forms are representable as a "four-group."

Returning now to Example 1 and the compositional manifestations of the work's set structure, the opening—completely linear—statement of the S delineates the importance of its hexachordal structure by articulating, through a rest, this set division. (An identical use of a rest can be found in the first linearly explicit statement of the set of *Moses und Aron*, in Aron's vocal line, on page 32 of the orchestral score (B. Schott's Söhne, Mainz, 1958). The end of the second H, and of the S, is articulated by a change of instrumental texture from a four instrument unison to a single instrument statement, by a change of register from that available to all four instruments to that uniquely available to the cello, and by an extreme dynamic change. The combinatorially related form that follows (T_5RI) often is selected by Schoenberg to succeed S (for example, in the statement of the theme in the Variations for Orchestra, the opening of the Concerto for Piano and Orchestra, and in the continuation of the passage from *Moses und Aron* cited above) since $SH_6 + T_5RIH_0 = A$. (This temporally successive compositional representation of set segments forming an A is termed a "secondary set," since—compositionally—it fulfills the set condition of total ordering; the term "aggregate" will be reserved for those compositional cases where the segments are not linearly ordered in relation to each other. Context will discriminate the uses of the term "aggregate" in the compositional and systematic senses.) Also, the intervallic identity between any two RI related forms provides immediate intervallic repetition. In Example 1, the H structure of the T_5RIS, and—therefore—the extent of the secondary set, is articulated by the instrumental partitioning of H_0 into (2^21^2) while H_6 is partitioned into only one part, stated unaccompanied by the first violin. The entrance of the next combinatorially related form, R, is in the other three instruments which present H_0, but then H_6, again, is assigned to the first violin alone. Here is a manifest, if simple, instance of what can be termed accurately "structural orchestration," a vast and important aspect of twelve-tone composition. After the statements of S and T_5RI, the progression through secondary sets necessarily ends (only a repetition of S could continue it); the H_0 of the R that now follows (as would also have been true of T_5I) taken together with T_5RIH_6 cannot create such a set, rather, $T_5RIH_6 + RH_0 = H$; but, therefore, $T_5RIH_6 + RH_6 = A$, and—with H's ordered—a secondary set; it is this hexachordal succession which is presented by the first violin.

After the statements of S, T_5RI, and R, the remaining related form T_5I is not stated; it is reserved for a more definitive role, to be discussed later. An I form is stated next, however, as one component of the first simultaneous statement of combinatorially related forms, temporally juxtaposed to provide a succession of aggregates. This measure, also, will be discussed in detail below.

The opening statement of S is characterized most strikingly by the repetition of the dyad (G♭, F), isolated by rests, as the sole deviation from the direct linear statement of the set members; similarly, the dyad (C, B) is repeated in the complementary H of T_5RI, and isolated instrumentally. The choice of these dyads for such singular treatment creates a direct association between the two set forms by so identifying ordered adjacencies which are common to the two sets, almost unique adjacencies, since they are the first two members of the unique, ordered trichords: (C, B, G) and

(B♭, G♭, F). The use of the total trichord in this function is delayed until a later stage of the movement; see—for instance—m. 636-7. These dyads serve to articulate the beginning and end of the two-set complex, since (G♭, F), repeated in the first set, is the final dyad of the second set, and (C, B), repeated in the second set, is the initial dyad of the first set.

Fixed adjacency structure, since it is a matter of ordering, essentially is independent of H structure. For a succession of p. c. nos. (a, b) in any S to remain fixed under, for some t, T_tI, S must contain the succession (c, d), where $a + c = b + d$, for $12 - a + t = c$; $12 - b + t = d$; $t = a + c$ (and $b + d$). Under this t, $a \to c$, $b \to d$, $c \to a$, and $d \to b$. If T_tRI is substituted for T_tI in this expression, the order of c, d must be reversed. Thus, here, (c, b) maps into (G♭, F) under T_5RI because the sum of the p. c. nos. of C and $F = 5$, and similarly the sum of b and G♭ $= 5$. And $t = 5$ is, of course, the H combinatorial value of t.

The repeated (A, B♭) and (E, D) in 621-2 are statements of dyadic adjacencies of the preceding T_5RIH_6, but they are not adjacencies in R, but compositionally secured through the instrumental partitioning of RH_0, which partitioning is also an obvious reflection of the registral disposition of T_5RIH_6.

The general treatment of the question of adjacency invariance in connection with H structure is handled most efficiently with the notation and methods of permutations. Thus, the H_6 of a specific S can be regarded as a permutation of the order nos. of a T_tIH_0 where t satisfies (1.1). In these terms, for the case here (0 1 2 3 4 5), with the upper row representing

(3 2 1 5 0 3)

the order nos. of T_5IH_0 and the lower their ordering in H_6 (of S), the adjacency structure preserving the (here) reversed trichord is, at once, obvious.

In Example 1 the first element of T_5RI creates, with the final two elements of S, a trichordal succession (E, A, A♭) which is a form of a trichord stated and repeated within S: (G, A♭, E♭) and (F, E, A). An immediate "motivic" repetition is created by the overlap of this (F, E, A) with (A, A♭, D♭). This immediate means of joining the successive set statements is very much a result of the order structure of S; one need but reverse the final two elements of S to secure $(S_{10,9}, S_{11,4}, T_5RI_{0,1})$, a trichord form not present in S.

Before devoting virtually the remainder of this article to a consideration of the transpositional choice in m. 623, I shall touch summarily on a few other aspects of this passage.

The registral disposition of an S or A statement is independent, systematically, of set structure; indeed, questions of specific instrumental limitations aside, any S or A can be ordered spatially in 12! ways. This alone emphasizes how consequential musically is the compositional choice of registral arrangement, both from a standpoint of internal structure and from that of progression, with its attendant linear-registral considerations. Although references have been made to Webern's procedure of maintaining a contextually established disposition over an extended part of a work, this facet of Schoenberg's music has been neglected. I restrict myself here to one aspect of the registral structure of m. 614-23. S is registrally disposed in the minimum possible space, the extrema defining an (absolute, non-modular) interval of 11; the mid-pitches of this particular disposition are C and D♭. That they are literally stated is trivial here, because of the minimal registral span of S, but—significantly—they are the pitches of greatest duration in the statement of S. This association of some type of musical emphasis with the explicitly stated mid-pitch (or pitches) of a registral disposition is conclusively characteristic of this passage. The following statement of T_5RI is disposed over an interval of 45, the mid-pitches are the explicitly stated (this is not trivial here), uniquely emphasized C and B in the viola, held fixed registrally from S. Similarly, the statement of R, defining an interval of 32, has as its mid-pitch the explicitly stated, repeated A of the second violin. Any lingering suspicion of fortuitousness should be dispelled by m. 623. Consider, first, the disposition of the total set pair, the T_9S in the cello and the combinatorially related T_2I partitioned (9 3) by the viola and second violin. The registral interval is 21, the mid-pitches are C♯ and D, the only two pitches held registrally fixed between the two aggregates of the measure. To achieve this Schoenberg made one, and only one, change in the registral disposition of S when stated here as T_9S: the E♭ in the cello of 623 is an octave lower than the element of the same order number in S, thus making this the lower extreme of the measure. If the original disposition had been maintained, then D alone would have been the mid-pitch, and—if it were to be emphasized uniquely by registral repetition—then the C♯ of the cello would have to be changed registrally, thus becoming the lowest (or highest) note of the measure, altering the disposition. It should be noticed, also, that the mid-pitches of the individual aggregates are the same D, C♯; this is trivial in the case of the second aggregate, which contains both extrema, but not so in the case of the first aggregate, whose interval number is 19. The change of the registral disposition of S as T_9S now makes the first two notes of the cello, the A and G♯, the mid-pitches of this set; the importance of this dyad in other respects is discussed below.

Correspondingly, I will restrict myself to but one observation on the "rhythm" of this excerpt, sufficient however to serve as a counterexample to the assertion that Schoenberg's rhythm is "unrelated" to the twelve-tone structure of his pitches. Consider the temporal duration of the successive set statements: $S = 4\frac{3}{4}$ measures, Secondary Set 4 (approx.), $T_5RI = 2\frac{3}{4}$, $R = 1\frac{3}{4}$ (approx.), and $T_9S + T_2I = 1$. I am not concerned with the absolute values of the durations, but with the use of the sets as units of durational definition, effecting a successive durational reduction to and including the first point where different set forms are combined simultaneously. Obviously, set (or aggregate) rhythm in this sense is employed as an analogue of harmonic rhythm in the triadic sense.

Associative harmony in the small is employed in this passage much as in, for example, such a non-twelve-tone work as Op. 23/3. These identities are virtually self-evident: that of the aggregate-formed simultaneity on the second beat of m. 623, and the set-formed simultaneity on the second beat of m. 619; the exact inversional identity of the trichord on the first beat of m. 623 with that of the fourth beat of m. 621 (and the first beat of m. 622); the preparation of the "obligatory" combinatorial interval 5 (stated explicitly by the initial notes of the cello and viola in m. 623) by the explicitly attacked, simultaneous dyads (G, C) on the second beat of m. 619, (B, E) on the first beat of m. 620, and (E, A) in m. 621; the vertical intervals (5, 8) associated with the A and B♭ of the second violin in m. 621-2 repeated in succession with the next two pitches of the second violin (B, C), created by the second violin and viola, again.

Now, at last, I shall examine the choice of $t = 9$ for the statement of S in m. 623. Most immediately, there is the identification of the first note of T_9S with the last of S. This identification is combined cyclically through a circuit of pitch classes by successive transpositions of S, defining—as initial and terminal p. cs.: $C — — A$ (in S), $A — — F\sharp$ (in T_9S), $F\sharp(G\flat) — — E\flat$ (in T_6S, m. 626-7), and $E\flat — — C$ (in T_3S, m. 628); the next statement of a T_tS is S itself in the following section of the movement (m. 633). This cyclical connection of similar set forms ("similar" signifying identity to within transposition) is available regardless of the structure of S; the interval of transposition is determined by $S_{0,a}$ and $S_{11,b}$, and the number of sets required to construct the circuit is $\dfrac{12}{b - a}$ or, equivalently, $\dfrac{12}{a - b}$. However, if there are other bases for choosing the transposition number, then the relation of the first and last p.cs. of S can be so determined. In the example here, the choice of $t = 9$ creates initial-terminal succession C-A-F♯-E♭, a "diminished seventh" outline which reflects still another characteristic of the structure of S. If the p.cs. of S are written mod. 3, the following results:

$$0, 2, 1, 2, 0, 1, 2, 1, 0, 2, 1, 0,$$

Each disjunct trichord contains one, and—thus—only one, element from each residue class, mod. 3; informally, it can be said that each trichord contains one element from each of the three "diminished seventh chords" which are available among the twelve pitch classes. These trichords, which play an explicit compositional role in the work (the very opening of the first movement, for example), then define a progression through the "diminished" seventh, as do the transpositions of S in the third movement. A similar succession could be achieved by setting $t = 3$, but this could not be also the basis of a terminal-initial succession, since p.c. numbers 0 and 3 are both in the first hexachord of S.

The immediate identificatory function of the initial note A in m. 623 is extended to the dyad of which it is the first member, for the succession $(A, G\sharp)$, phrased together, it should be noticed, continues the pitch identity with m. 618, where $(A, A\flat)$ is the dyadic join of S and T_5RI. For this to be available in a S, $S_{0,0}$ and $S_{1,a}$ must define an interval "a" equal to that defined by $S_{11,b}$ and T_tRI_0, $12 - b + t$; if the t determines a (1.1) combinatorial relation, then it is itself a function of $S_{0,0}$. The dyad $(A, G\sharp)$ is stated simultaneously or successively (in this order, or reversed) once or more in each succeeding measure of this section of the movement, culminating with the $(A, G\sharp)$, each pitch under a fermata, the highest pitches of the section (the same registral placement of these pitches occurs also four measures earlier), at the end of the section (m. 629). The A, G$\sharp$ as mid-pitches have been mentioned above. Identification of the cello A of m. 623 with the terminal A of S is clarified further by the simultaneous statement of C $(R_{11,0})$ in the first violin, thus providing a simultaneous presentation of the first and last notes of S, the former even in its original register.

But the choice of $t = 9$ in m. 623 effects more complete and fundamental associations, if sonically less immediate ones, instancing more general principles than those just observed. Since the sum of the pitch members of all pairs of elements with the same order numbers in I related sets is the same, the distribution of the elements of an S into such pairs for any $T_{t_1}S$, $T_{t_2}I$ juxtaposition is determined completely by the pitch numbers of S, since $S_{m,a}$ and $S_{n,b} \rightarrow T_{t_1}S_{k,a}$, $T_{t_2}I_{k,b}$ and, of course, $T_{t_1}S_{1,b}$, $T_{t_2}I_{1,a}$ if, and only if, $a + b = t_1 + t_2$. More specifically, two successive pitch numbers (a, b) of S are associated with the same order nos. of the I related sets if $a + b = t_1 + t_2$. In the Quartet S, the pitch number sum of the pitch successions (C, B), and (F, G$\flat$) is, in both cases, 11. (The importance of these dyads in previously discussed regards must not be forgotten.) The "identification" of these "horizontals" as "verticals" in I related sets requires that the $t_1 + t_2$ associated with these sets sum to 11. If, as here, $t_2 - t_1 = 5$ to effect H combinatoriality between the I related sets, then t_1 must satisfy the expression: $t_1 + t_1 + 5 = 11$, and therefore $t = 9$ or 3; the first value is that chosen in 623, the second that occurring in the last set of the circuit (see m. 628 in the score).

The procedure, as a determinant of transpositional choice, plays a fundamental role in other works of Schoenberg, for instance, in the Phantasy for Violin. The initial S and (H combinatorially related) T_5I are:

$$S: \quad 0, 11, 3, 1, \quad 7, 9, \quad 6, 2, 10, 5, 8, 4$$
$$T_5I: \quad 5, \quad 6, 2, 4, 10, 8, 11, 3, \quad 7, 0, 9, 1$$

At measure 21, the first transposition of S occurs, with its associated I; $t = 9$, and the t associated with I then must be 2, and their sum $= 11$, which is the value of the sum of the first two pitch numbers of S and T_5I. Thus, these successive elements become simultaneities:

$$S_9: \quad 9, 8, \quad \underline{0}, 10, 4, \underline{6}, 3, \underline{11}, 7, 2, \underline{5}, 1$$
$$T_2I: \quad 2, 3, \underline{11}, \quad 1, 7, \underline{5}, 8, \quad \underline{0}, 4, 9, \underline{6}, 10$$

The initial successive dyads of S_9 and T_2I, since their sum is 5, were simultaneities in the statements of S and T_5I.

The next (m. 25) transposition of the pair of sets proceeds similarly, by another interval of 9, so that in T_tS, $t = 6$, and in T_tI, $t = 11$; this constitutes a return to the simultaneous dyads of the initial statement, since $6 + 11 = 5$:

$$T_6S: \quad 6, 5, 9, \quad 7, 1, 3, 0, 8, 4, 11, 2, 10.$$
$$T_{11}I: \quad 11, 0, 8, 10, 4, 2, 5, 9, 1, \quad 6, 3, \quad 7.$$

In the Fourth Quartet, the total intervallic structure of H_0 (and, therefore, of H_6 as well) possesses a characteristic highly relevant to the choice, $t = 9$. One, and only one, interval occurs only once: 6. The G and D♭ of H_0, and the B♭ and E of H_6 (which, incidentally, combine to form a "diminished seventh chord," again), therefore, define H_6 as a transposition of H_0 by the interval of 9 or 3 (since the interval 6 is its own complement, no choice between these complementary intervals can or need be made). This is analogous to characterizing the G major scale as a transposition by a perfect fifth of the C major scale, solely in terms of the intervallic relation between the unique intervals (coincidentally, also 6) of the two scale pitch collections. In these terms, T_9S is to S, as SH_6 is to SH_0. The significance of this aspect of the structure of S is revealed more directly when it is seen that, therefore, under T_9: (G, D♭) → (E, B♭) and (B♭, E) → (G, C♯); under T_6: (G, D♭) → (C♯, G) and (B♭, E) → (E, B♭); and, under T_3: (G, D♭) → (B♭, E) and (B♭, E) → (D♭, G). Thus, the circuit of transposed S's may be described as defining an imprimitive system with regard to the pitch content of the tritones contained in disjunct hexachords. These sets form a group of order four (but not a "four group"), and there are three such isomorphic groups each associated with a so-related pair of tritones, and generated by the four members of the residue classes, mod. 3. Thus, in m. 614-29, every disjunct H contains either the tritone of H_0 or that of H_6, in the same or reversed order, regardless of the set form involved; this, of course, follows from the above by the very nature of IH combinatoriality. Such an instance is but a slight indication

of the profound importance of the intervallic content of an H, and—
therefore—of the intervallic relations between complementary two part
partitions of an S (or A).

Now, also, the significance of $t = 3$ as determined by the inversional
relation between H_0 and H_6 when H_0 is stated in normal form is obvious.

The instrumental partitioning (9 3) of T_2I in m. 623 not only places
in the second violin a permutation of the fifth, sixth, and seventh pitches
of T_9S, relating these trichords by RI, but the remaining pitches of T_2I,
in the viola, relate the first four note, sixteenth note succession to the second
according to the following intervallic patterns: 1, 4, 12-1; 4, 1, 12-4; and
the first four elements of T_9S, supplying—necessarily—the interval succession: 12-1, 12-4, 1, are now identical—in totality—with the last four of
T_2I, while the remaining two attacks of the viola reverse the final dyad
of T_9S.

Example 2

Example 2 demonstrates Schoenberg's use of combinatorially determined criteria as determinants of external structure: "form," in the sense
of the deployment of areas of thematic, textural, rhythmic, and com-
parably manifest similarities. Example 2 is a return, the only return, to
the unison statement, the tempo, the rhythmic structure (with one tiny
exception), and the metric of the movement's opening. The set form is
T_5I, the one form H combinatorially related to S omitted, as observed
above, from the opening succession of set statements. This "functional
transposition" of S assures that (F, G♭) now occupies the positions held
by (C, B) in S, and (B, C) those of (G♭, F). Now, the repeated notes of
the set statement in this "isorhythmic" repetition are (B, C), and those
of the following RI related form (R) are (G♭, F). The terminal and initial

notes of these so related forms are the familiar (A♭, A), etc., etc. All of these features are results of the principles discussed above. This successive statement of what, in simultaneous statement, would produce a note-against-note combinatorial presentation of two, pitch dyad identical, successive aggregates is time-congruent "form" of the most definitive sort.

If many of the topics investigated in this paper have been treated only cursorily, one entire domain of the relation of set structure to compositional structure has been omitted entirely: the combinatorial areas associated with the subsets of S, through derivation (see SA, p. 59–60). This omission has been dictated by the asserted concern with the Schoenberg example (Schoenberg never employed derivation explicitly and independently, for all that—for example—the secondary set formed by SH_6 and T_5RIH_0 can be regarded as derived from SH_6), and the enormous scope of the subject, which conjoins the techniques of Schoenberg and Webern in a generalization whose compositional implications are comprehensive, vast, and challenging.

TWELVE-TONE RHYTHMIC STRUCTURE
AND THE ELECTRONIC MEDIUM

MILTON BABBITT

TO PROCEED from an assertion of what music has been to an assertion of what music, therefore, must be, is to commit a familiar fallacy; to proceed from an assertion of the properties of the electronic medium to an assertion of what music produced by this medium therefore must be, is not only to commit the same fallacy (and thus do fallacies make strange bedfellows), but to misconstrue that compositional revolution of which the electronic medium has been the enabling instrument. For this revolution has effected, summarily and almost completely, a transfer of the limits of musical composition from the limits of the nonelectronic medium and the human performer, not to the limits of this most extensive and flexible of media but to those more restrictive, more intricate, far less well understood limits: the perceptual and conceptual capacities of the human auditor. Therefore, although every musical composition justifiably may be regarded as an experiment, the embodiment of hypotheses as to certain specific conditions of musical coherence, any electronically realized composition which employs resources singularly obtainable by electronic means, in addition, will incorporate—in that *Gedankenexperiment* which is the mental act of composition—certain premises that are either severely circumscribed by the limited confirmed knowledge of the nature of these capacities or by isolated facts of musical perception, themselves obtained mainly with the assistance of electronic media, for incorporation into the premises of the particular work. Even the composer who employs the RCA Synthesizer, which most conveniently permits the merging and interaction of the "Gedanken" and the "Actual" experiments by allowing immediate aural test of the prescribed events at each stage of compositional realization, cannot employ the medium fluently and efficiently by so doing without a sacrifice of all but the most local points of continuity and interrelationship. If more securely founded and ambitiously structured electronic composition is not, then, to halt to await those perhaps long delayed investigations which may, in turn, produce adequately general results only in an unforeseeably distant future, it probably must hypothesize in a more traditional manner, by incorporating into its postulates widely tested and confirmed statements regarding the perception of music, derived from successful past experiments, that is, from musical compositions. In this consequential respect, electronically produced compositions can differ among themselves and from non-electronically produced compositions in terms of the extent to which the hypotheses they exemplify already have been widely tested and confirmed, that is, the degree to which they incorporate "traditional" laws into the postulates of the work, and also the degree to which these "traditional" laws are incorporated into the scope of the rule of substitution[1] for descriptive terms, founded either on validated properties of similitude or on hypothesized properties of similitude, so that in the latter case these properties are themselves being tested by the composition, while in the former case of validated properties it is rather the significance of the similitudes with regard to a specific property that is being tested. At the extreme of "nontraditionalism" is the selection of an uninterpreted formal system, no interpreted instances of which have been musically validated, along with coordinative rules which, likewise, have not been validated independently. In such a case, the probability that such an unrestricted choice from such a large number of possibilities at both stages will yield a significant result is extremely small, or the result itself is likely to be virtually trivial, that is, hardly to admit nonverification.

In constructing a musical system for an electronically produced work, whether this system be exemplified in but a single work or a body of works, there is a particular temptation to proceed in this "nontraditional" fashion, since one can presume as the values associated with notationally separable components (the range of discrete values that each component of the musical event may assume) those which are obtainable as the result of the medium's providing measurable and regulable values of frequency, intensity, duration, and spectrum to a degree of differentiation far exceeding the, at least, present discriminative capacity of the auditory apparatus under the most generous temporal conditions, and further providing those values at time points whose precise specifications similarly can produce measurably different quantities which surpass the discriminative and memorative abilities of the most appropriately qualified observers. Surely it is in the domain of temporal control that the electronic

---

[1] The rule of substitution may be regarded informally as providing the transformation of a validated statement into a statement which is less validated by virtue of the incomplete knowledge of the object designated by the substituted terms or of the relations among the objects designated by the terms, for the purpose of testing the second statement.

medium represents the most striking advance over performance instruments, for such control has implications not only for those events
which are normally and primarily termed "rhythmic" but for all other
notationally apparently independent areas: speed and flexibility of
frequency succession, time rate of change of intensity, and important
components of what is perceived in conjunction as tone-color, such
as envelope—which is merely the time rate of change of intensity
during the growth and decay stages—and deviations of spectrum,
frequency, and intensity during the quasi or genuinely steady-state.
Indeed, it is this imposition of time control upon timbral components
which is, at least partially, responsible for the emphasis, the exag-
gerated emphasis, on the purely sonic possibilities of the electronic
medium; but whereas not even the number of relevant dimensions
of tone color are generally known (in the sense of reproducing the
dimensionality, not the identical characteristics, of non-electronic
timbre) the basis of perceived homogeneity of timbre over an extended
registral span—fixed, or limitedly variable input signal subjected to
the resonance influence of a fixed formant—is known, and is synthetically verifiable and easily obtained electronically. But the precise
placement of time points and their associated durations, though easily
and exactly specifiable, takes one into the area of rhythm, which is not
only of central concern in contemporary compositional thought, nonelectronic as well as electronic, but the most refractory and mysterious
perceptually. There are very few useful results available concerning
the correlation between specified and perceived duration; even specified
identity appears to be not necessarily perceptually invariant with
regard to a contextual situation, and those bases of similitude of durational succession inferred from traditional contexts—multiplication of
the constituent durational values by a positive constant, usually an
integer or its reciprocal—are not of general applicability when the
associated pitch succession or pitch contour is altered, or the durational succession is not endowed with obvious cues. With so little
information of these types to provide the postulates of a rhythmic
system, applicable to nonelectronic music and extrapolable to the
electronic realm, it is more fruitful to examine a musical pitch-class
system, one which by now can be regarded as "traditional," which
incorporates qualitative time properties into its very rule of formation.
For, in the extensive discussions which have surrounded the twelve-
tone system, be they those which have concerned themselves with
inferring or imposing rhythmic schemata, "serial" or non-"serial,"
from or upon twelve-tone compositions, or those questioning the associative, articulative role of rhythm as a function of characteristics of

the pitch structure, there has appeared to be little awareness of or concern with the immanently temporal nature of the twelve-tone pitch-class system. To the end of examining this temporal nature and deriving a quantitative temporal interpretation of the system, I propose to consider a few structural properties of the system which incorporate different modes of dependency upon temporal factors.

A twelve-tone set can be characterized as a collection of twelve different pitch-classes[2] (or, more conveniently, as the integers from 0 to 11 inclusive, denoting these classes) ordered by the relation of temporal precedence (designated $<$) or, equivalently, temporal subsequence(designated $>$). The collection is strict simply ordered with regard to this relation; that is, the relation is asymmetric, transitive, and connected (and, of course, irreflexive)[3] in the collection, and—therefore—is indeed a relation which induces a "serial" ordering. (It should be emphasized that this is the total meaning of the term "serial": it implies nothing with regard to the operations upon such an ordering, or the nature of the elements ordered.) This ordering is the basis for the assignment of order numbers to the pitch class numbers, for these integers of order (0-11 inclusive) are strict simply ordered with regard to the usual interpretation of $<$ as less than, and $>$ as greater than.

At this point, as a means of informally evaluating the temporal constraints imposed by the principle of formation of a twelve-tone set, I shall assume on purely empirical grounds that there are eleven qualitatively significant temporal relationships which can hold between two musical (say, pitch) events. Let x and y designate these events, and let a left parenthesis signify the time point initiation of the event and a right parenthesis signify the time point termination. Then, the eleven relationships are:

1. x) $<$ (y. [that is, the termination of x precedes the initiation of y]
2. (x $<$ (y; x) $<$ y); but x) $\not<$ (y.
3. (x $<$ (y; x) $\not<$ y); y) $\not<$ x).

[2] For terms and notation not fully explained here and later in this article, see my articles: "Twelve-Tone Invariants as Compositional Determinants," the *Musical Quarterly*, April 1960, pp. 246–259 (henceforth abbreviated: TT); "Set Structure as a Compositional Determinant," above, pp. 129–147 (henceforth abbreviated: SS).

[3] A relation R is irreflexive on a collection: if for any element x of the collection, xRx does not hold, i.e. x cannot have the relation (such as temporal precedence) to itself.

R is transitive: if for any elements x, y, z: if xRy and yRz, then xRz.

R is connected: if between any two elements, x and y, of the collection, either xRy or yRx.

R is asymmetric: if xRy, then yRx cannot hold.

4. $(x < (y; \quad y) < x)$.

5. 6. 7. 8. are derived from 1. 2. 3. 4. respectively by substituting x for y, and y for x.

9. $(x \not< (y; \quad (y \not< (x; \quad x) \not< y); \quad y) \not< x)$.

10. $(x \not< (y; \quad (y \not< (x; \quad x) < y)$.

11. $(x \not< (y; \quad (y \not< (x; \quad y) < x)$.

Given any two pitch classes of a twelve-tone set, only four of the eleven possibilities can be made to hold without violating the meaning of the order numbers.

The collection of ordered pairs: order number, pitch-class number, each of which uniquely determines an element of a set, is a function, in which the order numbers may be considered as defining the domain, and the pitch-class numbers the values of the domains; in this sense, pitch-class is, not inconsequentially, a "function" of a relative time point, designated by the order number. The function is biunique,[4] possessing—therefore—a unique inverse, which defines a twelve-tone set, and the ordered pairs associated with the elements are alternatively to be considered as defining a mapping[5] of the ordered chromatic scale onto itself in terms of either order numbers or pitch-class numbers (the two are equivalent in this, and only this, case). The pitch-class numbers themselves can be regarded as interval numbers, numerically characterizing the interval class by the unique integer arrived at by subtracting (mod. 12) the pitch-class number associated with order number 0 from the pitch-class number of the element in question. This definition of interval is extended to define the directed pitch class distance between any two elements, and when applied to successive elements (those elements whose order numbers differ by one) yields the familiar interval class number succession, which when associated with the appropriate order numbers is also strict simply ordered. Conventionally, the order number associated with the interval class number determined by the larger of the two order numbers associated with the pitch class numbers involved in the determination of the interval will be that interval's order number. This collection of ordered pairs (order number, interval class number) is, similarly a function, but only in the case of an all-interval set is it a biunique function; in all other cases, it is a mapping of the integers 1-11 into, rather than onto, themselves. It is this succession which is preserved under transposition, but before considering the usual twelve-tone operations upon the defined relations, I shall examine

---

[4] In the sense of a one-to-one relationship between order number and pitch number.

[5] A mapping is a law that associates with any element of a domain an element of another domain, which may be itself, as in this instance.

further the structure of the set in terms of temporal precedence and antecedence relations. In strict analogy with pitch-class or interval class interval numbers, one may speak of order interval numbers, defining the directed temporal distance between pitch-classes, or interval classes, in terms of the number of intervening pitch or interval classes. Although the succession of numbers so determined by successive set elements is trivially a succession of 1's for any form of the set, the order interval number associated with a particular pair of pitch-classes or interval classes is significant for a large number of used and useful compositional techniques. Consider first a given set, presented at least twice, on each occasion partitioned (instrumentally or registrally or dynamically or etc.) on the principle of identical extracted interval sequences. Total pitch order is preserved, and the succession in each part preserves ordered interval content, but the durational rhythm in each part is not, in general, preserved or preservable. The very fact and the nature of the number of different ways of such a presentation are entirely determined by the ordering of the particular set.

These are (3^2) (2^3) partitions of a set,[6] with the constituent parts represented linearly. The case of such an ordering which preserves the order interval numbers of each extracted part is obtainable only when the set has been constructed originally through the identification of order intervals with pitch-class intervals, not merely those determined by successive pitch-class elements. The rhythmic implications of such interval associative procedures are as obvious as is their dependence upon the order number interval fulfilling the role of a metric.

Invariants under transposition similarly involve temporal order criteria. While pitch interval succession is preserved, and no order number, pitch number couple can be, one of the most general, and least obvious of such invariants is the equal number of order inversions associated with transposed sets whose transposition numbers are complementary. This measure of the derangement of the order numbers of sets in relation to a reference set also serves as a reminder that, for any given set, a transposition of that set can be represented equivalently as a permutation of pitch-class numbers or order numbers, for indeed a permutation, in this context, is an operation on relative temporal positions.

The identification of different transpositional forms of a set through identity of extracted pitch sequences creates, as in the related case

6 Two 3-element and three 2-element partitions.

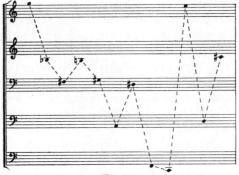

Ex. 1a

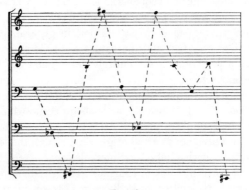

Ex. 1b

of interval sequences, a rhythmic situation, with the temporal attributes of the set determining the precise nature of such identities.

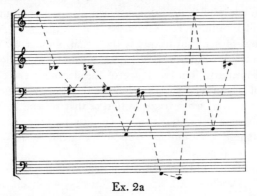

Ex. 2a

is the same partitioning as Ex. 1a, with

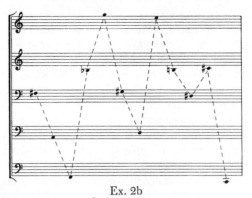

Ex. 2b

the transposition at 11, identically partitioned with regard to pitch sequences.

Somewhat different in nature, but familiarly consequential, is the temporal role of the combinational identification of a collection within a set with a content identical collection in another transposition of the set. This property can be considered either by observing those collections whose content is held fixed by a transposition number (that is, as a general invariant) or by considering the specific set structure required to enable such collections to remain fixed in pre-assigned order positions. For a simple instance, any collection of four pitch-classes containing two tritones must map into itself under transposition by 6. Thus (Ex. 3a), the pitch-class collections repre-

Ex. 3a

sented in each set form by order numbers 0, 2, 8, 11, are identical while the temporal permutation of the four elements within the collection—of 0, 2, 8, 11 into 11, 8, 2, 0—can be represented cyclically: (1 4) (2 3); similarly the collections represented by order numbers 1, 3, 7, 9 and 4, 5, 6, 10. The similarity of permutations within the collections can be seen to be a result of set structure, and is not a general invariant.

The order interval number associated with any given pitch dyad of a set undergoes, under transposition, an alteration—or non-alteration—of value depending upon the specific pitch ordering of the set. Thus, in the set of Ex. 1a, the undirected order interval number associated with the pitch dyad G-C♯ for each transposition number is: $t_0 = 11$, $t_1 = 6$, $t_2 = 4$, $t_3 = 8$, $t_4 = 1$, $t_5 = 6$, $t_6 = 11$, $t_7 = 6$, $t_8 = 4$, etc. The temporal aspects of such properties of set structure, particularly in their more complex, but easily inferred, extensions are as manifold as they are inescapable, but since the desire here is to examine selected, representative manifestations of a rhythmic nature rather than to attempt to exhaust the subject, I turn to those, in some respects strongly dissimilar, temporal factors involved in some of the primary invariants associated with the operation of inversion.

The fundamental interdependence of temporal order and inversion can be inferred immediately from the possibility of defining the inversion of a linear dyad in terms of interchange of order numbers; any pitch dyad can be mapped into itself under inversion and transposition by the interval determined by the dyad in its original order. Stated in another way, the intervallic result of reversing the order of pitch-class elements is complementation, which is of course the intervallic result of inversion.

The most familiar invariant under inversion, made so by its constant and varied application by Webern, is that which necessarily obtains under transposition by an even transposition number: the retention of those, and only those, order number, pitch number couples of the S which are a tritone apart and whose pitch numbers are equal to one half of the transposition number (TT, p. 254). The generalization of this criterion provides a means of defining 12 equivalence classes[7] of 12 inversionally related set pairs each, among the 144 so related pairs; each pair within a so-determined class establishes a succession of pitch dyads consisting of pitch-classes of the same order number, which is a permutation of the similarly arrived at succession of each of the other pairs of the class. Obviously, such a given pitch dyad appears in one and only one equivalence class, so that such a class is uniquely identified by a single so-constructed pitch dyad. The 12 pairs of sets of such a class are closely analogous to those 12 pairs of transposed related sets which produce a succession of dyadically determined interval numbers, all of which are equal; in the present case, the sums of the pitch numbers of each pair are equal. This unique (for each equivalence class) number is called the "index" of the equivalence class.

---

[7] An equivalence relation R is a relation that is reflexive, transitive, symmetric, and connected.

In contradistinction is that partitioning into equivalence classes of the 144 pairs with regard to the 12 total transpositions of a set pair which preserve the succession of intervals determined by pitch-classes of the same order number, or, perhaps more simply, the coupling of a fixed, so computed interval number with a duplicated order number. Exactly two pairs from each of six such equivalence classes here belong to the same equivalence class formed according to the previous criterion.

All such 144 pairs reveal the same *pattern* of intervallic repetition, that is, the order intervals determined by repeated intervals are invariant, since this property is determined by the tritone related pitch-classes in S. If we let the first six letters of the alphabet denote the six intervals which can occur (even, when the transposition interval between the components of the pair is even; odd, when it is odd), then the pattern of repetition of the set of Ex. 3a is: a, b, c, d, e, f, f, d, c, b, e, a. The order interval 11, for instance, is associated with a different pitch interval for each set pair in an equivalence class determined by the first criterion above, that dependent on the sum of the pitch-numbers, and—naturally—is associated with the same pitch interval for each set pair in an equivalence class determined by the second criterion, that dependent on total transposition. But the pattern of pitch dyad repetition, and, therefore, the associated order intervals, are determined not by the structure of the set, but by the interval between pitch numbers of the same order number. For the set of Ex. 3, the pattern of identical dyad repetition for transposition interval 3 (as determined by elements of order number 0) is: a, a, b, b, c, c, d, e, e, f, d, f; for interval 9 it is: a, b, c, d, e, f, e, c, d, a, f, b (Ex. 3b and 3c). The pattern is identical for pairs belonging to the same equivalence class in the second sense (although the actual pitch content of these intervals is different in each case); the pattern is the same for exactly two pairs in each equivalence class in the first sense.

Closely related to these characteristics which impose rhythmic patterns of repetition with associated qualitative values of duration on pairs (and, by simple extension, to any number) of inversionally, and—therefore—transpositionally related sets, is a property which is difficult to characterize informally in its most general application. (See TT, pp. 256-257.) However, both for purposes of later discussion and for its significance as a temporal aspect of the twelve-tone system an instance of this property must be displayed.

Ex. 3a

Ex. 3b

Ex. 4b is a duplication of the succession of three-part simultaneities of Ex. 4a, although the temporal relation of the transpositionally related dyads and the inversionally related single line has been exactly interchanged; this is an instance of intervallic structure invariance under a prescribed alteration of the temporal order and a consequent alteration of the pitch content of the successive simultaneities. The property generalizes to any number of inversionally related components, with any number of transpositionally related lines constituting a component, and—of course—to any total transposition.

The identification of inversionally related sets through extracted interval or pitch sequences is again dependent on the temporal structure of the set and the statement of conditions for such a representation in a pre-defined number of parts with a specified number of

Ex. 4a

Ex. 4b

elements in each part must incorporate a condition upon the order relations of S.

That the representative properties that have been and shall be discussed are not to be construed as compositional imperatives or prescriptions to the end of securing temporal characteristics from the properties of the twelve-tone system, but as temporal attributes which inhere in the system and must, therefore, be manifest compositionally, is most apparent in the next case: the interval succession of retrograde-inverted related sets is identical to within complete order reversal. I shall forego further discussion of this property beyond the indication that the succession of simultaneously formed intervals determined by RI related sets symmetrically ordered is intervallically symmetrical about the midinterval (or intervals). The following is a characteristic pair:

Ex. 5

The means of formation of equivalence classes of pairs by the application of this principle is obvious.

As a final observation, in order to indicate the dependence of a concept which is not normally regarded as temporal in character upon temporal considerations, I shall use the concept of combinatoriality. (See SS, p. 129ff.) Whatever the number of set forms contained in an aggregate, and whatever the number of pitch elements each form contributes to the aggregate, qualitative temporal constraints are necessarily involved. In the simple case of hexachordal inversional combinatoriality, so often encountered in Schönberg's music, the formation of an aggregate by two inversionally related hexachords requires the statement that the pitch-class with order number 6 in one hexachord may not be stated until after the statement of the pitch-class with order number 5 in the other hexachord, and vice versa; this is a necessary condition for such a hexachordal construction.

The license of simultaneous statement of pitch-classes whose order interval number is 1, which has been stated verbally and employed compositionally is—most strikingly—a temporal condition. Such a statement of a set can be regarded as a strict partial ordering (a serial ordering minus the property of connectivity) with regard to the relation of $<$, or a simple ordering with regard to $\leqq$ (the equals sign

here denoting simultaneity). The admission of this possibility increases from four to seven the number of temporal relationships
which can obtain between two events, from the total of 11 listed
above, and allows a twelve-tone set to be stated totally in terms of any
number of order numbers ranging integrally from 0 to 11 inclusive.
With relation to the serial ordering of the set, such a procedure can
be regarded as a mapping of the order numbers into themselves,
subject to the condition that if order number m maps into order
number n (with n $<$ m) then order number m $+$ 1 maps into n or
n $+$ 1. The absence of any constraint on spatial ordering makes possible, as in the related case of the spatial distribution of a set or
aggregate in any time distribution, the representation—spatially—of
any set by any other set; this overidentification suggests that a serious
study of this question is crucially necessary. (David Lewin's article
below does present a solution to one aspect of this problem, and suggests paths for future investigation.—*Eds.*)

The construction of a quantitative temporal system by interpreting
pitch numbers as temporal values, since order numbers themselves
are "ordinal" temporal values, and thus constructing a "twelve-tone
rhythmic system" can be viewed either as a reinterpretation of pitch
numbers so as to assure isomorphism between the two systems, or as
assigning temporal interpretations to the uninterpreted terms of the
finite numerical equal difference structure of which both the pitch
and rhythmic systems will be exemplifications. It seems reasonable to
require, in the light of the preceding discussion, that such an interpretation satisfy a number of general conditions. It must not reduce
the possibilities or range of applicability of such qualitative temporal
characteristics as those discussed above; it should provide only a
substitution for the relation of precedence and antecedence of a
relation of measured precedence and antecedence. It must interpret
the entire extensional meaning of pitch-class numbers and those concepts which are formulated in terms of pitch-class numbers. It must
provide for such concepts being endowed with an interpretation
tenable in terms of musical perception, so that the system so constructed will be autonomously closed, not merely by formal analogy
with the pitch-classes, so that the totality of, at most, 48 temporally
founded sets which can be formed from a given set will be justifiably
separable from the 12! permutations of the temporal equivalents of
pitch-class numbers, and so that the invariants associated with the
transformations of the pitch system will have independent analogs in
the temporal system.

Manifestly, the interpretation of set numbers as multiples of a durational unit does not satisfy these minimal conditions, however acceptable duration may appear as the primitive constituent of a description of temporal perception. There is no apparent basis for constructing duration classes by designating as elements of the same durational equivalence class those durations which differ by a multiple of 12 or any other number. The temporal analog of pitch interval is translatable only as "the difference between durations." Even without arguing the dubious perceptual status of this notion, the ordered succession of such differences remains invariant under transposition if and only if one assumes difference classes as a result of applying transposition modularly, and therefore embracing the assumption of duration classes in its most unrealistic form, so that the succession of, say, a quarter-note duration followed by a dotted quarter-note duration creates an "interval" equal to that created by a dotted half-note followed by a sixteenth. Naturally, the same result is obtained whether one ostensibly avoids this dilemma by interpreting a given transposition as a permutation of order numbers, or faces it fully by modularly adding to each duration a duration equal to the unit duration multiplied by the transposition number. (This is precisely what has been done compositionally and stated verbally by those who most vehemently and precipitously have since renounced the twelve-tone system as "old-fashioned serialism" and "exhausted." They have revealed significantly their profound comprehension of the nature of the system by "inventing" the notion of "double series" to accomplish what has just been described. The "two" series are totally equivalent representations of a set, one in terms of pitch numbers, the other in terms of order numbers.)

This unsatisfactory analog of interval, in all of the ramifications derivable from the earlier discussion of invariants, should suffice to close the discussion of this interpretation. But a few other deficiencies perhaps should be noted briefly. The analogy of pitch properties dependent upon correlation of equal order numbers of two (or more) set forms cannot, in general, be fulfilled under this interpretation. Combinatorially related durational set forms must depend upon equality of the sum of durations of the constituent set segments, and therefore combinatoriality, almost contradictorily, does not hold in general under total transposition of the component set elements.

The apparent insistence upon the necessity of the temporal interpretation translating completely the attributes of the pitch system into temporal terms must not be regarded as an insistence upon complete analogy for analogy's sake or as an unawareness of the differences

between temporal and pitch elements. On the contrary, it is to justify
the construction of a system which will impose constraints upon the
temporal elements of a composition with a comparable effect upon the
nature and extent of the inter-event influence in the rhythmic domain
to that of the pitch system in its domain. As a system, it should possess
unique properties independent of pitch association, as the pitch system
possesses properties independent of quantitative temporal values.

To this end, since duration is a measure of distance between time
points, as interval is a measure of distance between pitch points,
we begin by interpreting interval as duration. Then, pitch number is interpretable as the point of initiation of a temporal event,
that is, as a time-point number. If this number is to be further interpretable as a representative of an equivalence class of time points and
the durational interval with regard to the first such element, it is
necessary merely to imbed it in a metrical unit, a measure in the usual
musical metrical sense, so that a recurrence of succession of time
points is achieved, while the notion of meter is made an essential part
of the systematic structure. The equivalence relation is statable as
"occurring at the same time point with relation to the measure." The
"ascending" ordered "chromatic scale" of twelve time points, then, is
a measure divided into twelve equally spaced time points, with the
metrical signature probably determined by the internal structure of
the time-point set, and with the measure now corresponding in function to the octave in the pitch-class system. A time-point set, then,
is a serial ordering of time points with regard to $<$. At the outset, I do
not wish to attempt to avoid the manifest differences between the
elements of the pitch system and those of the time-point system, that is,
perceptual—not formal—differences. A pitch representative of a pitch-
class system is identifiable in isolation; a time-point representative
cannot conceivably be, by its purely dispositional character. But an
examination of a time-point set will clarify the systematic meanings,
and the reasonable musical meanings associated with these new
concepts.

S: 0,0 1,3   2,11   3,4   4,1 5,2   6,8 7,10

          8,5   9,9   10,7   11,6

Ex. 6

Ex. 6 is a time-point set analog of the pitch set of Ex. 1, whose
numerical representation as number couples is indicated. The metrical

signature is chosen in the light of the hexachordal combinatorial structure of the set. Since duration is simply the directed distance between time points, the notated durations are not obligatorily the "actual" durations of the event, be it represented in terms of pitch or register or timbre or dynamics, etc., initiated at a time point; the notated duration, under this interpretation, may represent an actual duration followed by a rest to complete the duration between time points.

Ex. 6 is but one possible representation of this set, the unique representation in the minimal total temporal duration. Obviously, the minimal number of measures required for the statement of a given time-point set is determined by the non-modular sum of the intervals divided by 12, and is equal to the number of octaves required for a statement of the analogous pitch set stated as an ordered simultaneity. (The minimal statement of a pitch set as a succession is trivially the same for all sets, the interval of 11.)

In strict conformity with the present interpretation, the initial three measures of the set are presented in two different ways in the following examples:

Ex. 7a

Ex. 7b

Both preserve the order of time points of Ex. 6. The first durational interval of Ex. 6 is 3 (interval units; the unit here being the duration of $\frac{1}{12}$ of the measure); of Ex. 7a it is 15, which equals 3 (mod. 12). A durational interval, then, represents a class of intervals equivalent to within an integral number of measures difference, and there can be no unique maximal statement of a time-point set. In Ex. 7b the first time point is repeated before the statement of the second time point, thus creating a first interval equal to the measure (this resource of "octave" statement can serve compositionally to present the meter of reference employed). All three representations must be regarded as "all-interval"; no durational class other than the 0 class is repeated.

The differences between Exx. 7a and 7b suggest the necessity for examining the nature of repetition in a time-point set, and it may be easily—too easily—assumed that the repeated time points of Ex. 7b derive their "justification" from the principle and practice of permitted repetitions of a single pitch in the pitch system. However, it should be observed that pitch repetition is not a pitch procedure, but a temporal procedure, independent of considerations of the pitch system, and, if a time-point system is assumed, the temporal placements of such pitch repetitions are determined by the time-point structure, not by pitch considerations. Therefore, the repeated time points of Ex. 7b must not be regarded as analogous with pitch repetitions; only real time duplication of time points (simultaneous statements of the same time point) is analogous, for the absolute interval between the first time point of Ex. 7b and the third is 15, between the second and third, 3. Pitch repetition does not alter the absolute pitch interval between the pitches repeated and the eventual successive pitch. The repetitions of Ex. 7b are analogous to the representation of a pitch class by different "registral" members of the class. It should be recalled that the concept of register in the twelve-tone pitch system with regard to all available pitches, founded merely on the assumption that no two non-identical elements of the same pitch-class can be regarded as in the same register, and that transposition which preserves absolute intervals must be regarded as preserving the registral relations among all the constituent pitch elements, is characterizable as irreflexive, symmetric, nontransitive, and not connected, with regard to the relation of "is not a member of the same register as"; so, too, is time-point "register" in the above sense.

The time-point analogs of Ex. 1a and 1b (Exx. 8a and 8b) indicate not only the results of interval (here, durational) sequence extraction but, necessarily, the meaning of "transposition" of time-point sets. Each transposition preserves the duration class succession, while effecting a particular permutation of the twelve time-point classes, and may be thought of as a translation of each time point a number of time-point units (sixteenths in these examples) to the right (i.e. as notated) equal to the transposition number. The result is metric reorientation of the set.

Ex. 9 is a transposition of the set of Ex. 6 with $t = 6$; the properties revealed in Ex. 3 are here evident. It follows that the number of order inversions of time points for complementary transpositions is equal, and that—indeed—all the properties of pitch transposition are translated into equally apparent properties of rhythmic transposition.

The inversion of a time-point set maps durations into their complements, mod. the measure. To verify that a time-point dyad maps into itself with interchange of order number, under inversion, the first two time points of Ex. 6 are displayed with the set inverted, and $t = 3$, in Ex. 10.

The preservation of order number, time-point number couples

Ex. 8a

Ex. 8b

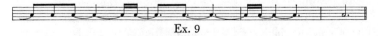

Ex. 9

Ex. 10

under inversion and an even transposition number, in this case, $t = 2$, is exhibited:

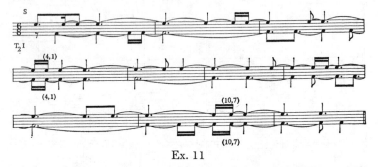

Ex. 11

The duplicated time-point numbers are, again necessarily, 1 and 7. Ex. 12 displays the resultant rhythm created by these two set forms. It indicates that such a rhythm created by set pairs belonging to the same equivalence class of pairs, under the criterion of equal sums associated with the time-point numbers of the same order number, will be permutations of the durations formed by disjunct time point dyads (beginning with the first); the resultant rhythms created by set pairs which are members of the equivalence class determined by total transposition are simply metrical displacements of one another. In Ex. 12 the succession of durations is to be regarded as: 2, 8, 4, 6, 0, 10, 10, 6, 4, 8, 0, 2. If the first time-point number of the set were—say—$4(T_4S)$, and thus the associated inversion's first time-point number were $10(T_{10}I)$, the succession would be: 6, 0, 8, 10, 4, 2, 2, 10, 8, 0, 4, 6. This demonstrates also that the distribution of equal durations in the resultant rhythm depends upon the distribution of time points in the set which are related by the time-point interval (duration) 6, while the specific durational values associated with these equal pairs are determined by the transpositional relationship between the two sets; since the distribution of complementary durations bounded by the same time points is determined by the transposition number, this distribution is the same for pairs belonging to the same equivalence class by total transposition.

The further exemplification in time-point and durational terms of inversional invariants, and the quantification of qualitative order properties so arrived at may seem superfluous in an introductory discussion such as this. But the temporal analog of Exx. 4a and 4b may not be immediately obvious, since the property involves invariance under temporal alteration; that the resultant durational successions associated with such presentations can be identical is demonstrated in the following example,

Ex. 13a   Ex. 13b

where the first two "interval" complexes of the succession are displayed in linear redistributions, with durationally equivalent components stated side by side. The complements of the intervals of Exx. 4a and 4b are displayed here, for the sake of simplicity.

The following example displays a retrograde form of the set of Ex. 6, with $t = 2$:

Ex. 14

The lower line of the following example

Ex. 15

displays a retrograde-inversional form, with $t = 7$. Both forms present the durations of their respective RI related sets in reverse order. The upper line of Ex. 15 is Ex. 6 repeated (mod. the measure), and the

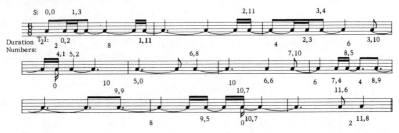

Ex. 12

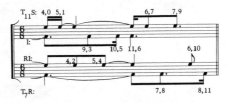

Ex. 19

two RI related lines display, in their resultant rhythm, a symmetry
of intervallic occurrences such as that discussed with regard to Ex. 5.
It now should be apparent that the "twelve time-point class system" is
structurally isomorphic with the twelve-tone pitch-class system. It
can be regarded as an interpretation of that permutation group of
order 48 at most, where the group elements are the permutations of
the twelve time-point classes specified by the transformation of the
system, or by the associated permutation matrices, with the group
operation, matrix multiplication. Therefore, such special characteristics of set structure as those permitting, say, the "combinational"
concept of combinatoriality, in time-point terms, simply involves the
construction of time-point aggregates by the components of appropriately related set forms. The structural characteristics of the set that
assures such resources are directly translatable from the pitch domain.
The first hexachord of Ex. 6 and the first hexachord of the combinatorially related inversion are so translated:

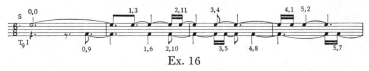

Ex. 16

Each time point occurs once and only once; beyond this contrapuntal
condition, the time-point aggregate—as the pitch aggregate—has no
unique representation. Indeed, even a minimal representation is not,
in general, unique. For example, in Ex. 16, the inversional component
requires four measures for its minimal representation, while the set
component requires only three; therefore this latter component can be
presented in a number of different ways within this totally minimal
representation. As in the analogous pitch situation, the time point 0
can be re-presented at the beginning of measure two without altering
the order structure of the component; then the aggregate, if presented
linearly, as a resultant, contains a non-immediate repetition of time
points. This is but an instance of the extensive compositional issue
arising from the circumstance that there are an unlimited number of
representations of an aggregate, both in the time-point and pitch
domains. If constituent pitch set segments are undifferentiated compositionally—presented, for example, as a single line in a single instrument without registral differentiation—then the set origins of the
aggregate are made ambiguous to the point of virtual undetectability.
In compositional practice, the constituents normally are differentiated
timbrally and/or registrally and/or dynamically and/or rhythmically;

similar methods clearly are required in the case of time-point aggregates.

The extension of time-point combinatoriality to all types and orders, to partitions of the aggregate into more than two equal parts, unequal parts, as well as to incomplete aggregates or weighted aggregates is immediate (SS, pp. 136–38). The basis of compositional decisions as to the length of a time-point aggregate—which may itself function as a large scale rhythmic unit, the exact distribution of time-point components within an aggregate, and the temporal progression of such aggregates is beyond the scope of this article, but I conclude this part of the discussion with Ex. 17, in which each part consists of two derived sets,[8] creating secondary sets (SS, p. 140), the upper two parts derived, through the operations of the system, from the first three time-point classes of Ex. 6, the bottom two from the succeeding three classes. Each of these pairs of lines is a rhythmic canon by inversion; the total rhythmic progression is in disjunct aggregates. Other properties, clearly revealed in the resultant rhythm and familiarly encountered in the pitch domain, will be apparent to the experienced observer. One property, however, should be mentioned, since it is a particularly significant temporal equivalent of a characteristic of inversionally related sets (SS, p. 144). For each of the inversionally related lines, the set numbers of elements of the same order number sum to 3; therefore any elements of the reference set (Ex. 6) whose set numbers sum to 3 will appear here as elements of the same order number. Thus, for example, the time-point succession associated with order numbers 5 and 6 in Ex. 6 appears here as a resultant rhythm formed by the upper two voices in measure eight, followed by the time points associated with order numbers 4 and 3, followed by those associated with order numbers 1 and 2. Many of the techniques of delinearization of a linear rhythm (the distribution of time points associated with a single set form among two or more linear representations of that form), and linearization of a resultant rhythm reside in this property, which—in turn—is but another facet of the inversional equivalence class property of the first kind mentioned above (p. 166); the modes of applicability for a given composition depend wholly on the structure of the compositional set.

It must not be inferred that this time-point system merely because it is equivalent to the twelve-tone pitch system, and for purposes of explanatory simplicity has been described by analogical reference to

[8] For an explanation of derived sets in the pitch sense, see my article: "Some Aspects of Twelve-Tone Composition." *The Score and I.M.A. Magazine*, June 1955, p. 59.

Ex. 17

the pitch system, implies a one-to-one compositional application of the two systems. The rhythmic system is closed, and as its structure is independent of pitch clarification, it can be applied as independently as the pitch system. Thus, a time point of a set can represent the point of initiation of a single pitch, the repetition of a pitch, or a pitch simultaneity, but it can fulfill also this function with regard to timbre, register, dynamic level, etc. Indeed, it is the polyphonic structure, not the simple coordination, between the pitch system and the time-point system that the formulation of this latter makes most valuable, and the structured rhythmic counterpoint of these dimensions is a question of compositional applications, and is a subject for, at least, another article. The brief, incomplete exposition of the system as here presented is merely to suggest a traditional premise for a temporal approach to the electronic domain.

It might be asserted that, although the principles of formation and transformation of the time-point system could have been suggested entirely by the appropriate formal system and adopted by virtue of the properties which maintain under this interpretation, the assumption of "twelve" time points is an arbitrary derivative of the pitch system. Obviously, the time-point system is applicable to any number of set elements, and has been applied compositionally to a smaller number; the pitch system did suggest the number twelve. But having suggested it, it is a suggestion well worth adopting independently, for many of the resources of the system (the time point, as well as the pitch) arise from the properties of the number 12, particularly the property of integral factorization by so large a number of integers, represented by the totient of 12 being equal to 4 (1, 5, 7, 11). Nor is it surprising or irrelevant that the compositions which apply this temporal system employ, as the time-point set, the exact analog of the pitch set of the composition; one might say, with equal justice, that the pitch set is the analog of the time-point set. So, such a composition is the point of conjunction and presentation of the two independently coherent yet deeply related structures.

The temporal constraints imposed by the rhythmic system, the degree and extent of the inter-event influence so determined, depend upon—at least—two contextual considerations: the particular temporal phenomenon desired, and the structure of the specific time-point set. With regard to the paradigm of the preceding examples, the composer might desire, and could achieve, any one of the 2^{11} possible compositional representations of the twelve time-point measure as a resultant rhythm, but the means of arriving at and departing from a predefined

measure depend upon set structure. Consider that simplest of measure representations:

Ex. 18

which, nevertheless, was not arrived at by any of the combinations of
Ex. 17. If the set of the work were the time-point "ascending chromatic scale," this measure would be easily available, and would
impose no conditions on approach and departure by virtue of set
structure. But if this measure were to be arrived at from the set of
Ex. 6, then the simultaneous statement of a number of set forms
is required.

Ex. 19 is one such presentation; the linear components, reading
from top to bottom, are the fifth, sixth, seventh, and eighth elements of
$T_{11}S$, the tenth, eleventh, and twelfth elements of I, the fifth, sixth,
and seventh elements of RI, and the—say—eighth and ninth elements
of T_7R. This presentation then imposes specific conditions on the
time points preceding and following this aggregate. (The further
implications for the total rhythmic structure of this conjunction of
sets are well worth considering, for all that they cannot be discussed
here.) In short, any rhythmic configuration is "possible," but any
such state of the composition must influence, to a greater or lesser
extent, other states of the composition. The unavoidable inference
that not everything is possible independently at every state of the
composition is merely to observe that the system is not constructed to
induce, in a relatively strict sense of the word, "randomness": the
absence of inter-event influence.

But, it may be asked, how can "any" possible rhythmic event be
made to occur in a system which assumes a minimum duration
between successive time points, and admits no durations other than
those which are integral multiples of this unit duration? I shall combine the answer to this question with the answer to another: what
does this rhythmic system have to do with the electronic medium,
particularly since it has been employed in, and is—therefore—applicable to, nonelectronic works? Clearly, the system crucially depends
upon the maintenance of an isochronous durational unit and its
multiple, the measure, the modular unit. To secure this, with nonelectronic media, is not only to court the terrifying and cumulative
hazards associated with the presentation of ensemble rhythms of any
complexity, but to be obliged to assume a quite coarse quantization
of the temporal continuum. But, with the electronic medium, the

maintenance of the isochronous unit is assured mechanically, and the accuracy of the ensemble rhythm is obtainable to any degree of exactness; in addition, the fineness of quantization available answers the first question above. To be sure, the examples so far presented do not contain, and could not have contained, triplet, quintuplet, and similar subdivisions in the usual sense; but such notational means are required only when the practical exigencies of rhythmic notation and tempo indication prevent the rhythmic structure from being notated in terms of a least common multiple durational unit. But, if it be assumed that each 16th note duration in the above examples represents a time duration of $\frac{1}{32}$ of a second, a common unit in Synthesizer programming, then the tempo of the examples would be: $\downarrow. = 320$. If the resultant of the combination of Ex. 16 is notated in terms of the reasonable tempo, $\downarrow. = 80$, the result would be:

Ex. 20

More extended answers to the two questions scarcely seem demanded if one requires merely the assurance that satisfactory answers exist.

Nevertheless, it is possible to answer the first question by showing another technique within the system. One of the fundamental empirical differences between the pitch and time-point systems is that the "octave" of the time-point system is determined only contextually, by metric signature and tempo indication; therefore, without altering the meaning of "octave" in this systematic sense, the two set components of Ex. 16 can be represented in their unique minimal form by equating, as total durations, three measures of the S component and four measures of the T_9I component:

Exx. 21a and 21b

Here, however, there is no aggregate construction; if the concept of aggregate is applicable at all, it must be in terms of the twenty different time-point values available in the resultant measure (Ex. 21b). Also, different time-point values in the components become identical values in the resultant. Although this technique does overcome some of the difficulties associated with the quantization minimum of nonelectronic music, its most fruitful application is the achieving of different modular units in association with different interpretations of the rhythmic structure, and where—therefore—aggregate structure has no particular relevance.

The use of the aggregate as the unit of temporal progression (in a sense similar to that in which Schönberg employed the pitch aggregate) makes the single, total set representation a constituent of a multiple of such aggregate units as in Ex. 17, with the multiple dependent upon the number of parts in the partitioning of the aggregate complex. This suggests that the compositional time-point set need not (in this case cannot) appear as the explicit, foreground rhythm. The determination of still another level of foreground, derived directly from the unique characteristics of the set, by the imbedding of new time points through the subdivision of the set-determined durations, is demonstrated:

Ex. 22

The first temporal hexachord of Ex. 6 (now displayed in a 3/4 meter) is here subdivided into eleven durations, which represent the durational succession of the inversion. The first three of these durations are placed between the first two time points of S, and each successive pair of durations occurs between the successive time-point pairs of S. The effect is that of changing the modular unit with each successive time point of S, with the critical requirement being that no new, so arrived at time point occupy a temporal position corresponding to that of the fundamental division of the measure, here, 16th-note durations. It is this avoidance of ambiguity that creates the appearance of complexity in conventional notation, but for all this forbidding appearance it is easily recognized that any such imbedded succession is merely a "diminution" or "augmentation" of a segment of S, and should be readily perceptible as such when associated with identities or similarities in other dimensions. The avoidance of auditory confusion of such derived time points with time points of forms of S is a matter of compositional clarification, solvable usually by the availability of superposed comparison of the two levels of time points (like a length comparison by superposition), accomplished by assigning different timbral or registral lines to the different levels of time points; the limits of such differentiation are then at the limits of discrimination between attacks (or, in general, initiations), making them therefore dependent upon such phenomena as envelope characteristics, absolute and relative frequencies, spectra, and dynamics. These limits, then, need not be determined by essentially memorative considerations.

If even so cursory a discussion of temporal levels suggests unavoidably the need for electronic realization, and a host of questions regarding temporal perception, it also suggests—perhaps less obviously—a brief excursion into the domain of frequency. This excursion is prompted by (and it shall not be allowed to exceed the immediate implications of this prompting) the fact that the examination of temporal systematization began with and originated from the traditional principles of the twelve-tone pitch-class system; the results of this examination return us to the area of pitch by a comparable mode of reasoning by analogy. Certainly, the electronic availability of the frequency continuum does not entail the imperative that this continuum be totally employed, any more than does the fact of the similar availability on the violin. But, likewise, it does not entail the consequence that it not be employed, particularly since new selections from this continuum need not be derived from independent premises, but from the attributes of traditional systems, or extensions of these systems. A combinational system (such as the traditional tonal system), founded on the selection of an unordered sub-collection from the total pitch-class collection, but with a *prime* number of equal parts to an octave, possesses the possibility of generating the complete collection of pitch classes by any non-zero interval, whereas this collection, in the familiar twelve-part division, can be generated only by intervals 1, 11, 5, and 7: numbers prime to twelve. Every such interval, then, will generate a maximal sub-collection (the number of pitch-classes in this sub-collection will be $n/2 + 1/2$, for primes greater than 2, where n is the total number of pitch classes) in which each non-complementary interval occurs with unique multiplicity; thus, a "circle" generated by each interval is obtainable, defining a unique hierarchy among the transpositions of the so generated sub-collections (transposed by the generating interval), a hierarchy founded on the traditional criterion of intersection of pitch class content between such sub-collections. In the usual system of temperament, only the content corresponding to the major or minor scales, and to the half chromatic scale, can be so generated. A division of the octave into, for example, 11 equal parts would yield five such non-complementary sub-collections of six pitch classes each.

The means of providing the physical basis of a permutational system by the extension of octave division to multiples of twelve equal parts will not be discussed; on the one hand, the properties of the twelve-tone system are extendable immediately to this new collection, while—on the other hand—the regarding of the traditional twelve-tone system as a permutational sub-system within such a total collection is too large and complex a subject to be discussed here.

A contextually determined division of the octave, thus varying from work to work and within a work, is suggested by the pitch analog of the final rhythmic procedure discussed (Ex. 22). Within the fixed, twelve part equal temperament, the interval between any two such pitch elements is divisible into an interval succession of the pitch set, with the similar restriction that there be no ambiguity of identification of a frequency so derived with a frequency of the fixed temperament.

The most elaborate extrapolation from the principle of construction of the twelve-tone pitch set is to a twelve-tone frequency scale, in which the frequencies chosen for an individual composition make available an exact reflection of the interval structure of the compositional set. For example, corresponding to the set of Ex. 1, such a "frequency set" would be (say, in the fifth octave): 262.6 (cps); 273.5; 302.6; 320.8; 353.5; 357.1; 378.8; 386.1; 411.5; 426.0; 462.3; 502.3; (525.2). If a twelve-tone set is now formed by serially ordering the classes of which these frequencies are representatives, an examination of the simplest invariants under the normal rules of transformation will reveal surprisingly new consequences; I shall mention merely that transposition is not, in general, interval-preserving, assuming that "interval" has its usual designation. Under this system, the properties associated with the normal systematic operations are dependent on the *frequency* materials of the particular work.

If there can be little question that such pitch and rhythmic extensions of the twelve-tone system carry music to the point of purely electronic feasibility, there still remain large questions that return this discussion to its beginning. Do such extensions maintain those characteristics of differentiation and identification which endow the principles of formation and transformation with their empirical justification in the traditional system? And, on the other hand, do such constraints, however extended their domain of application, not eliminate, unnecessarily and undesirably, certain electronically available resources?

The answer to the first question is, obviously, that such extensions well might not, in a significant sense. Even though one is not prepared to state general laws with regard to those complex, multiple correlations between the acoustic and auditory domains, so that the precise auditory effect of a particular acoustical specification may be difficult of useful prediction, electronic instruments have made certain specific kinds of consequences predictable. Even with regard to only the normal frequency materials of conventional temperament, the identification of interval succession appears impossible beyond, electronically, quite modest speeds, to the point where even the mere number of different intervals cannot be identified; two, specified as equal, frequencies will be heard as different pitches beyond a certain durational minimum, with the minimum determined by the associated spectra, among other things. Here, then, the bases of traditional musical hearing disappear, for both the tonal and twelve-tone systems rest upon the assumptions of pitch invariance with regard to time, timbre, loudness, and duration, and of intervallic invariance with regard to transposition under similar conditions of alteration of other dimensions. The ordering principle of the twelve-tone system, which embodies the "new" memorative demands of the system (although the very conception of "theme" or "motive" in any music assumes the significance of order, but not as a primitive of the system), is also made inapplicable when a pitch succession, whose internal pitch ordering is clearly identifiable in a certain contour presentation, is altered in contour and registral range, so that the order becomes not completely identifiable. Similarly, a succession of pitches, clearly identifiable at a particular speed, cannot be perceived as containing even the same number of pitches at a critically greater speed, this critical point being dependent upon not only the acoustical characteristics of the components, both individually and in relation to one another, but the compositional context of the event.

But all of this is merely to say that the necessary characteristics of the system must be preserved in the auditory domain, and not merely in the domain of notational specification. Indeed, it is the fact of systematic presuppositions that makes it possible for the composer to determine the acceptability of a presented event, independent of its electronic specification. To say that, for example, a specified frequency lasting $\frac{1}{8}$ of a second does not represent the same pitch as the same specified frequency lasting $\frac{1}{32}$ of a second is merely to assert that the two different pitches have different notations with regard to duration. Any electronically specified event will have its aural correlate, even if this correlate be silence or a click; the compositional question is simply whether silence, or a click, is what is required at that moment. The relation between notation and aural event has never been one-to-one traditionally, and the increase of the values of the "many" in the many-to-one relationship does not alter the fundamental situation. If the properties crucial to a composition's being perceived as an instance of a particular system are embodied only in the input specifications of the composition, these properties may be destroyed by perceptual "limitations," for—indeed—one can speak of such "limitations," as opposed to "characteristics," only with regard to systematic presuppositions; that a perceived alternation of pitches 30 times a second in the eighth octave becomes a perceived repetition of a single pitch in the third octave cannot be termed a perceptual "limitation" without an initial assumption of intervallic invariance under transposition. Systematically determined similarity relations, particularly when reinforced by identity of other components, are in fact powerful perceptual aids; two isolated events, specified as similar but (for a reason such as those stated above) perceived as dissimilar, may be perceived as similar when made components of larger contexts whose relationship as totalities is inferrable under the presented constraints of the system.

As for the second question as to whether systematic constraints do not eliminate the use of available resources, it should be clear from the preceding that the twelve-tone extensions into the electronic domain do not necessarily eliminate any auditory event or complex of events. In any case, a collection of available physical materials—in this case, the area of materials made available electronically—does not entail a particular system. If musical structure can be presumed to address itself to the "ear," and to be founded on criteria of relatedness, purely "contextual" electronic music must either deny all past experience and criteria of similitude, or disallow it as irrelevant on the grounds that each event is unique by virtue of its (non-modular) time-point value; but even uniqueness is a relational property, for it assumes criteria of differentness, and—thus—relatedness. A musical system can provide only the possibility of musical coherence in its own terms; the question of the perceptual and conceptual significance of these terms is the issue with which we began. Perhaps a system founded on the unique resources of the electronic medium, and on premises hitherto unknown and not as yet even foreseeable, will be discovered and vindicated. Meanwhile, if it is only meanwhile, there is still an unforeseeably extensive domain in which the electronic medium uniquely can enrich and extend the musical systems whose premises have been tested, and whose resources barely have been tapped.

A THEORY OF SEGMENTAL
ASSOCIATION IN TWELVE-TONE MUSIC

DAVID LEWIN

I: *Introduction*

A: Examples and discussion

SEGMENTAL relations between different forms of a row can and
often do play an important constructive role in much twelve-tone
music. In any of Schönberg's "hexachordal" pieces, for instance, many
significant consequences of the hexachordal construction of the rows
are apparent upon even the most cursory examination of the music.

The row $\emptyset_0$ of the Violin Concerto Op. 36 is of typical hexachordal
structure (Ex. 1): there is an inverted form, I_0, such that the segment
consisting of the first six pitch-classes of $\emptyset_0$ is also a segment (the
last six pitch-classes) of I_0; likewise, the segment consisting of the last
six pitch-classes of $\emptyset_0$ is also a segment (the first six pitch-classes)
of I_0.

Ex. 1

This relation is not the only segmental correspondence of importance in the piece, however. For instance, note that I_{11} "preserves the
trichords of $\emptyset_0$" (Ex. 2).

Ex. 2

We may see two conspicuous exploitations of the latter relation in and about the cadenza of the first movement. (The music, from the upbeat to m. 230 through m. 235, is reproduced on pp. 115-116.) First, notice that at the formal conclusion of the cadenza (m. 234), the solo violin plays a presentation, not of $\varnothing_0$ (as one would "expect"), but of I_{11}. Nevertheless, this presentation of I_{11} is deployed so as to stress, among other things, the trichords of Ex. 2. In this respect, then, it associates strongly with $\varnothing_0$.[1]

A more complex exploitation of the trichordal relationship appears at the opening of the cadenza. After the first three 3-note chords, a brief 64th note figure is presented; there then follows a literal transposition of the three 3-note chords a semitone higher. Since the row form used for the opening 3-note chords was $\varnothing_3$: (C-Db-Gb-D-G-A-Eb-E-Bb-B-F-Ab), one naturally tends to hear a certain "$\varnothing_4$-ishness" when the chords appear transposed. Actually, the transposed chords do not arise from $\varnothing_4$, but from RI_3: (A-C-F♯-G-C♯-D-Ab-Bb-Eb-B-E-F). Thus the trichordal relation between $\varnothing_4$ and $(R)I_3$ (Ex. 3) is exploited very strongly, in spite of the fact that $\varnothing_4$ itself is never explicitly presented in the passage.

Ex. 3

These examples are of considerable value in cautioning us against the naïve but plausible assumption that all effective associative relations in such music as this must be presented explicitly. The reader is urged to keep this moral in mind throughout the sequel. Of course, the extent to which we will recognize any such relations, whether explicit or not, is heavily dependent on the extent to which the compositional presentation of the notes involved supports or obscures the abstract relation, and/or the extent to which the sonorities involved have been explicitly established as referential.[2]

---

[1] Since $\varnothing_0$ itself does not appear in the immediate environs, a critical evaluation of the "success" of the exploitation of the trichordal relation here would become involved with the question of how firmly the trichords of $\varnothing_0$ have been established, in the large, as a referential sonority-group. That is, we "accept" the trichordal presentation of I_{11} at least to the extent that we would "accept" a trichordal presentation of $\varnothing_0$ at this point, as far as the trichords themselves are concerned.

[2] Milton Babbitt ("Set Structure as a Compositional Determinant," above, pp. 129–147) has pointed out that the row of Schönberg's Fourth Quartet

It will be noted that the segmental relations I have discussed so far have been such as to involve the entire row (two hexachords, three tetrachords [in footnote 2], four trichords).[3] However, isolated segments of rows may also function associatively, and often do. For instance, in Schönberg's *Violin Phantasy* Op. 47, the row forms shown in Ex. 4 are such that the last three pitch-classes of the first form are the same, *in toto*, as the first three of the second form.

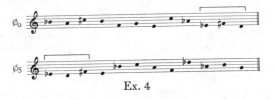

Ex. 4

possesses significant trichordal and tetrachordal structures, as well as the commonly recognized hexachordal structure:

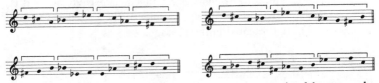

I have heard the musical relevance of this observation questioned by some, who point out that trichordal and tetrachordal equivalences are not to be found conspicuously exploited *explicitly* in the piece. It seems to me, however, that this criticism does not really come to grips with the issues involved. For the most important implication of the observation, I feel, is that whenever a trichordal or tetrachordal texture is heard, a potential enriching structural ambiguity is manifested.

Thus, e.g. in the opening section of the first movement, there is a prominent trichordal texture in the accompaniment which persists at least until m. 21, where the hitherto vertically presented trichords become linearized. First we hear trichords from $\emptyset_0$: (D-C♯-A-B♭-F-E♭-E-C-A♭-G-F♯-B), then trichords from I_0: (G-A♭-C-B-E-F♯-F-A-C♯-D-E♭-B♭), then trichords from $\emptyset_0$ again, and then trichords from I_0 again, all presented vertically.

Note, however, that the trichords of I_0 could also have been derived from $\emptyset_1$:

Similarly, the trichords of $\emptyset_0$ could have been derived from I_{11}. I would certainly not like to claim that I hear the "trichords from I_0" *more* as inversions of the "trichords from $\emptyset_0$," than as transpositions of them, as I am listening to this passage. In this sense, they are structurally ambiguous. The permutations of the orders of succession of trichords in the passage strengthen this viewpoint.

[3] For a more complete and penetrating discussion of these types of segmental relationship, the reader is referred to Babbitt, *op.cit.* That article also contains much other material of relevance to the present discussion.

This relation is conspicuously exploited in mm. 32-34 of that piece:

Ex. 5

The positions of the segments (at the end of the first form and at the beginning of the second) make the association especially strong here, as do the compositional factors of texture and registration. But even segments which occur within the middle of a row may easily become involved in associative relations, particularly if rhythmic and metric factors are propitious. For instance, the row forms of Ex. 6, from Schönberg's Fourth Quartet Op. 37, are not only related hexachordally, but also have the indicated trichordal segments in common.

Ex. 6

In mm. 25-28 of the quartet (Ex. 7), I find the associative effect of the corresponding trichordal groups quite audible.

Ex. 7

This example also demonstrates that more than one segmental relation between two row forms may be functioning in a given passage (above, not only the hexachords but the trichordal segments imbedded within them).

A further example of segmental association, one in which *none* of the segments involved appears either at the beginning or at the end of either row form, is provided by the opening of Schönberg's Piano Suite Op. 25. This passage presents two row forms, the second of which is the tritone transposition of the first; the rows have in common four two-element segments: two "tritones" and two "minor thirds":

Ex. 8

In the music (mm. 1-2½, Ex. 9), the tritone segments are deployed in such a way as to interact strongly with rhythmic and metric factors. Rhythmic support for the establishment of the meter is provided by the fact that the only two places in the first one and a half measures where two notes are attacked simultaneously are on the fourth beat of m. 1 and on the first beat of m. 2 (both metrically "strong"). Interacting is the association of the tritone G-D♭ in the right hand in the last half of m. 1 with the tritone D♭-G in the left hand in the first half of m. 2. Observe that no other pitch-classes appear more than once in the opening one and a half measures, a fact which strengthens the segmental association.

Ex. 9

The association of the tritone A♭-D in the right hand, m. 2, with the tritone D-G♯ in the left hand, m. 3, is aurally clear because of the strong metric position of the D and ancillary rhythmic position of the A♭ (G♯) at both places (in each case, the tritone is heralded by a crescendo); in addition, the tritone appears at both places as the final (and falling) interval of a linear phrase, particularly conspicuous because the strict melodic imitation breaks off after the tritones.

The segment C-A in the left hand, m. 2, is clearly associated with the C-A in the right hand, m. 3, through the meter. There does not seem to be any aurally prominent exploitation of the common G♭-E♭ segment.

There are two reasons why I have drawn all these examples from works of Schönberg. First, his production displays a great variety of structural utilization and compositional deployment of segmental relationships. Second, his segmental relations are generally such that the order of succession of pitch-classes within the corresponding segments of the row forms is not simply preserved or retrograded, but is permuted in more complex fashion. This tends to emphasize the "harmonic" aspect of any associative exploitation of the relationships; it is that aspect to which the following discussion will be devoted.[4]

[4] In contrast to Schönberg's practice in the latter respect, e.g. most segmental relations *exploited* by Webern either preserve or retrograde the ordering of pitch-classes within the segments. The following examples are typical:

Footnote 4 continued

In these cases, the "harmonic" aspect of the segmental structures, while obviously significant, is complicated by, and to some extent ancillary to the serial correspondences.

An interesting example of Webern's attitude toward the compositional exploitation of segmental relations is provided by mm. 56-63ff. of the third movement of the Piano Variations Op. 27. Here the trichords B-Bb-D and F-A-G♯ act as "pivot chords" in relating presentations of the following rows and their retrogrades:

Note that although the trichords are presented vertically in the music, the order of pitch-classes within them, in the row forms involved, is preserved or retrograded.

In contrast, the latent hexachordal relation between the above two row forms, which does *not* preserve or retrograde the order of pitch-classes within the hexachords,

is not exploited here (nor is any hexachordal relation between any analogously related pair of row forms ever exploited conspicuously in the piece). The hexachordal structure of the row may perhaps have an aural effect in the large, but it clearly does not have as basic a function in the piece as do Schönberg's hexachordal structures in his hexachordal music.

B: Prolegomena

In the preceding section, I have discussed examples of compositional and structural exploitation of segmental relations between row forms. Compositionally, we have observed that segments in common between two row forms can supply a natural basis for connecting the musical presentations of those row forms by "associative harmony." Structurally, we have observed that certain aspects of the internal structure of a row may be manifested through segmental relations with various other row forms; conversely, every segmental relation between two twelve-tone related row forms may be viewed as a manifestation of some properties of that internal structure which they, and all other rows related to them through any twelve-tone operation, share. For instance, in connection with Ex. 2, the statement: "I_{11} preserves the trichords of $\emptyset_0$" is equivalent to the statement that any row derived from $\emptyset_0$ by transposition, inversion, retrogression, or any combination of these operations will be such that its group of four trichords can be inverted into itself. In connection with Ex. 4, the statement that the first three pitch-classes of the second row form are the same, *in toto*, as the last three pitch classes of the first form is equivalent to the statement that the last three pitch-classes of any twelve-tone related row will be a transposition of its first three pitch-classes.

The general importance of segmental associations[5] as constructive

[5] I use the word "associations" here (rather than "relationships"), because segmental relations may be and have been exploited in other than associative ways. In particular, the "combinatorial" aspect of segmental relations is of great importance in the literature and theory of twelve-tone music.

(Segments from two or more rows may be said to be in a "combinatorial" relation when no two of the segments have any pitch-classes in common, and when the segments collectively "add up to" an aggregate of *a priori* structural significance, such as the total chromatic, a Babbitt source set, *et al.* The reader is referred to Babbitt, *op.cit.*, and to his earlier article "Some Aspects of Twelve-Tone Composition," *Score*, June 1955; also to George Rochberg, "The Harmonic Tendency of the Hexachord," *Journal of Music Theory*, November 1959; finally to Donald Martino, "The Source Set and Its Aggregate Formations," *Journal of Music Theory*, November 1961, the most thorough and exhaustive study of generalized combinatoriality in print to date.)

In cases of what Babbitt calls "6^2, 4^3, 3^4 and 2^6 combinatoriality," it is possible for a given segment of a row to be functioning both combinatorially and associatively. These are situations in which the segments entering into a combinatorial relation are transposed or inverted forms of one another (as collections of pitch-classes).

E.g. in Ex. 1, the first six pitch-classes of $\emptyset_0$ are in *combinatorial* relation with the first six pitch-classes of I_0; they are also in *associative* relation with the last six pitch-classes of I_0. In the chart of row forms from Webern's Opus 24, presented in footnote 4, the first three pitch-classes of $\emptyset_0$ are in combinatorial relation with the first three pitch-classes of I_0 (they add up to a Babbitt source set, the "chromatic hexachord"), they are in associative relation with the last three pitch-classes of I_0.

I recommend the study of Babbitt's song cycle "Du" as fruitful in this connection: within a framework of 3^4 and 6^2 combinatoriality, the compositional deployment of elements in twelve-tone music, it seems to me, lies precisely in this duality between their compositional and structural aspects. That is: any associative exploitation of a segmental relationship may be viewed simultaneously as an exploitation of some aspect of the structure of the row. Or, taking the dual point of view: any aspect of the segmental structure of a row can potentially be exploited by means of a compositional association.

From the former viewpoint, we may distinguish, in the analysis of a given piece, certain compositional associations (arising from segmental relations) from others, as possessing a peculiar type of structural significance. Other associations may possess other types of structural significance, or they may be purely "formal."[6]

From the latter viewpoint, it is interesting to note that through the exploitation of segmental relations it is possible to expose aspects of a *serial* structure by *"harmonic"* compositional techniques.

With these considerations in mind, I believe that a precise and systematic study of segmental associations, both as they have been exploited compositionally and in their abstract relation to serial structure, will be of interest.

Part II of this article will develop synthetically the theoretical tools and concepts that are desirable for the project. Since their desirability may not become fully apparent until Parts III and IV, I must ask the reader's indulgence for a certain amount of formalism and new terminology which this derivation will entail.

In Part III, I hope to show that the "precision tools" developed in Part II are useful in illuminating certain aspects of Schönberg's compositional technique.

In Part IV, I shall discuss two theoretical topics arising from the concepts developed in Part II; the material is highly speculative but, I think, suggestive. Once more, there will be a good deal of formalism; I shall try to intersperse it with indications as to its possible relevance, but the reader can omit this section without missing much that is pertinent to the central argument.

---

the combinatorially functioning segments at times supports and at times obscures potential segmental associations.

[6] Thus, e.g. the association from the *Violin Phantasy* displayed in Ex. 5 is structural in our present sense. In contrast, turning again to the opening of the cadenza in the first movement of the Violin Concerto, the association there of the Db-G-Bb immediately preceding the cadenza with the Db-G-Bb in the upper "voice" of the opening 3-note chords is not structural in our present sense. Since, however, the Db-G-Bb which precedes the cadenza *is* a presentation of a segment, we might call this association "semi-structural"; as we shall see later, the diminished triad-as-segment plays a strong structural role in the piece.

II: *The "Nesting" Concept*

A: Definition and derivation

Since in the following I will deal with both *ordered* and *unordered collections* of pitch-classes, they will be distinguished from each other as follows: *ordered successions* of pitch classes will be hyphenated; e.g. "A-B♭-E♭" denotes that specific succession of those three pitch-classes. In contrast, when I refer to *unordered collections* of pitch-classes, I shall enclose their names in parentheses. Thus, "(A B♭ E♭)," "(A E♭ B♭)," "(B♭ A E♭)," "(B♭ E♭ A)," "(E♭ A B♭)," and "(E♭ B♭ A)" all denote the same thing: the unordered collection of those three pitch-classes.

If P, then, is some unordered collection of two or more pitch-classes, and if Ø is some twelve-tone row, "P is a segment of Ø" means that the elements of P appear consecutively, in *some* order of succession, within Ø. Thus (A B♭ E♭), (C♯ G), (C F♯ C♯), (E♭ B C F♯ E), et al., are all segments of the row A-B♭-E♭-B-E-F♯-C-C♯-G-A♭-D-F.

We are to be concerned with segments which two given rows have in common. Although in all of the specific cases we shall examine, the two given rows will be related via a twelve-tone operation (transposition, inversion, retrogression, or some combination thereof), we can carry out a good deal of the following work without making this assumption. It seems fruitful to do so, in light of the use, in some twelve-tone works, of relations between rows other than the "classical" ones mentioned above.[7]

Hence, let us suppose that Ø and Ø′ are *any* two rows. The pattern of segmental relations between Ø and Ø′ may be quite complex. There may be "segments within segments" in common (see the discussion of Ex. 6 and 7 on p. 92); also some of the segments in common may "overlap" (Ex. 10).

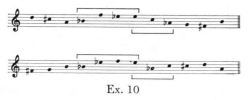

Ex. 10

It may then be difficult to be sure we have ascertained *every* segment in common between two given rows by merely inspecting

[7] See, for instance, George Perle, "Evolution of the Tone-Row: the Twelve-Tone Modal System," *Music Review*, II, 1941.

them in a haphazard way. For this reason, it is worthwhile to have
a systematic method of finding all the segments in common between
two given rows.

Such a method is available. Rather than describe it abstractly, I
shall illustrate its operation in a specific example. The reader will
then, I think, be able to apply the method to any other specific case.

For this example, then, let Ø and Ø′ be the rows shown in Ex. 11.
We wish to find every segment which Ø and Ø′ have in common.

Ex. 11

(A B♭), the collection of the first two pitch-classes of Ø, is *not*
a segment of Ø′. (B♭ E♭) is not a segment of Ø′. (A B♭ E♭) is not
a segment of Ø′.

(E♭ B) is not a segment of Ø′. Nor is (B♭ E♭ B). Nor is (A
B♭ E♭ B).

(B E) is not a segment of Ø′. Nor is (E♭ B E). But (B♭ E♭ B
E) *is* a segment of Ø′, and so is (A B♭ E♭ B E).

Again, (E F♯) is not a segment of Ø′, etc.; but (A B♭ E♭ B
E F♯) is.

Going on in this fashion, we see that the two rows have in common
the segments (B♭ E♭ B E), (A B♭ E♭ B E), (A B♭ E♭ B E
F♯), (C C♯ G A♭), (C C♯ G A♭ D), and (C C♯ G A♭ D F); and
we know that they have no other segments in common.

It will be observed that some of the above collections are sub-
collections of others. The following "spatial" array (Ex. 12) displays
these relations among the collections.

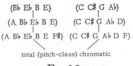

Ex. 12

I shall call the array of Ex. 12 *the nesting*[8] *of the total (pitch-class)
chromatic with respect to the rows Ø and Ø′*. It will be denoted symbolically by *N(Ø,Ø′)*.

[8] The word "nesting" has a mathematical meaning which is not being used precisely
here. I choose the word in order to have some term with which to denote the type of
array of which Ex. 12 is an example, and "nesting" seems intuitively plausible.

Observe that Ex. 12 may be regarded from two complementary points of view: it shows us what segments the two rows of Ex. 11 have in common, but also represents, as it stands, a certain "harmonic idea." Any compositional exploitation of any segmental relation between the rows of Ex. 11 will, in its associative aspect, be a part of this "harmonic idea."

The nesting format is well suited to displaying overlapping segments in common between rows. For instance, let us now take, as "Ø" and "Ø'," the rows of Ex. 13. We see that these rows have in common (among others) the segments (A B♭ E♭ B E F♯) and (B E F♯ C C♯ G), which overlap.

Ex. 13

Ex. 14 displays the nesting of the total chromatic with respect to the rows of Ex. 13. Notice that the overlapping segments fit in quite naturally.

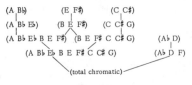

Ex. 14

B: Interactions between nestings and the twelve-tone operations

As a preliminary remark, I should point out that the nesting of the total chromatic with respect to two given rows Ø and Ø' is, of course, the same as the nesting with respect to Ø' and Ø. For we are involved only with the segments that the two rows have in common; which of the rows we happen to *mention* first is irrelevant.

Thus, although the algorithm we went through following Ex. 11 seized on one of the two rows as a point of departure and reference, the result would have been the same had we used the other row as a basis for carrying through the work.

In terms of our symbolic notation, this observation is written:

$$1: \ N(\emptyset, \emptyset') = N(\emptyset', \emptyset)$$

Now note that, since segments are conceived as *unordered* collections, every segment of a given row $\emptyset$ is also a segment of its retrograde $r(\emptyset)$. Thus, any segments which $\emptyset$ has in common with any other row $\emptyset'$ will also be segments in common between $r(\emptyset)$ and $\emptyset'$; conversely, any segments which $r(\emptyset)$ has in common with $\emptyset'$ will also be common to $\emptyset$ and $\emptyset'$. Therefore the nesting with respect to $r(\emptyset)$ and $\emptyset'$ will contain exactly the same collections as does the nesting between $\emptyset$ and $\emptyset'$. Similarly, we can retrograde $\emptyset'$ *ad lib.* without affecting the nesting. In symbolic notation, we write:

$$2: \ \ N(\emptyset, \emptyset') = N\big(r(\emptyset), \emptyset'\big) = N\big(\emptyset, r(\emptyset')\big) = N\big(r(\emptyset), r(\emptyset')\big)$$

Nestings can be transposed and inverted by transposing and inverting the constituent collections of pitch-classes. For instance, Ex. 15 shows the nesting of Ex. 12 transposed by the pitch-class interval $(+)2$; Ex. 16 shows the nesting of Ex. 12 inverted, with B♭-and-A (or E-and-E♭) as center of inversion.[9]

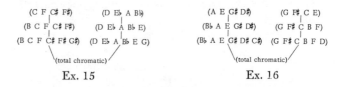

Ex. 15   Ex. 16

As one would suppose, the new array obtained by transposing or inverting a nesting with respect to two given rows is, in fact, the nesting with respect to the correspondingly transposed or inverted forms of those rows. For example, Exx. 15 and 16 arose, respectively, by transposing Ex. 12 through the interval 2 and inverting Ex. 12 about B♭-and-A. Ex. 12 was the nesting of the total chromatic with respect to the rows of Ex. 11. If we transpose the rows of Ex. 11 by the interval 2 (Ex. 17), we see that Ex. 15 is indeed the nesting of the total chromatic with respect to the new rows so obtained.

[9] A *pitch-class inversion* can be determined by fixing a center of inversion, just as a pitch-inversion can be. Thus, the operation of "pitch-class inversion about B♭-and-A" interchanges B♭ with A, B with G♯, C with G, C♯ with F♯, D with F, and D♯ with E.

Hence, the collection (B♭ E♭ B E) of Ex. 12 inverts, via this operation, into the collection (A E G♯ D♯) of Ex. 16: B♭→A, E♭→E, B→G♯, E→D♯. Likewise the collection (C C♯ G A♭) of Ex. 12 inverts into (G F♯ C B) of Ex. 16: C→G, C♯→F♯, G→C, A♭→B. And so on.

Ex. 17

And if we invert the rows of Ex. 11 about B♭-and-A (or E-and-E♭) (Ex. 18), we see that Ex. 16 is the nesting with respect to those new rows.

Ex. 18

In general, if *t* is any transposition-operation (defined by the interval of transposition), or if *i* is any inversion-operation (defined by the center(s) of inversion), the array obtained by applying the operation to a nesting with respect to two given rows will be the nesting with respect to the correspondingly transposed or inverted forms of the given rows. In symbolic notation:

$$3a: \quad t\left(N(\emptyset, \emptyset') \right) = N\left(t(\emptyset), t(\emptyset') \right)$$
$$3b: \quad i\left(N(\emptyset, \emptyset') \right) = N\left(i(\emptyset), i(\emptyset') \right)$$

From laws No. 1 and No. 3, we can deduce two corollaries which are not intuitively obvious. Let us suppose we are considering two rows which are related inversionally (that is, for some inversion-operation *i*, defined by its center(s) of inversion, we can write the two rows as Ø and i(Ø)). Then the nesting with respect to those two rows will be inversionally symmetrical with respect to the inversion *i*—that is, *i* applied to the nesting yields back the nesting itself.

For example, the two rows of Ex. 11 are inversions of each other, the centers of the inversion being F-and-F♯ (or B-and-C). Observe that the associated nesting (Ex. 12) is inversionally symmetrical about F-and-F♯ (or B-and-C). For that inversion, when applied to the nesting, interchanges (B♭ E♭ B E) with (C C♯ G A♭), (A B♭ E♭ B E) with (C C♯ G A♭ D), and (A B♭ E♭ B E F♯) with (C C♯ G A♭ D F).

Again: the two rows of Ex. 13 are inversions of each other, the center of inversion being B (or F). The associated nesting (Ex. 14) is inversionally symmetrical about B (or F).

What this "means" is that the "harmonic idea" arising from segmental relations between two inversionally related rows is itself inversionally symmetrical.[10]

In symbolic notation: if i is any inversion-operation, and $\emptyset$ is any row, then

$$4{:}^{11}\; i\left(N\left(\emptyset,\ i(\emptyset)\right)\right) = N\left(\emptyset,\ i(\emptyset)\right)$$

In analogous fashion, if t_6 is the operation of "tritone transposition," and if $\emptyset$ is any row, then $N\left(\emptyset,\ t_6(\emptyset)\right)$ will remain unchanged if its constituent collections are all transposed a tritone. Symbolically:

$$5{:}\quad t_6\left(N\left(\emptyset,\ t_6(\emptyset)\right)\right) = N\left(\emptyset,\ t_6(\emptyset)\right)$$

Of course, in the light of law No. 2, retrograding any of the rows involved in No. 3, No. 4, and No. 5 does not affect the result.

III: *Analytic Applications of the Nesting Concept*

In this section, I hope to exhibit, in studying some of the music from in and about the cadenza of the first movement of Schönberg's

10 The nesting for the two rows of Ex. 6 is

The music of Ex. 7, as we saw, exploits both the hexachords and the trichords. In addition, the texture differentiates the dyads whenever they appear within the trichords. Thus Ex. 7 exploits the entire nesting. The resulting inversional harmonic symmetry seems to me very strong. It is supported by, and supports, the rhythmic symmetry.

11 As stated above, this fact follows deductively from No. 1 and No. 3. For those who are interested, I give a proof.

Given $\emptyset$ and i, we observe first that $i\left(i(\emptyset)\right) = \emptyset$. This is so because i, as an operation, interchanges pitch-classes in pairs, except for those it may leave fixed. E.g. if the center of i is C, then i leaves C fixed, leaves F♯ fixed, interchanges B with C♯, interchanges B♭ with D, etc. Thus if one application of the operation is followed by a second application, any pitch-classes which were left fixed the first time remain fixed (e.g. C→C→C, F♯→F♯→F♯); and any pitch-classes which were changed the first time are "re-interchanged" back to where they started (e.g. B→C♯→B, D→B♭→D, etc.).

Armed with this lemma, we can simply write out:

$$\begin{aligned}
i\left(N(\emptyset,\ i(\emptyset))\right) &= N\left(i(\emptyset),\ i\left(i(\emptyset)\right)\right) &\text{(No. 3b)}\\
&= N\left(i(\emptyset),\ \emptyset\right) &\text{(lemma)}\\
&= N\left(\emptyset,\ i(\emptyset)\right) &\text{(No. 1) q.e.d.}
\end{aligned}$$

Violin Concerto (see the excerpt on pp. 115-116) evidence of the utility of the nesting concept as a tool for examining some of Schönberg's compositional techniques.

Throughout Part III, "$\emptyset_0$" and "I_0" will denote the rows of Ex. 1. These are also the "$\emptyset$" and "$\emptyset'$" of Ex. 11. Ex. 12, then, displays $N(\emptyset_0, I_0)$.

Transposed forms of $\emptyset_0$ and I_0 will, as in Part I, be denoted by "$\emptyset_n$" and "I_n," where n is the interval of transposition. Retrograde forms of $\emptyset_n$ and I_n will be denoted by "R_n" and "RI_n."

A: Trichordal structure of the row

The row-form I_{11} "preserves the trichords of $\emptyset_0$." This was noted in Ex. 2.

$\emptyset_0$ and I_{11} were the "$\emptyset$" and "$\emptyset'$" of Ex. 13; hence Ex. 14 gives the complete nesting $N(\emptyset_0, I_{11})$.

In the discussion following Ex. 2 in Part I, two examples of conspicuous compositional exploitation of the trichordal structure were noted in the music: in the solo part beginning at m. 234, and in the 3-note chords opening the cadenza. The nesting array of Ex. 14 gives us further information about the segmental relations between $\emptyset_0$ and I_{11}. Note, in particular, that Ex. 14 highlights the structural distinction between the "diminished triad" and the other three trichords.

Evidence for the fact that Schönberg was aware of this distinction can be found in both the musical passages mentioned above. In the solo part at mm. 234ff., observe that the compositional presentation of the diminished triad is differentiated from the presentation of the other three trichords both rhythmically and timbrally (harmonics are used to demarcate the first notes of the presentations of the other three trichords, but not of the diminished triad). See, incidentally, mm. 52-55 in the solo part, where $\emptyset_0$ was exploited "trichordally" (Ex. 19)—the trichords, of course, being the same as those of I_{11}.

Ex. 19

And in the opening of the cadenza, observe that the diminished triads are sharply differentiated from the other trichords rhythmically, texturally, and dynamically.

B: A study in local association

From the upbeat to m. 230 up to the beginning of the cadenza, a strong linear presentation of $\emptyset_5$ is made. The cadenza then presents $\emptyset_3$, RI_3 and I_3 up to *lento, sul G*, at which point a strong linear presentation of I_6 appears which associates with the earlier presentation of $\emptyset_5$ through its rhythm and contour.[12] If we compute $N(\emptyset_5, I_6)$ (Ex. 20), we see that the *only* segment these rows have in common is (B F). Note that in each of these rows, that tritone connects the two hexachords appearing therein (of course, the nesting cannot tell us this). As both linear presentations of $\emptyset_5$ and I_6 in the music articulate the hexachords (in the first case, through a change of instrument and register; in the second, through a rest, timbre change, and phrasing), the (B F) relation may have some aural effect.

$$\frac{N.(\emptyset_5, I_6)}{(B\,F)}$$
$$|$$
$$\text{(total chromatic)}$$

Ex. 20

I should like to examine here certain techniques of "harmonic" association that are displayed in the intervening music which, I think, serve further to bridge the presentations of $\emptyset_5$ and I_6. I shall restrict my attention to the portion of the cadenza from the first *presto* up to *lento, sul G*, as the preceding parts of the cadenza contain trichordal, tetrachordal, and dyadic relationships which would complicate the discussion. It should, however, be borne in mind that, by the time the first *presto* is reached, both $\emptyset_3$ and RI_3 (which is segmentally equivalent to I_3) have been firmly established.

The row forms involved in this portion of the music are $\emptyset_3$ (first *presto* to *feroce*), I_3, and $\emptyset_3$ again. I shall refer to that point in the music where the last of the above forms is presented as *feroce* (a). It will be convenient to tabulate the various nestings involving $\emptyset_5$ (point of departure), $\emptyset_3$, I_3 (intermediate points), and I_6 (immediate destination) (Ex. 21).

12 The association is particularly potent because the rhythm and contour are strongly thematic. They refer to the solo part in m. 20, which was conspicuously established as the first climax-point of the piece. (That climax is supported very powerfully. Registrally: the E♭ is the highest note of the piece, and particularly of the solo line, so far. It is made even more conspicuous as such by the stepwise preparation B♭→C→C♯→D in mm. 18-19. Dynamically: the ff, reached after the long crescendo from m. 17, is the loudest dynamic indication so far in the piece.)

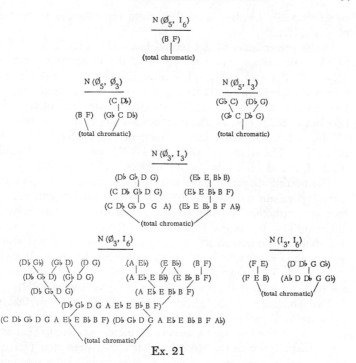

Ex. 21

Examining the presentation of $\emptyset_3$ beginning at the first *presto*, we see that its hexachordal segments are articulated by a rest, and emphasized by the parallelism between their presentations.

Within the presentation of the first hexachord (C Db Gb D G A), the tetrachord (Db Gb D G) is rendered conspicuous through registration. The C is attached to this tetrachord as a "drone," and the A is detached from the resulting pentachord (C Db Gb D G) rhythmically, timbrally, and registrally. Observe, by inspecting $N(\emptyset_3, I_3)$, that the hexachord, the pentachord, and the tetracord are all segments of both $\emptyset_3$ and I_3. In fact, they constitute "half" of the nesting; that is, within a presentation of the first half of $\emptyset_3$, it is impossible to have any more segmental association with I_3.

Note, in addition, that the tetrachord (Db Gb D G) is also a segment of I_6 (the local goal); i.e. that tetrachord is also part of $N(\emptyset_3, I_6)$. More: observe that the dyads (Db Gb) and (D G), into which that tetrachord is divided by the compositional presentation, are also constituents of $N(\emptyset_3, I_6)$.

Finally, note that the trichord (C Db Gb), which is brought out compositionally by the slur and staccato repetition, is a constituent of $N(\emptyset_3, \emptyset_5)$.

In the presentation of the second hexachord (E♭ E B♭ B F A♭) of $\emptyset_3$ which follows (second *presto*), the constituent pentachord (E♭ E B♭ B F) of $N(\emptyset_3, I_3)$ is brought out compositionally. However, the tetrachord (E♭ E B♭ B) of that nesting is *not* brought out here (as would be structurally analogous to the presentation of the first hexachord); instead, the presentation emphasizes the tetrachord (E B♭ B F). The latter is a constituent, not of $N(\emptyset_3, I_3)$, but of $N(\emptyset_3, I_6)$. The dyads (E B♭) and (B F) are also constituents of $N(\emptyset_3, I_6)$, and (B F) is also a constituent of $N(\emptyset_3, \emptyset_5)$.

The nesting diagrams have helped us to see that, in spite of the formal parallelism between the two hexachord presentations, the harmonic structure (in our sense) of the presentations is slightly different. That is, speaking very loosely: the presentation of the first hexachord maximized structural harmonic relation to I_3, and also had quite a bit of relation to I_6. The presentation of the second hexachord preserved the same amount of relation to I_6 while somewhat weakening the relation to I_3. Both presentations related somewhat to $\emptyset_5$.

The advantage of the nesting diagrams, of course, is that they allow us to formulate the above rather vague statements quite precisely and with reference to specific harmonies involved. That is, we can actually diagram the structural harmonies presented (Ex. 22). In connection with this, it is wise to keep in mind the positions of the presentation of $\emptyset_5$ (original point of departure), $\emptyset_3$ (where we are now), I_3 (immediately following; also note the earlier presentations of RI_3), and I_6 (eventual goal).

	first hexachord presentation	second hexachord presentation
constituents of $N(\emptyset_3, \emptyset_5)$	(C D♭ G)	(B F)
constituents of $N(\emptyset_3, I_3)$	(D♭ G♭ D G) (C D♭ G♭ D G) (C D♭ G♭ D G A)	(E♭ E B♭ B F) (E♭ E B♭ B F A♭)
constituents of $N(\emptyset_3, I_6)$	(D♭ G♭) (D G) (D♭ G♭ D G)	(E B♮) (B F) (E B♭ B F)

Ex. 22

In the presentation of I_3 beginning at *feroce*, the hexachordal segments are again stressed by the formal parallelism.

Within the presentation of the first hexachord (F E B E♭ B♭ A♭), the constituent tetrachord (E♭ E B♭ B) and pentachord (E♭ E B♭

B F) of N(I₃, Ø₃) are stressed. None of these is a constituent of
N(I₃, I₆). However, note that, whereas the opening trichord
(C D♭ G♭) of the preceding presentation of Ø₃ related back to Ø₅,
the opening trichord (F E B) of this presentation of I₃, which is again
brought out by the slur, now relates ahead to I₆ . . . i.e. it is a
constituent of N(I₃, I₆).

The dyads (E B) and (E♭ B♭) are not constituents of any nesting
under consideration.

In the following presentation of the second hexachord (D D♭ G
G♭ C A) of I₃, the emphasized pentachord (D D♭ G G♭ C) is a
constituent of N(I₃, Ø₃); the emphasized tetrachord (D♭ G G♭ C),
however, is not. It is, rather, a constituent of N(I₃, Ø₅).

Thus, whereas the opening trichord of this presentation of I₃
related to I₆ rather than to Ø₅ (as did the opening trichord of the
presentation of Ø₃), the tetrachord within the second half of the
presentation of I₃ relates to Ø₅ rather than to I₆ (as did the analogous
tetrachord of Ø₃). Observe that the dyads (D♭ G) and (G♭ C) here
are also constituents of N(I₃, Ø₅).

The strong accent on the A♭ (but not on the A) seems a puzzling
feature of this presentation of I₃. I advance, with some diffidence, the
following suggestion: the creation of an artificial downbeat on the
A♭ seems to rob the following D of what would otherwise be its downbeat character. To my ear, one result of this is to associate the A♭
more strongly with the notes that follow it (as being within the A♭'s
"measure") than with those that precede it. In this connection it may
be relevant that (A♭ D D♭ G G♭) is a constituent of N(I₃, I₆).

We go on now to the following presentation of Ø₃ at *feroce* (a).
The hexachords are no longer as strongly stressed compositionally.
Thus, perhaps the most characteristic aspect of N(Ø₃, I₃) is liquidated
in preparation, presumably, for the subsequent change from "3-forms"
to a "6-form." That is: the appearance of the hexachord-and-its-com-
plement at a certain transpositional level [(C D♭ G♭ D G A) and
(E♭ E B♭ B F A♭)] is characteristic of the exploitation of row forms
Ø₃, I₃, R₃, and RI₃. Within the form I₆, the hexachord-and-its-comple-
ment appear at a *different* transpositional level. Thus the liquidation
of the hexachord at its "3-level" makes for a smoother harmonic
transition. The pentachord (C D♭ G♭ D G) and the tetrachord
(D♭ G♭ D G) are also liquidated by the new texture.

Note, however, that the opening trichord (C D♭ G), relating to
Ø₅, is still prominent compositionally. And the dyads (D♭ G♭) and
(D G), constituents of N(Ø₃, I₆), are also prominent.

The dyads (E B♭) and (B F) and the tetrachord (E B♭ B F)

are prominent; all are constituents of $N(\emptyset_3, I_6)$; none are constituents of $N(\emptyset_3, I_3)$. Among the constituents of the latter nesting, the most prominent in this presentation is probably the pentachord (E♭ E B♭ B F), but it is, even so, much weaker than it has been at its previous appearances (second *presto* and *feroce*).

A further point which I think is of interest: in the presentation of $\emptyset_3$ at *feroce* (a), note that the voice-leading in register is all *ascending* until the final A♭ (C→D→E♭, D♭→E→F, G♭→A→B♭→B). This accentuates the differentiation, prominent also rhythmically, of the low A♭ from the other notes of the presentation. Observe, correspondingly, that (everything but A♭) is a constituent of $N(\emptyset_3, I_6)$. One might, of course, say merely that $\emptyset_3$ ends with A♭ and I_6 begins with A♭; this formulation, however, does not suggest any rationale for the compositional *differentiation* of the A♭ from everything else within the presentation of $\emptyset_3$.

It is interesting to observe that Schönberg exploited almost every constituent of every nesting listed in Ex. 21. Naturally, it would be extravagant to assert that these "structural harmonies" carry the passage by themselves. Other factors are potent, including some that operate very strongly in a larger context.[13] Nevertheless, I feel that the harmonies are functional.

Again, I would not claim that the structural harmonic techniques we have examined are to be found employed to as great an extent everywhere in Schönberg's twelve-tone music. I chose the passage, obviously, precisely because I found it one in which the techniques were employed particularly conspicuously. I think it does indicate that the nesting construct is useful in illuminating one of Schönberg's technical resources.

IV: *Two Theoretical Conceits*

A: What kinds of harmonic ideas can be nestings?

It was pointed out in Part II that every nesting may be viewed not only as an aggregation of segments in common between two given rows, but also as a harmonic idea *in se*. Evidently it is possible to construct harmonic ideas of this sort merely by selecting a certain aggregate of collections of pitch-classes and drawing the appropriate lines to indicate which collections are included in which other collections. Exx. 23a-23e, for instance, are harmonic ideas of this sort.

---

[13] Especially, e.g. the thematic variant D♭-D-F♭-F latent in the texture at the first *presto*, followed by the latent E-E♭-C♯-C at *feroce*. See the opening eight measures of the piece, and also the last *lento* of the cadenza.

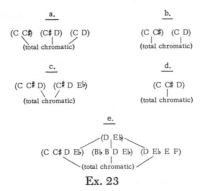

Ex. 23

It seems evident to me that in any totally chromatic music in which associative harmony plays a role, such harmonic ideas will often be manifested. Even in twelve-tone music, such ideas may easily emerge without necessarily being derived from segmental relations.

The obvious question arises: is there anything particularly characteristic about those harmonic ideas which are nestings, by means of which we can distinguish them *in se* from those harmonic ideas which could not be nestings? More precisely, we ask:

QUESTION 1: Given a certain harmonic idea H (such as those of Ex. 23), under what conditions is it possible to find two rows Ø and Ø', such that H = N(Ø, Ø')?

I believe that this question, in spite of its generality (we do not demand any serial relation between Ø and Ø'), is of musical interest. For there is much music being written now (especially in the United States) in which passages of more or less "free" total chromaticism alternate with passages of more or less "strict" serial treatment. An investigation of question 1 might shed some light on how some harmonic ideas arising in a "free" context might "pull" in a serial direction, while others might not. In this connection, naturally, one would have to examine specific pieces. I feel that Sessions' Third Symphony, for example, will repay such study; it would be out of place, however, to launch an analytic examination of such scope here.

Question 1 as a mathematical problem is extremely non-trivial. As yet, I have been unable to solve it (that is, to find properties which will completely characterize nestings from among all possible harmonic ideas). I have found several properties which all nestings must possess, but I have not been able to show that any harmonic idea which possesses all these properties must be a nesting. To give the reader an idea of the various sorts of complications which can arise in attempting to solve the problem, I shall show that none of the harmonic ideas of Ex. 23 can be a nesting.

As far as Ex. 23a is concerned, there can not be even one row in which (C C♯), (C♯ D) and (C D) are all segments, much less two. For if Ø were such a row, then since (C C♯) and (C♯ D) would be segments, either the succession C-C♯-D or the succession D-C♯-C would have to appear within Ø; in either case, (C D) could not also be a segment.

Concerning Ex. 23b: if there were two rows Ø and Ø′ such that this diagram were N(Ø, Ø′), then, as in the discussion of Ex. 23a, either the succession C-C♯-D or the succession D-C♯-C would have to appear within Ø; likewise, one of these successions would have to appear within Ø′. In any case, the trichord (C C♯ D) would be a segment both of Ø and of Ø′. As this trichord does not appear in Ex. 23b, the latter cannot be N(Ø, Ø′).

Now suppose we could find a Ø and a Ø′, such that Ex. 23c was N(Ø, Ø′). Since (C C♯ D) and (C♯ D E♭) would be segments of Ø, one of the following successions would have to appear within Ø: C-C♯-D-E♭, C-D-C♯-E♭, E♭-D-C♯-C, or E♭-C♯-D-C. In any case, (C♯ D) would be a segment of Ø. Likewise, that dyad would be a segment of Ø′. Since it does not appear in Ex. 23c, that array cannot be N(Ø, Ø′).

Turning to Ex. 23d: there are only six possible orders of succession for the three pitch-classes within any putative Ø: C-C♯-D, C-D-C♯, C♯-C-D, C♯-D-C, D-C-C♯, and D-C♯-C. Similarly, one of these successions would have to appear within any putative Ø′. The reader may verify that, no matter which of the possible cases arose, either (C C♯), (C♯ D), or (C D) would also be a segment of both Ø and Ø′. Since none of these dyads appears in Ex. 23d, the latter is not a nesting.

As far as Ex. 23e is concerned, as in the case of Ex. 23a, there cannot be even one row Ø such that all the collections of Ex. 23e would be segments of Ø. For since (D E♭), (C C♯ D E♭), and (B♭ B D E♭) would all be segments, some succession such as C-C♯-D-E♭-B-B♭ or B-B♭-E♭-D-C-C♯, etc. would have to appear within Ø. That is, the (D E♭) segment would be "surrounded," in some fashion, by (C C♯) and (B B♭); thus (D E♭ E F) could not also be a segment.[14]

---

[14] After the rather lofty claim for the value of answering question 1, the reader may be somewhat annoyed by the picayune discussion of Ex. 23. I should probably explain why I do not consider my position inconsistent.

I believe that music theory is most fruitfully regarded as an attempt to construct intellectual models for general modes of hearing. As such, it should be as thorough as possible. To the extent that question 1 reflects a valid problem concerning a general

Two special cases of question 1 would naturally be of more specific relevance to twelve-tone music:

QUESTION 2a: Given a harmonic idea H, under what conditions is it possible to find a row $\emptyset$ and a transposition t such that H $= N \left(\emptyset, t(\emptyset) \right)$?

QUESTION 2b: Given a harmonic idea H, under what conditions is it possible to find a row $\emptyset$ and an inversion (-operation) such that $H = N \left(\emptyset, i(\emptyset) \right)$?

The conditions for questions 2a and 2b would naturally include the conditions for question 1; it seems fruitless to attack the special problems until the general one has been solved.

B: Nestings as row-defining

In Part IB, I noted that ". . . through the exploitation of segmental relations, it is possible to expose aspects of a *serial* structure by '*harmonic*' compositional techniques." In other words, every nesting which involves a given row yields a certain amount of structural information about that row. More exactly: the nesting will inform us that the collections displayed are all segments of the row. It will not, of course, tell us *where* in the row these segments appear. Nevertheless, a knowledge of sufficiently many segments of a row will enable us to infer certain conclusions about the order of succession of some of its elements; see the discussions of Ex. 23.

Now, the "knowledge" and "inference" referred to above are evidently of an intellectual nature. Nevertheless, the "knowledge" can obviously mirror a musical experience: the apprehension of a harmonic idea. And to the extent that, in certain contexts, we tend to organize our musical sensations in serial terms, the "inference" reflects a genuine aspect of a certain mode of hearing. To the extent that that mode of hearing is operative in a given musical context, it is plausible

---

mode of hearing, it is a legitimate theoretical question; the more thoroughly we investigate question 1, the more sensitive we should become to that mode of hearing.

Any composition, however, although it will reflect certain assumptions about or predispositions toward certain general modes of hearing on the part of the composer, always unfolds in specific musical contexts. At any point in the music, it is possible that several modes of hearing may be operative, including some which have not as yet been abstracted into a body of theory.

To me, question 1 represents an inquiry into one aspect of a very broad mode of hearing. It would be presumptuous to suppose, even if question 1 were to be answered, that one would immediately find striking and "pat" examples of its relevance throughout the literature. What I would hope to be able to find would be examples in which, in a "free" totally chromatic context, those harmonic ideas which were *more* "nesting-like" (i.e. violated few of the conditions demanded by question 1, and violated them in relatively inconspicuous ways compositionally) tended to "pull" the music in a serial direction.

that we should tend to hear the constituent collections of harmonic ideas as putative row segments. In fact, if we hear sufficiently many and varied harmonic ideas, it is possible that the putative segments will be many and varied enough so as to actually define one specific row. What I mean, in musical terms, by "define" is obviously vague. The topic is highly speculative; nevertheless, I believe that it is suggestive enough to warrant closer investigation. Even in cases where we do not have sufficient harmonic information to "define" a row, I feel it is legitimate to conceive of several harmonic ideas as being collectively highly definitive or not very definitive in serial terms.

For example, let us consider the Violin Concerto once more. We have observed that the nestings $N(\emptyset_0, I_0)$ and $N(\emptyset_0, I_{11})$ are of significance in the piece. Considering these nestings now purely as harmonic ideas, let us call them H_1 and H_2 respectively (Ex. 24).

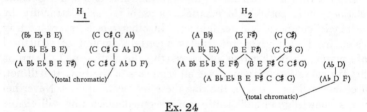

Ex. 24

I will show that these harmonic ideas *almost completely determine* $\emptyset_0$ (or its retrograde); that is, any row which includes as segments all the constituent collections of H_1 and H_2 must be "nearly" $\emptyset_0$ or R_0.

Let $\emptyset$ be any row which includes all these collections as segments. Obviously $r(\emptyset)$ will be another such row. We are to show that $\emptyset$ must be "nearly" $\emptyset_0$ or R_0. We reason as follows:

(A B♭) is a segment of $\emptyset$ (H_2). Hence either the succession A-B♭ or the succession B♭-A appears within $\emptyset$. Since we are willing to accept $r(\emptyset)$ as readily as $\emptyset$, we may assume that A-B♭ appears within $\emptyset$.

(A B♭ E♭) is a segment (H_2). Hence either A-B♭-E♭ or E♭-A-B♭ appears within $\emptyset$. But if the latter were the case, then (B♭ E♭ B E) (H_1), which does not contain A, would not be a segment. Hence A-B♭-E♭ appears within $\emptyset$.

(B♭ E♭ B E) is a segment (H_1). Hence either A-B♭-E♭-B-E or A-B♭-E♭-E-B appears. But in the latter case, (E F♯) could not be a segment (H_2). Hence we infer A-B♭-E♭-B-E and, since (E F♯) is a segment, A-B♭-E♭-B-E-F♯.

(C C♯) is a segment (H₂). Hence either C-C♯ (subcase 1) or C♯-C (subcase 2) appears.

Subcase 1: If C-C♯ appears, then, since (C C♯ G) is a segment (H₂), we must have C-C♯-G or G-C-C♯. Then, since (C C♯ G A♭) is a segment (H₁), we must have either C-C♯-G-A♭ or A♭-G-C-C♯. And since (A♭ D) and (A♭ D F) are segments (H₂), we will then have either C-C♯-G-A♭-D-F or F-D-A♭-G-C-C♯.

Recalling that we have already established A-B♭-E♭-B-E-F♯, we now observe that (B E F♯ C C♯ G) is a segment (H₂). Hence the only possibility for collocating the two hexachords is A-B♭-E♭-B-E-F♯-C-C♯-G-A♭-D-F, and Ø = Ø₀.

Subcase 2: If C♯-C appears, we follow the same procedure, and conclude that Ø must be the row: A-B♭-E♭-B-E-F♯-C♯-C-G-A♭-D-F; that is, Ø is the same as Ø₀, only with the adjacent C and C♯ interchanged. In this sense, then, H₁ and H₂ "practically" define Ø₀, or are "highly definitive" of Ø₀.

An important structural aspect of Ø₀ which we have not yet mentioned is the inclusion, within it, of a six-element segment which is an all-combinatorial hexachord (Ex. 25).

Ex. 25

A complete discussion of this aspect of the row would be outside the province of the present paper;[15] for our purposes it is sufficient to note that Ø₆, I₃, and I₉ preserve that hexachord (Ex. 26).

Ex. 26

Ex. 27 shows the complete nestings N(Ø₀, Ø₆), N(Ø₀, I₃), and N(Ø₀, I₉). Note that every constituent of N(Ø₀, Ø₆) is also a con-

[15] See Babbitt's discussion of the all-combinatorial tetrachord in the row of Schönberg's String Trio, above, pp. 129–147.

stituent of $N(\emptyset_0, I_9)$. Hence the former nesting gives us no more information than does the latter.

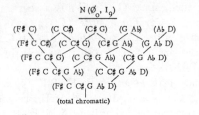

Ex. 27

The reader may verify for himself that $N(\emptyset_0, I_0)$, $N(\emptyset_0, I_3)$, and $N(\emptyset_0, I_9)$, considered purely as harmonic ideas, collectively define $\emptyset_0$. He should start by observing that (everything-but-A) is a seg-

ment; hence A must be the first or the last pitch-class of any putative
∅. Since r(∅) is equally acceptable, it may be assumed that A is
the first pitch-class of ∅.

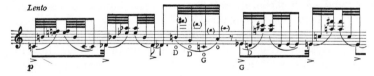

OPERATIONS ON WAVEFORMS

J. K. RANDALL

─────────────────■■■■■■─────────────────

[*Read to the Fall Joint Computer Conference, San Francisco, 11/8/66.*]

However useful the concept of "timbre" may be for music in which relations of spectrum, vibrato, tremolo, and so forth, are less elaborately structured compositionally than are relations of pitch and rhythm, new possibilities for articulating musical structure (that have arisen specifically by virtue of the control given us, by electronic media, over each "ingredient" of timbre separately) are rendering this concept, if not useless, then at least misleading and inhibiting both to current research and to current composition. If we contend, for example, that vibrato is a component of timbre; and that to exert beneficent influence upon a timbre, a vibrato must be moderate in speed (say, several cycles per second, not several per minute or several hundred per second) and well within the boundary of the chromatic semi-tone in width, with both speed and width of course somewhat randomized; then we must recognize that such contentions invoke, at least tacitly, our generalized rememberance of what vibrato "sounds like" (or, worse, *ought to* "sound like") in familiar musical contexts—that is, in contexts where vibrato is not among the most highly compositionally structured aspects of sound. I am concerned here not with the demonstrable[1] irrelevance of this generalized remembrance even to those contexts which our remembrance generalizes upon; I am concerned here rather with the musically useful results of considering, say, vibrato as a perceivable, structurable, and electronically controllable musical continuum in its own right: that is, with perceptions which only the music of the future and the very recent past can induce us to make. Please keep in mind that such refinement and extension of our abilities to perceive, and more importantly of the very modes in which we perceive, is one of the more basic and traditional roles of the art of music.

In compositionally exploiting vibrato as such a continuum, let's consider what it would initially seem reasonable to *avoid*. First, I would recommend avoiding techniques which reduce vibrato to the least struc-

[1] Cf. above, p. 122ff.

turally relevant of its traditional roles: namely, the role of subliminally "lushing-up" tone quality. Second, I would avoid segmenting my continuum on the model of generalized remembrance: identifying a particular segment as the good stuff or the real thing and everything outside that segment as "too" this or "too" that can only stultify my compositional imagination at the outset, and thereby prevent me from ever inducing those very perceptions I ought to be most solicitous about. Instead, I would simply ask myself in moving along this continuum: what kind of musical structures can I imagine that would most strikingly exploit, and thereby make most perceptible to me, the relations I think I ought to be able to hear? My most interesting problems will arise not where I think "normal" passes over into abnormal vibrato; but rather where vibrato itself seems to pass over, first, from a wiggling *of* pitch into some sort of noise *around* a pitch, and then over into a complex mode of pitch-*production* in which the center frequency, the speed of the vibrato, the difference between the two, the sum of the two, the frequencies which delimit the width of the vibrato, and individual frequencies of the spectrum to which the vibrato is applied, all participate as principal components. And these problems will not necessarily be "resolved" by my determining, democratically or otherwise, just where within my continuum each boundary lies—rather, I would expect that, just as the right musical context could fully articulate, for my perception, one of these boundaries, so some other musical context could either dissolve that boundary or reduce to contextual irrelevance the very terms in which it was defined. In short, these seeming boundaries might well prove to be musical structural relations internal to and dependent upon specific musical contexts—and not psycho-acoustical "facts" about the "materials" of music. And third, I would avoid saturating individual tones with additional, contextually nonsignificant, ingredients, chosen to instrumentalize, i.e., lush-up, electronically generated timbres. Instead, I would devote my attention to musically developing however few or many timbral ingredients a compositional idea may suggest in somewhat the sense that I would try to musically develop basic configurations of pitch and rhythm. The often-deplored uniformity, monotony, or outright nastiness of electronic timbres seems to me more properly analyzed as a failure of some existing electronic compositions adequately to structure and develop their timbral components as elements of the composition, rather than as any inherent debility in current technology or any musical dullness "inherent" even in the balder electronic timbres. It is of course simply true that we can produce an electronic tone each of whose components remains uniform from the beginning of the tone to the end; and that a composition which spends 15 or 20 minutes, or even 1 or 2 minutes, celebrating this truth courts triviality. But a composition which meets the threat of triviality with a barrage of irrelevancies is at least as feeble a composition; and perhaps a feebler one, in that it explicitly presents so many things which—specifically by virtue of electronics—could have been musically developed. If I am willing, in instrumental music, to put up with that hopefully rather small percentage of the total sound which *can't* fairly be said to participate constructively in any "local open-ended agglomeration of musical developments in progress"—that is, with these musical irrelevancies which lush-up the tone—this is no reason why I should be willing to put up with them in electronic music where we have become for the first time free to build into individual tones precisely what the musical contexts may suggest *and no more;* that is, free to treat the individual tone as something which need resemble in no degree whatever an extra-structurally prefilled garbage-can.

Now vibrato is just one of the many potentially structurable aspects of sound which have been too often, in effect, written off as ingredients of something more vague. I would like to discuss specifically a few of the characteristics of sets of partials, harmonic and nonharmonic, which composers including myself have tried to release from subliminal influence upon "timbre," and to develop musically as compositional elements.

In the right musical context, it becomes quite easy to perceive and relate sets of partials in the following terms:

1. Registral position: that is, position of any set in the pitch continuum —regardless of the pitches of perceived or unperceived "fundamentals."

2. Intervallic spread: that is, the musical interval defined by the highest and lowest frequencies in any set.

3. Density: that is, the average number of elements in a set which lie within some relevant standard musical interval.

4. Total number of elements in a set.

5. The distribution of relative amplitude over any set.

6. Physical place or places from which any set, or any element of a set, seems to emanate.

This list could obviously be extended; but it is already sufficiently detailed to provide a basis for defining some musical operations on sets of partials—operations many of which may be viewed as attempts to capitalize upon the capacities of electronic media in order to subject to elaborate and continuous musical structuring aspects of sound which the composer for instrumental media cannot risk reliance upon except for rather gross general contrasts and rather subtle local articulations. For example, we know that certain instruments can noticeably transform their tone-qualities in the course of single notes: strings, say, by sliding and tilting the bow; winds, say, by slowly inserting or removing a mute. We know that, in percussion instruments especially, different components of the spectrum fade out at different rates; that most instruments have some junk in the attack; that the component partials, even during "steady state," fluctuate in amplitude; that many instruments can, in a highly limited degree, vary their speeds and widths of vibrato and amplitude modulation; that certain percussion instruments produce sounds which lie in a tantalizing no-man's-land between definite and indefinite pitch; and that the physical positions of several instruments relative to one another can be of structural musical, as well as of acoustical, consequence. But because of the severe limitations imposed upon the compositional exploitation of all these facts of instrumental sound by the physical limitations of instruments and the human body, it is computers, and not conventional instruments, that have the capacity to really capitalize even upon instrumentally-suggested transformations of waveform, [2] whether over the course of a whole composition, from note to note, or within single notes. Partly in this connection I have welcomed the chance offered by computers to try using exclusively sets of partials (harmonic and nonharmonic) derived from one another and pitch-configurations basic to a composition by operations appropriate to that composition; and certain operations have been sufficiently appropriate to a composition I am now working on for me to have incorporated them as alternative branches in a Music IV subroutine. These operations upon sets of partials, in the use of which I lean heavily on the assumption that in the right musical context we can perceive the characteristics I have listed, are the following:

1. Mappings of basic sets of partials onto enlarged and compressed spaces:

(My subroutine does this by preserving the proportions among the component musical intervals of the basic set of partials while gradually changing the intervals themselves. In the continuum thus generated, the basic set itself corresponds to the point of zero enlargement of the total space.)

2. Mappings of basic sets which preserve frequency differences while gradually changing the musical intervals:

[2] I ask the reader's indulgence for my continuing to include physical places of origin among the "properties" of a waveform and hence among its transformables.

(My subroutine does this by adding a constant to each of the partial numbers. In the continuum thus generated, the basic set itself corresponds to the constant zero. I should perhaps here emphasize that the relation between a set of partial-numbers and its corresponding musical intervals and the relation between a set of frequency-numbers and its corresponding musical intervals is one and the same relation: specifically, a given ratio, whether of partial-numbers or frequency-numbers, corresponds to the same musical interval. Hence my subroutine—whose variable arguments are largely operation-codes and musical intervals—treats partial-numbers with impunity as if they were, in effect, frequency numbers.)

3. Mappings of basic sets which exponentiate the partial-numbers by a constant:

(In the continuum thus generated, the basic set itself corresponds to the constant *one*. Since it is not intuitively obvious to me what the musical intervallic result might be of exponentiating partial-numbers by, say, the constant 3.508, the relevant variable argument for this (as for any other) operation in my subroutine is a desired intervallic spread of the result: the subroutine computes whatever mysterious constant it needs to get that intervallic result.)

4. Mappings of basic sets which treat partial-numbers themselves as exponents for a constant base:

(This operation is suggested by the rather well known effects of using the twelfth-root of two as a base for integral exponents. However, it should be noticed that this operation has one characteristic which fundamentally distinguishes it from the other operations I have discussed: in the continuum thus generated, the basic set itself does not in general appear at all.)

5. Mappings of basic sets onto their total inversions—intervallic, frequency-differential, or exponential.

(In order to retrieve for me my control over the assorted registral positions of the assorted new spectra generated by sequences and combinations of these operations applied to derived as well as to basic sets of partials, my subroutine accepts a transposition-number as one of its variable arguments: for example, any derived set at transposition zero will have the same weighted center as the set from which it was derived. I hope it is clear without illustration that, because of the sheer messiness of the calculations required, the computer is as necessary in deriving the new sets of partials in the first place as it is in simulating soundwaves resulting from their use. And yet the results of appropriate musical use of these operations seem to me quite readily perceivable as various kinds and degrees of intervallic distortion, while quite distinguishable in musical function from "chords.")[3]

In compositionally using any such derivations as these, we now have, realistically, the chance to structure developments within any single note exclusively in ways that reflect developments, or the principles of development, in a composition as a whole. There is no longer any gross physical limitation upon the particular ways in which, during a single note, one set of partials may become transformed into another; upon the particular rhythms in which structurally relevant chunks of a total spectrum may fade out—whether immediately following the attack or more gradually during an eminently unsteady state; upon the relevant permutations of amplitude-values which any single set of partials occupying an entire note may undergo; upon the range over which speeds and widths of vibrato and amplitude modulation may change during a single note; upon particular ways in which a single note may fluctuate between definite and indefinite pitch; or upon the complexity of arrangement of moving and stationary sources from which various stereophonic sounds seem to emanate.

If I have repeatedly directed my discussion from electronic possibilities in general toward possibilities for single tones in particular, it is in order to suggest a realistic alternative to the stultifying concept of "timbre": I think that concern with electronic "timbre" should be replaced by, and indeed probably has as its only salvageable inspiration, the compositional exploration of modes of musical development within single tones. The new electronic possibilities may even lead us to the belief that the concept of "timbre" was really never much more than the repository of some notion that individual tones have "moods." We long ago quit talking about "happy melodies" and "pungent harmonies" in favor of contextual musical analysis of developing musical structures of, primarily, pitch and rhythm; and I would hope that we could soon find whatever further excuse we still need to quit talking about "mellow timbres" and "edgy timbres," and "timbres" altogether, in favor of contextual musical analysis of developing structures of vibrato, tremolo, spectral transformation, and all those various dimensions of sound which need no longer languish as inmates of some metaphor.

[3] Notice the injustice of claiming any more radical distinction between sets of partials and sets of simultaneous notes (i.e., "chords") in the case, say, of an orchestral performance of a Mozart symphony: it's not that we *can't* hear those individual overtones *if we try:* on the contrary, it's by succeeding in the attempt that we most convincingly reinforce our musically well-founded determination *not* to. Somehow our musical intelligence persuades us to absorb these overtones as qualifications of fundamentals; much as it persuades us to absorb an assortment of messages traceable to balky (plastic) gut, slithering (plastic) horsehair, dental protuberance, and salivary dispersion as qualifications of attack. In these cases as normally, our ears admirably perceive in modes conducive to musical sense.

THE CONCEPT OF UNITY IN
ELECTRONIC MUSIC

(Die Einheit der musikalischen Zeit)

KARLHEINZ STOCKHAUSEN

ON SEVERAL previous occasions, when I have been asked to explain the composition of electronic music, I have described four characteristics that seem important to me for electronic composition as distinguished from the composition of instrumental music:

1) the correlation of the coloristic, harmonic-melodic, and metric-rhythmic aspects of composition
2) the composition and de-composition of timbres
3) the characteristic differentiation among degrees of intensity
4) the ordered relationships between sound and noise

Here, I would like to discuss only the correlation of timbre, pitch, intensity, and duration. In the past, it has been customary to regard these correlative properties of sound as mutually independent, as belonging to fundamentally distinct spheres. They have appeared increasingly separate as our acoustical perception developed along such lines.

Similarly, the means employed for the production of sound, as well as the compositional process itself, were consequent upon this conceptual separation. To generate sound-events having single perceptible pitches, we used the so-called sine tone, square-wave, or saw-tooth generators, which produce periodic oscillations. Sound-events of indeterminate pitch, those that are more or less noise-like, were produced by means of noise generators.

We varied such sound- or noise-colors by means of electrical filters, with which one can strengthen, attenuate, or suppress entirely individual partials or whole frequency-bands—the so-called formants, or bands of noise—of the spectra.

Intensity was controlled by regulating, with the aid of a voltmeter, the voltages recorded on tape (whereby the spectrum itself automatically varied with the variations in intensity), whereas duration was determined simply by the length of tape on which a sound was recorded.

Compositionally, in terms of the production and manipulation of sound, these individual sound-properties had to be dealt with separately. But, on the other hand, we perceive a sound-event as a homogeneous phenomenon rather than as a composite of four separate properties. At a relatively early stage of my work in electronic composition, I had already considered the possibility of equating this unity of perception with an analogous unity in composition itself. In the preparatory work for my composition *Kontakte*, I found, for the first time, ways to bring all properties under a single control. I deduced that all differences of acoustic perception can be traced to differences in the temporal structure of sound waves. These temporal relations enable us to distinguish the many different manifestations of pitch, timbre, simultaneity, sound-mixture, and noise: their speed of oscillation, their particular intervals—either equal and regular or more or less irregular—their density, and the frequency with which pulsations reach the ear. It seemed to me that the differences in intensity among sounds ultimately derive from the latter property: when pulsations of equal value follow one another in closer temporal succession, the over-all intensity increases; to effect this, the density would, in fact, have to be so great that the individual pulses were no longer conveyed as a succession of equal perturbations of the atmosphere but rather as mutually interfering sound-waves: the particles of air agitated by the initial pulses would thus be reactivated by further pulses before they have become quiescent and are, so to speak, "shaken up," so that the impression given is of an increase in over-all intensity. The total complex thus appears as a *single* greater wave rather than *several* smaller ones. The faster the succession of pulses, the stronger will be the appearance of the resultant wave.

A periodic sound wave, such as a simple tone, fluctuating regularly in intensity, would thus be the result of a succession of pulses that alternately accelerate and decelerate within each period. The difference between the fastest and slowest rates of speed of the pulses in each period would define the direction of its intensity (its "intensity envelope") and its amplitude. The distance between periodically recurring equal rates of speed would determine the pitch.

.. . . etc.

Ex. 1

If a succession of pulses of this kind were to be accelerated so that between the periodic recurrences of the highest speed there were a time interval of, say, 1/440 sec., one would hear a simple tone with the pitch of A-440.

If the rate of speed of the pulse-succession did not fluctuate regularly (～～～) but consisted instead of periods of several unequal parts within each equal time-span (as, for example, ⋀⋀⋁⋀⋁⋀⋀), the so-called "color" of a steady sound would vary according to the wave crests. A "period" divided into two parts would be represented as follows:

Ex. 2

In a more or less noiselike sound-event the periods would no longer be regular; i.e. the time intervals between recurrences of equal rates of speed would not remain constant but would vary irregularly between a given fastest and slowest speed. These extremes determine the limits of a frequency band, a so-called "colored noise" band. If the rate of speed of the pulse succession were so widely varied that the smallest interval between pulses were ca. 1/16,000 sec., and the longest ca. 1/20 sec., occurring at regular time-intervals, and everything between these extremes occurred in a highly aperiodic fashion (in a manner that one might term "aleatoric") the result would be "white noise."

For most musicians, these considerations may seem specifically related to acoustics rather than to music. Actually, however, a musical composition is no more than a temporal ordering of sound events, just as each sound event in a composition is a temporal ordering of pulses. It is only a question of the point at which composition begins: in composing for instruments whose sounds are predetermined, a composer need not be concerned with these problems. On the other hand, in electronic music, one can either compose each sound directly in terms of its wave succession, or, finally, each individual sound wave may be determined in terms of its actual vibration, by an ordering of the succession of pulses.

If, in fact, all of the experiential properties of sound could be traced to a single principle of ordering—such temporally composed successions of pulses—compositional thought would have to be radically reoriented. The distinction between the "acoustical prearrangement" *within* the material and "musical ordering" *using* this material would now have to be discarded. The prevailing additive, or "synthetic" compositional procedure, in which the different properties are bound together, would now be expanded through a protogenerative and more unified approach. One would not proceed from sound properties that had already been experienced and then allow these to determine temporal variations; instead, one would compose the temporal arrangements of pulses themselves, and discover their resultant sound properties experimentally.

After my first, relatively simple, attempt at such a procedure, I was able to predict roughly the particular temporal orderings of the pulses. I then prcceeded to record fixed successions of pulses on tape within a relatively low speed range (using pulsation intervals of between 1/16 and 16 secs.) and then increased the speed until I arrived at the "field" of frequencies and color that I desired. This was done by means of a pulse generator with which the speed of the pulse succession was regulated by hand. Thus, for example, if I wished to generate a periodic wave—that is, a sound of constant pitch—from a succession of pulses lasting eight seconds whose speed variations are fixed, I would have to accelerate the rhythmized eight-second succession 1,024 times, that is, transpose it ten octaves upwards, reducing its duration from eight to 1/128 sec. In order to sustain this pitch of 128 cps. for 10 sec., I would have to re-record the original succession 128×10, or 1,280 times, which can easily be done by means of a tape loop. The "color" of the resulting sound would be determined by the variations of speed among the pulses of the original succession, which are now determined by the periodic duplications and accelerations of the wave form within each time span—i.e. the "intensity envelope."

With such a compositional procedure, then, one must proceed from a basic concept of a *single, unified musical time*; and the different perceptual categories, such as color, harmony and melody, meter and rhythm, dynamics, and "form," must be regarded as corresponding to the different *components* of this unified time, as follows:

1. Harmony and melody correspond to periodic waves (that is, to sound-events of constant pitch) whose individual periods should not be greater than ca. 1/16 or less than ca. 1/6,000 sec. because beyond these limits they are no longer audible as "pitches."

2. The color of harmonic spectra corresponds to the whole number fractions which, as "fundamentals," refer to periods of between ca. 1/13,000 and ca. 1/16 sec.; the color of nonharmonic or noiselike spectra corresponds to more or less aperiodic successions of periods.

3. Between ca. 1/30 and 1/16 sec. our perception of duration gradually changes into perception of meter and rhythm; i.e., *periodic periods* may then be considered as *meters*, and the *internal intervallic relationships* of the distances between pulses within any given meter—that which determines the tone color for periods shorter than ca. 1/16 sec.—may here be considered as "rhythm."

Aperiodic relationships of periods, which are considered *"noises"* in the sphere of color, correspond, when the periods are longer than ca. 1/16 sec., to *aperiodic rhythms* having no recognizable meters—i.e. no recognizable periodicity (just as a deviation from simple periodicity in the sphere of frequency—*"dissonance"*—corresponds, in the sphere of duration, to *syncopation*).

Although many of the new compositions have been criticized for their alleged "lack of rhythm," they may actually be considered to have "pure rhythm" without meter. This objection, moreover, is exactly analogous to that directed against the use of aperiodic sound waves, i.e. against "noises."

4. Meter and rhythm correspond to the time intervals whose order of magnitude is between ca. 1/8 and ca. 8 secs. At about 8 secs. our ability to distinguish durational relationships gradually breaks down. With values of greater length we are no longer able to remember the exact lengths of durations or perceive their proportions as accurately as we can those that lie between ca. 1/8 and ca. 8 secs.

"Form" in a special sense—the time relationships of longer events—corresponds to durations of the order of magnitude of from several seconds to about 15-60 minutes (for "movements" or whole "compositions").

The transitions and overlappings between all the time spheres are quite flexible, but this is especially so with reference to "form," which is most obviously an approximation (in the literature of music, of course, the durations of "movements" or *continuous* works vary from several minutes to ca. one hour).

Perhaps I should mention here that each of the three large musical time-spheres—*frequency duration, rhythm duration*, and *form duration*—are of approximately equal size: each has a compass of about seven "octaves" (where "octave" signifies a relation of 1:2). Between the highest note on the piano, whose fundamental wavelength is ca. 1/4,200 sec. and the lowest, whose wavelength is ca. 1/27 sec., there are just over seven octaves. Below this point sound waves gradually become audible as rhythms (a good illustration of this is the audible effect of the lowest notes on the organ), and from ca. 1/16 sec. to ca.

8 sec.—the span of rhythm durations—there are again seven octaves, as follows:

$$(2^1 \ - \ 2^2 \ - \ 2^3 \ - \ 2^4 - 2^5 - 2^6 - 2^7 \ - .)$$
$$1/16'' - 1/8'' \ - \ 1/4'' \ - \ 1/2'' \ - \ 1'' \ - \ 2'' \ - \ 4'' \ - \ 8''.$$

The sphere of form duration, from ca. 8 sec. to between ca. 900 secs. (15 minutes, the approximate traditional duration of single movements of a work) and ca. 3,600 secs. also includes seven-nine octaves, as follows:

$$(\ - \ 2^1 \ - \ 2^2 \ - \ 2^3 \ - \ 2^4 \ - \ 2^5 \ - \ 2^6 \ - \ 2^7 \ldots)$$
$$8'' - 16'' - 32'' - 64'' - 128'' - 256'' - 512'' - 1{,}024'' \ldots$$

Thus, the total musical time sphere encompasses the durations between ca. 1/4,200 sec. and ca. 900 secs., that is, 22(-24) "octaves," or 22-24 progressions of 1:2.

At this point I would like to demonstrate, with an example from my composition *Kontakte*, a continuous overlapping between the time sphere of "frequencies" ("sounds" and their "colors") and the sphere of "rhythms" (individually audible pulses within given time intervals). This overlapping will take place in the zone between ca. 30 and ca. 6 pulses/sec. To begin with, I fed a periodic succession of 16.6 pulses/sec. into a very narrow-band filter. This succession emerged as a sound wave of clear, recognizable pitch. Then, within one minute's duration, I continuously varied the frequency position of this filter from 40 cps to 300 cps—that is, over a span, from low to high, of about 3 octaves—in an ascending zigzag glissando pattern:

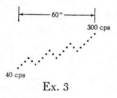

Ex. 3

These variations in filtering are heard as variations in the pitch resulting from the pulse-succession.

Next, I subjected this result to a tenfold acceleration, until 166 pulses/sec. sounded instead of 16.6 pulses/sec.; that is, one heard a steady pitch having a frequency of 166 cps (between $E\flat_3$ and E_3). The *pitch* variation between 40 and 300 cps, heard at the first stage, now appears as an intensification of the tone color of the 166-cps tone (now 6 secs. in duration). Because of the high speed, this pattern is no longer heard as an ascending "melodic line."

For the continuation of this sound, I generated a thirty-second succession of pulses whose speed decreased from 16.6 pulses/sec. to 4 pulses/sec. according to a zigzag pattern. Simultaneously, the filter was continuously varied downwards from 300 cps to 40 cps and then upwards again to 300 cps.

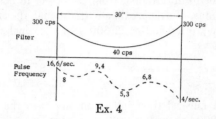

Ex. 4

During the next 45 secs., the speed was lessened from 4 pulses/sec. to 1 pulse/sec. according to a pattern of 4 zigzag alterations of the filter in the range between 300 and 54 cps. After 27 secs., the filter remained level at 54 cps.

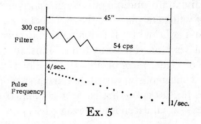

Ex. 5

In the third part of the pulse succession the speed was decreased regularly from 1 pulse/sec. to 1/4 pulse/sec. (within 45 secs. duration); the position of the filter remained constant at 54 cps for the first 15 secs., and then, suddenly, with each individual pulse, it was varied seven times in a fixed up-down, up-down "melodic" pattern, and then held constant at 44 cps.

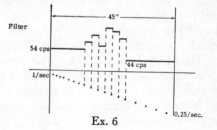

Ex. 6

Next, I connected the resultant parts, and the overall diminution of the speed amounted to 6 octaves (from 16.6 pulses/sec. to 1/4 pulse/sec., along with the abovementioned pitch variations between 300 and 44 cps). (60" + 30" + 45" + 45")

For the last pulses, I gradually altered the filter feedback time so that, at the end, the duration of each individual pulse is increased, and the "color" becomes somewhat "metallic."

At this point, I subjected the total result to an acceleration, which amounted, at the beginning, to a tenfold acceleration from 16.6 to 166 pulses/sec., and, by virtue of the continuous alterations, to a 2.5-fold acceleration at the end, so that the intervals between the final pulses amount to ca. 1.5 secs. The pitch of the final pulses is then steady at 160 cps, which is approximately the same as that with which the event began. Whereas the accelerated form of the original frequency variation is heard chiefly as tone-color variation, we gradually perceive it again as a succession of individual pulses, as pitch, because of the continuous dissolution of the sounds. The initial sound of 166 cps slides (in 6" + 32") about 7½ octaves downwards, passing through the zone where perception of pitch modulates into perception of rhythm, where perception of "tone color" merges into that of "melody," and thus the "color" is dissolved into a succession of individual "pitches."

At the conclusion of this pulse succession, the intervals between the individual pulses correspond to 45.5 cm., 48.5 cm., 52 cm., and 57 cm. of the tape (where 38.1 cm. = 1 sec.). I then added three more pulses with a pitch of 160 cps, between which the intervals were 89 cm. and 140 cm. This continued the gradual retardation and lengthening of the pulses. The third and final pulse was protracted into a continuous sound once again (by means of overmodulating the filter feedback). By means of amplification I made this sound increasingly "overtone-rich" and in five stages filtered continuously from the lowest to the highest portions of the sound. As a result, within 48 secs., its color first gradually brightened, then passed out of the range of audibility, "over the top," as it were.

OPPOSITE AND OVERLEAF:
Stockhausen, *Kontakte*, pp. 19 and 20

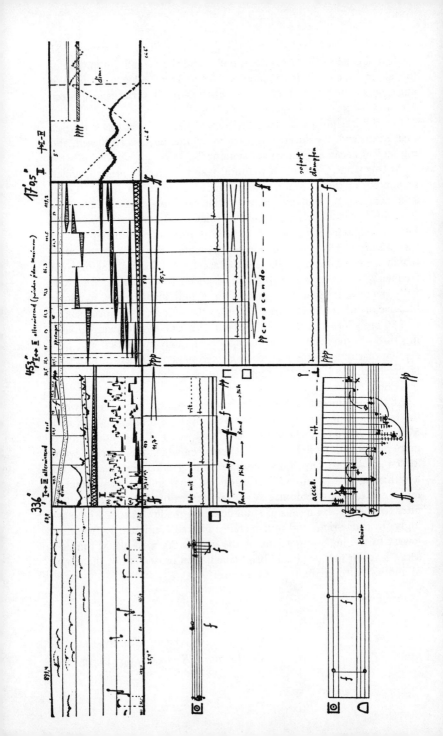

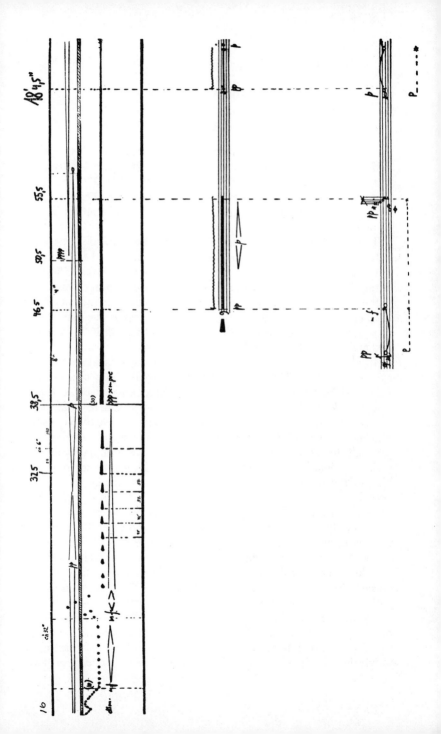

Beginning   200–300 cps
                450–600 cps (after 8″)
                800–1,000 cps (after 17″)
FILTER: 1,500–3,000 cps (after 26″)
                5,000–10,000 cps (after 35″)

The entire process of temporal transformation, as it was applied in *Kontakte*, is schematically represented in the score between the time coordinates 16′56.5″ (highest layer) and 18′26.5″ (pp. 19-20 in the score). Most of the events in *Kontakte*, like the one in the example, were composed by means of many temporal transformations of pulse structures.

I have already affirmed my belief that any drastic separation between acoustics and music is no longer meaningful where composition includes the synthesis of the sound waves themselves. The temporal process by which a sound is transformed into a rhythm can, without doubt, take a musical form. The aesthetic judgment of the listener can determine if the result of this process is successful, if it is significantly congruent with the total work, and if it has been accomplished with originality and imagination.

It is understandable that, in traditional Western music, where the spheres of harmony and melody dominate, only those sound-events were used that have periodic waves and clear, recognizable, constant "pitch." The way in which the laws of harmonic and melodic union of such tones, whose harmonic sound spectra are based on whole-number divisions of the sound waves of the fundamentals, corresponds precisely to the definition of consonant and dissonant intervals and their function, indicates the necessity of excluding noise from this kind of music. Similarly, in the sphere of duration, the *meters*, i.e. periodic time intervals (or measures) were filled in with rhythms—consequently, by whole-number divisions of the meters (tone color is to a fundamental as rhythm is to a meter)—and all of the variations and disruptions of the metrical periodicity were regulated according to the definition of syncopated and regular time intervals and their function. Correspondingly, in the sphere of form, such metrical successions were formed periodically into units of 2, 4, 8, 16 measures with "irregular" (or, better, "syncopated") variants of 3-, 5-, 7-, or 9-measure periods. All of musical time was unified under a common principle, and it was unnecessary to include in this scheme the actual sound wave structure of instrumental tones, since this was guaranteed in advance by the selection and construction of instruments of fixed pitch. If nowadays, on the other hand, it has become necessary to take into account factors such as those discussed here, to bring all the spheres of electronic music under a unified musical time, and to find one general set of laws to govern every sphere of musical time itself, this is simply a result of the condition imposed by electronic music that each sound in a given work must be individually composed.

(Translated by Elaine Barkin)

SOME PROBLEMS IN
RHYTHMIC THEORY AND ANALYSIS

PETER WESTERGAARD

WE KNOW LESS about the rhythm of contemporary music than the numerical precision of many fashionable descriptions would suggest.[1] Such descriptions usually consider the organization of "purely rhythmic" factors (such as duration) without respect to other factors.[2] We are, however, accustomed to hearing music in terms of the complicated interaction of many factors.

This difficulty is of course easily avoided in analyses of those special cases (so striking in Stravinsky) where nonrhythmic factors are used chiefly to differentiate between elements of a purely rhythmic design.[3] Such special cases only seem problematic in that they neither look nor sound like anything in the eighteenth or nineteenth centuries; they are in fact much easier to analyze than music based on more traditional rhythmic procedures. Special cases must be simple to be effective; an evolving tradition usually implies increasing complexity.

Analogous complexities of pitch organization in Bartók or even Schönberg have yielded to extensions of Schenkerian analytic concepts.[4] Yet the underlying structure (if not the detail) of Schönberg's

---

[1] Those in *Die Reihe* are only the most notorious.

[2] Except in so far as all factors are related to a common numerology. A classic example is György Ligeti's analysis of Boulez' *Structure Ia* (*Die Reihe*, 4, Universal Edition, pp. 38-64). It should be pointed out that Ligeti is describing not the piece but the composer's technique. Some of the consequences of this technique (or lack of it) are indicated in Ligeti's later "Wandlungen der musikalischen Form" in *Die Reihe*, 7; see particularly p. 6. This is, however, also a common failing for speculative theory (see the relation between the overtone series and rhythm in Henry Cowell's *New Musical Resources*, Alfred A. Knopf, New York, 1931, but first written in 1919) or the usual descriptions by composers of their own processes.

[3] See the analyses of Stravinsky's "Danse Sacrale" by Friedrich Petzold ("Formbildende Rhythmik," *Melos*, Feb. 1953, pp. 46-47) and Pierre Boulez ("Propositions," *Polyphonie*, 2ᵐᵉ cahier, 1948, pp. 66ff.) as well as of his *Symphony in Three Movements*, rehearsal numbers 7 to 13 by Arnold Elston ("Some Rhythmic Practices in Contemporary Music," *Musical Quarterly*, 42, 1956, p. 324). All three consider rhythm as "additive." (See Curt Sachs, *Rhythm and Tempo*, W. W. Norton & Company, Inc., New York, 1953, and see his connection of [tonal] harmony with "divisive"—as opposed to additive—rhythm, pp. 91 and 268.) Petzold finds neat terraces of metric types, Boulez a "rhythmic pedal" à la Messaien. Elston finds progressive growth of phrase length to a point of greatest tension but finds no "straightforward arithmetic progressions—this would be dreary" (p. 324); however, he does not analyze the specific choice of lengths.

[4] Analyses by Allen Forte (*Contemporary Tone-Structures*, Bureau of Publications, Teachers College, Columbia University, New York, 1955) and Roy Travis ("Toward a New Concept of Tonality?," *Journal of Music Theory*, III, 2, November 1959, pp. 257-285) explicitly use Schenker's procedures, but many others have used those Schenkerian concepts which now seem to have become common currency.

and Mozart's rhythm would seem to be closer than that of their pitch relationships. The point is, though, that no theorist has adequately handled Mozart's rhythm either. The problem of rhythm in contemporary music lies not in the difficulties of extending traditional analytic concepts to handle increasing complexity in new music, but in the inadequacy of traditional analytic concepts to handle any music. Thus, while I agree with Edward Cone that the crucial question for rhythmic analysis in new (or any other) music is "can we locate the structural downbeat?," I am alarmed at the ease with which he surmises that "if we can, then we can proceed with analytic concepts in some way analogous to those of the traditional rhythm and meter, phrase and cadence."[5]

To my knowledge the basic problem of the relationship of rhythm and meter, phrase and cadence to the location of the structural downbeat has not been solved in the literature of rhythmic theory. Those few writers who have considered the problem have characteristically been so concerned with their own particular universal that their solutions are of little general use.[6] A more flexible approach than most will be found in Grosvenor Cooper and Leonard Meyer's recent attempt at a general analytic method for rhythm: *The Rhythmic Structure of Music*.[7] This method uses concepts of accent and group as proposed by Mursell[8] in a hierarchy of "architectonic levels" possibly suggested

[5] "Analysis Today" in the *Musical Quarterly* for April 1960. I suspect that the problem lies in a confusion between that which intuitively seems so clear in "the Golden Age of functional tonality" (see Cone's "Music: A View from Delft," above, pp. 57–71) and the unclear state of our theoretical knowledge of the music of that age. I am deeply indebted to both of Cone's articles for the formulation of this article.

[6] Riemann (*System der Musikalischen Rhythmik und Metrik*, Breitkopf & Haertel, Leipzig, 1903) is certainly the ranking theorist to exhibit this widespread disease.

[7] *The Rhythmic Structure of Music*, University of Chicago Press, Chicago, 1960. An expansion of the method proposed by Meyer in his *Emotion and Meaning in Music*, University of Chicago Press, Chicago, 1956, pp. 102-124.

[8] James L. Mursell, *The Psychology of Music*, W. W. Norton & Company, Inc., New York, 1937, chs. IV, V. Mursell bases his theories on various turn-of-the-century experiments in which subjects tended to perceive a series of stimuli in groups when every second, third, or fourth stimulus was accented (i.e. emphasized either by intensity [volume] or duration); when the accent was produced by intensity, subjects tended to perceive groups with an accent at the beginning of the group; when the accent was produced by duration, they perceived groups with an accent at the end. Attempts were made to determine the degree of duration or intensity required to produce grouping, as well as the extent to which duration creates the illusion of intensity and vice versa. Mursell's groups "which are the basic constituent elements of the whole structure of musical rhythm [are]:

⌣ —	Iamb Type	⌣ ⌣ —	Anapest Type
— ⌣	Trochee Type	⌣ — ⌣	Amphibrach Type
— ⌣ ⌣	Dactyl Type	⌣ ⌣ ⌣	Tremolo Type

|—|—| Single Beat Type"

(Mursell, pp. 176-177)
Cooper and Meyer omit the last two types.

by Schenkerian structural levels although not really analogous to them. The format of their analyses should be clear from the following example:

Ex. 1

The chief attractions of this kind of method lie in:

1. the flexibility of the basic unit. (A group can have a variety of shapes;[9] there is no one "normal type" of which all others must be variants.[10] Nor is group tied to meter;[11] although expected length is one of the factors which help produce a sense of group, exact duration is not *the* distinguishing feature.)[12]

2. the nature of the hierarchy. (Presumably the first accent on level 1 in our example is in some sense more important—is more of a "structural downbeat"—than the second accent, because the group of

---

[9] Only the first five of Mursell's groups are considered as "basic rhythmic groupings" in their initial presentation (p. 6). Nor is it clear why ◡ ◡ ◡ — is not basic but the result of two levels (e.g.) while ◡ ◡ — is as basic as ◡ —. However, in the course of analyses of actual pieces, the vocabulary of groups becomes extended and distinctions between groups become less definite. This is particularly true where a number of groups form an extended upbeat on a higher level. (See their analysis of mm. 33-76 of Act II of *Tristan*.)

[10] See the Procrustean procedures of Riemann, *op.cit.* Riemann's well-known mania for upbeats is foreshadowed in Rudolph Westphal (*Allgemeine Theorie der Musikalischen Rhythmik, Leipzig*, Breitkopf & Haertel, 1880, pp. 116ff.).

[11] The traditional use of poetic feet, e.g. Westphal and Riemann. Even Theodor Wiehmayer (*Musikalische Rhythmik und Metrik*, Heinrichshofen's Verlag, Magdeburg, 1917) who realizes that the boundaries of poetic feet as applied to music need no more coincide with the bar lines than minimal sense units (*Wortfuesse*) coincide with metric units (*Versfuesse*, p. 22) reserves poetic feet for metric units of the same length. For phenomena which Cooper and Meyer present as simply

he must invoke other considerations. (See the section on *motiv*, p. 161.)

[12] See their concept of "morphological length" for higher levels. Contextually as well as stylistically produced expectations are considered, a welcome change from the "normal" four or eight measures.

which the first accent is the nucleus in turn forms the nucleus of the group on level 2.) [13]

Unfortunately, the authors fail:

1. to define adequate analytic criteria for the location of accent. ". . . [S]ince accent appears to be a product of a number of variables whose interaction is not precisely known, it must for our purposes remain a basic, axiomatic concept which is understandable as an experience but undefined in terms of causes."[14]

2. to consider the rhythmic structure of polyphony. (While much tonal music has little polyphonic interest in its surface texture, almost all tonal music of any stature has considerable polyphonic interest in its underlying structure.) [15]

Both failures are customary in the literature of rhythmic theory. The first failure might be remedied by a study of rhythmic detail which, instead of assuming the bar lines of the printed page, examines the interplay of notated compositional elements with the unnotated means the performer uses to project accent placement.[16] If Cooper and Meyer's hypothesis of the similarity of rhythmic action on various levels is as correct as it is attractive, exact information about just what the performer does at lower levels could provide valuable clues to what the composer does on higher levels.

The second failure might be remedied if someone were to act on Allen Forte's suggestion for "constructing a theory of rhythm for tonal music."[17] Forte points to Schenker's statements that there is no rhythm

[13] The authors never actually say as much. But this is clearly the great advantage of their method over those which summarize larger relationships simply by stating the number of measures per unit. (Cf. Wiehmayer's "Zifferschrift," op.cit., p. 228.)

[14] Such modesty is at least preferable to the usual discussions of *Wesen*. In the course of the book analytic choice at lower levels is evidently largely determined by metric position (even though originally meter was defined as being produced by accent), at higher levels intuitively, by the "feel" of the harmony. The inadequacy of the latter is demonstrated by the accent location at higher levels in the example first given (p. 84).

[15] As in most books on rhythm, the examples usually give only the melody. The reader is urged to "consult the original score to discover the ways in which the particular grouping is supported by such factors as harmony, texture, orchestration, and so forth" (p. 37). Two special aspects of polyphony are considered: "metric dissonance," 6/8 against 3/4 in a Dufay example, and completion of rhythmically incomplete fugue subjects by counter-subjects (pp. 162-165). The closest to a general principle for polyphonic rhythm is: ". . . weak beats having different functions [afterbeat in one voice, upbeat in another] may occur simultaneously without creating any ambiguity" (p. 56).

[16] Exact means of measurement of performance factors have long been available. See "Objective Analysis of Musical Performance," *Studies in the Psychology of Music*, IV, The University Press, Iowa City, 1936. Despite the title these studies do not constitute analysis in our sense, but only description. So far as I know no musical theorist of any stature has made use of this potentially valuable material.

[17] The first in his discussion of "five unsolved problems in music theory . . . [with an indication in each case of] . . . how Schenker's ideas could contribute toward a solution" in his article on Schenker in the *Journal of Music Theory* for April 1959.

at the *Ursatz* level, that rhythm first arises at the various middle ground levels from the counterpointing of structural voices against each other in a rhythmic ordering, and that this ordering becomes progressively differentiated as we approach the foreground. He suggests the following points of departure for an extended study: "(1) At what structural level do rhythmic events begin to determine the tonal structure of a given work? (2) What is the nature of the relationship between the constituent rhythmic levels in a given work?"[18]

In view of the almost entirely negative results of the foregoing survey of the state of rhythmic theory, it might be useful to examine a few measures of a specific piece in order to see how much can be done analytically in spite of this lack of a general theoretical basis. I can think of no more lively example of a complex extension of the already complex rhythmic tradition of tonality than the twelve measures that elicited Cone's question about the structural downbeat: the beginning of the third movement of Webern's *Piano Variations*, Op. 27.

Our analysis will attempt to show: I) the differential role of rhythm in creating pitch relationships, and II) some ways in which pitch relationships create a sense of rhythm, particularly large-scale rhythm. During I we must keep in mind Cone's remark, "Much of the vitality of the music of the Classical period derives from the constant interplay of meter and rhythm, the former determined by regular beats and measures and the latter by constantly varying motifs and phrases . . . [as well as the questions] . . . Is meter in Webern to be felt as a constantly present control? Is it a pure convention?"[19] During II we must examine the forces involved in locating the structural downbeat, the first E♭ in m. 12.[20]

I. *Differential Role of Rhythmic Factors*

A. Detail

As in most music, the differential role of rhythmic factors is clearest at the detail level.

---

[18] It should not be assumed that Forte's second question would lead to something resembling Cooper and Meyer's architectonic levels. Their conceptions of rhythm are diametrically opposed. Cooper and Meyer conceive of rhythm as "a summarizing aspect" of music (p. 182). Forte assumes "that rhythm plays a purely differential role in Western music" (*Contemporary Tone-Structures*, p. 9).

[19] Boulez singles out Webern (as opposed to Schönberg and Berg) for the fact that his regular meters represent only a notational convenience (*op.cit.*, p. 67).

[20] Cone states: ". . . I hear the downbeat as the E♭ at the beginning of measure 12; and I consider it no accident that it occurs at the beginning of a measure, preceded by a *ritardando*." ("Analysis Today," p. 45)

1. Phrase[21]

Phrases are demarcated by the traditional means of a) silence and b) dynamics. With one exception (the quarter note at the end of m. 11) there are no silences within phrases. With one exception (end of m. 10, beginning of m. 11) there is always a silence of from one to three quarter rests between consecutive phrases. With one exception (the *diminuendo* in m. 11) the dynamic level is marked as constant within phrases. With one exception (the *f* at mm. 5-6 and the *f* at mm. 7-8) the dynamic level of consecutive phrases is contrasting. The significance of these exceptions will be discussed later.

2. Texture

The two-note melodic units of the textural voices are differentiated by duration rather than by the more traditional register.[22] Thus in the first phrase, long but separated (a) (♩ 𝄾 ♩) is differentiated from short but legato (b) (♫); in the second phrase, long and legato (c) (♫) is differentiated from short and staccato (d) (♩ ♩).

3. Meter

While the 3 of the 3/2 signature is not evident at the detail level (except possibly at mm. 10-12), the 2 (the half note as beat) is evident because of the following consistent usages:

a. The rhythm of individual voices: although there is an odd number of quarter notes (one, three, five or seven) between attacks in each two-note melodic unit, and although the position of the ♩ ♩ is constantly varied, with respect to the ♩ beat, the position of the ♩ 𝄾 ♩ and ♩. ♩ is always such that the first note is off the ♩ beat and the second on. (exception: left hand, m. 10)

b. The rhythm of the combined attacks of all voices: all phrases end on the ♩ beat. The first six phrases begin off the ♩ beat. In the first six phrases quarter-note motion leads to a note on the ♩ beat. (m. 1 ♩. ♩ ♩ | ♩ , mm. 2-3 ♩ | ♩ ♩ ♩ ♩)

B. Higher levels

As in most music the differential role of rhythm at higher levels is less clear. Of greatest importance are the irregularities of detail which force our attention to longer range relationships.

[21] By phrase I refer to the smallest units that could be called phrases (the first four notes, the next five, the next three) because they are the most clearly demarcated. The demarcation of larger units will be discussed later.

[22] Register is thus freed to differentiate structural voices.

1. Meter

There is no measure-to-measure regularity until mm. 10-11. We may assume that the regularity at mm. 10-11 helps us hear the *ritardando* in m. 11 as such. May we also say that, despite the consistency with regard to the ♩ beat, because of the lack of larger metric regularity before m. 10, the listener is hindered from hearing a structural downbeat before m. 10? We must first see if there are any other regularities, hidden by the written meter and implying some other meter.

The first three phrases are isorhythmic with the next three. But note that the period is thirteen ♩s long. Since thirteen is a prime, other meters are as easily destroyed as 3/2. For example the 5/4 cross rhythm mentioned by Cone either a) becomes syncopated against itself in the second set of five 5/4 measures

Ex. 2

or b) must take on an extra quarter rest, making the fifth 5/4 measure a 6/4.

Ex. 3

If we could sense a), the effect might be to keep the second set of three phrases up in the air and thus avoid a structural downbeat until the last phrase. But do we have enough experience with 5/4 to handle such a situation—particularly when it is extended well into the next two phrases?

Ex. 4

Isn't it easier to hear the extra quarter rest of b) as an articulation between the two isorhythmic groups of three phrases each? These questions would be easier to answer if we had a clearer idea of the function of irregularity of the quasi-metrical organization of groups of measures in, say, Mozart.

2. Phrase length

We are on surer ground when we remove the difficult problem of beat placement implicit in meter and consider that of phrase length. What effect do the changes in duration between beginnings of consecutive phrases or between attacks of first and last notes of a phrase have?

Ex. 5

Presumably, the parallelism between the fourth phrase and the first phrase is brought to our attention by the unexpected shortness of the third phrase. The fourth phrase arrives too early. Does that keep the end of the third phrase from being too final? (from becoming the structural downbeat?)[23] At least the last attack of the third phrase is, like the last attacks of the surrounding phrases, equidistant from the surrounding phrase beginnings.

Potential finality is a greater danger at the end of the sixth phrase because of the rhyming effect of the isorhythm. But the even earlier entrance of the seventh phrase destroys, for the first time, the equidistant position of the final attack of a phrase. It is at this point that regularity with respect to the 3/2 meter finally takes over. The 3/2 meter was not, however, entirely inoperative during the first six phrases. Working against the AABAAB phrase length plan is an ABABAB for the metric position of the final note of a phrase. Each even-numbered phrase ends on the second or third beat of the measure, but each odd-numbered phrase ends on the downbeat. Furthermore these downbeats are three measures apart (mm. 2, 5, and 8). Presumably we should expect the seventh phrase to end on the first beat of m. 11. But the seventh phrase, despite its six notes, is too compact. The eighth phrase begins on the downbeat of m. 11. Presumably the expected downbeat is delayed until m. 12. The sense of delay is intensified by the *ritardando* and the mid-phrase rest. The downbeat note itself is emphasized not by being louder or longer, but by being softer (because of the exceptional > in m. 11) and shorter than expected (a staccato quarter not a whole note).

[23] The fourth phrase is not only early but loud. The fourth phrase is f while the first phrase was p. The other isorhythmic phrases are the same dynamic level, the second and fifth f, the third and sixth p. (*Cf.* the *tutti* entrances on the eighth or sixteenth measure of so many classical Allegros.) We are here of course prepared for the f by the previous dynamic alternation. It is only in retrospect that the fourth phrase is out of line.

II. *Pitch relationships as determining rhythm*

A. Detail

1. Texture

Only one interval class[24]—the minor second—is used for all two-note melodic units. Such consistency helps make the listener expect the completion of those two-note melodic units not completed within a phrase.

2. Phrase

When a phrase consists solely of such two-note melodic units (the first, fourth, seventh, and eighth phrases) the phrase is in some sense complete. However, when a phrase has an extra note which does not participate in such a two-note unit within the phrase (the E in m. 3, the D in m. 7), the phrase is in some sense incomplete. In both cases completion of the two-note melodic unit occurs in the next phrase (the F in m. 4, the C♯ in mm. 8-9) seven quarter-notes later.

3. Meter

Is there any consistency in intervallic usage with respect to metric position?[25] Because the attacks of all two-note melodic units are always an odd number of quarter notes apart there are only two possible positions of the melodic unit with respect to the ♩ beat. The consistency of position is with regard to rhythmic type, not interval. As stated before, the second note of the ♩♪♩ and ♩. ♩ figures always falls on the ♩ beat (exception: the nonlegato ♩. ♩ at m. 10). Does the habit of hearing prolonged melodic minor seconds as leading tones (upbeat) to stable tones (downbeat) help project the metric position of these figures? Or have the accented chromatic neighbors of *Tristan* long since changed all that?

Less problematic is the role of the unison. Presumably, given no other differentiating information, we would tend to hear the repeti-

[24] The interval class of the minor second includes minor ninths and major sevenths and any octave compound of these intervals.

[25] David Lewin in the *Journal of Music Theory* ("A Metrical Problem in Webern's Op. 27," Spring 1962, pp. 125-133) ingeniously establishes a correlation between interval classes (0, ±3, and 6 half steps) with even numbers of quarter-note distance between notes for the first six measures of the second movement of the Variations. While this might conceivably help establish some kind of quarter-note meter (already more simply established by the tempo proportion between the first movement's 3/16 at a dotted eighth = 40 and the second's 2/4 at a quarter = 160), it does not establish where the quarter-note beat falls. The more obvious forces at work to establish the half note as a unit of measurement in this movement have already been described. The above paragraph considers only those intervallic relationships which might affect the choice of which quarters fall on the half-note beat.

tions as strong-weak rather than weak-strong. There are no immediate repetitions in this section, but where a pitch is repeated in the immediate vicinity, the second note falls off the ♩ beat (the G♯'s in mm. 5-6, the A's in m. 9, the E♭'s in m. 12). Pitch repetitions such that the second note falls on the ♩ beat are more distant. (The G's in mm. 3 and 6 and the F's in mm. 7 and 10 are the closest.)

B. Larger considerations

1. Structural voices

The most strongly defined structural voice seems to be

Ex. 6

a. these widely separated notes form a voice in that

Ex. 7

i. they participate in a common rhythmic type.

ii. they are in the same register. Other notes in this register—the C♯ in mm. 8-9 and the F♯ in m. 10 do not participate in the 𝅝 𝄽 𝅝 rhythm and are presumably subordinated by their symmetrical relation to those notes that do.

Ex. 8

b. this voice is strongest because

i. it moves in half steps. Other voices equally well defined by register and rhythmic type do not move in half steps. Their sense of motion in a totally chromatic context is therefore less striking.

Ex. 9

ii. other possible voices that do move in half steps are less consistently defined by register.

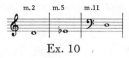

Ex. 10

2. Rhythmic effect of the structural voices

For the listener the advantages of the neighbor note motion Eb-E-Eb are

a. it is easy to hear and requires no further harmonic explanation (i.e. there is no need to consider a possible "tonic sonority" through which and with reference to which voices move. Such considerations occur only later in the movement.)

b. it is rhythmically well defined. If nothing in the rhythmic detail and nothing in the subsequent motion of the structural voice contradicts the impression it will be heard as stable-unstable-stable and hence probably strong-weak-strong. In fact, as has been pointed out, the rhythmic detail does a great deal to confirm that impression. In the subsequent motion of structural voices, while the Eb stays put (end of m. 12), the static F above the treble staff of the first eleven measures finally moves down a semitone to E (m. 12) and the voices which had moved solely in whole tones shift a half step.[26]

Ex. 11

What does the foregoing analysis not tell us? What important questions does it avoid? Such an analysis may show something of "the constant interplay of meter and rhythm" and indicate some ways in which the latter is determined if not "by regular beats and measures" in the traditional sense, in any case by a high degree of regularity. But does it show, for example, that meter is "felt as a constantly present control"? Webern's economy of materials makes it easy for the analyst to codify regularity. But is this regularity sufficient to induce in the listener the kind of expectation that is so vital to phenomena like meter or structural downbeats? Is there enough regularity for the irregularities to be recognized as such, and so to lead the listener to a larger context? Is the larger context regular enough to be comprehensible?

[26] The transition from consecutive quarters to simultaneous quarters is prepared by the simultaneous D-C♯ in m. 11, the first two-note attack in the movement. The

My answer to all these questions is yes, but I have insufficient theoretical grounds for my answer. On the other hand I have insufficient theoretical grounds for answering yes to the same questions asked about a few measures of Mozart. Admittedly, in Cone's words, "Webern's Piano Variations . . . present the metric problem in an acute form." But does not the following example also?[27]

Ex. 12: Piano Quartet, K.478

___

transition from legato to the prevalent staccato of the new section is announced by the structural downbeat e♭.

[27] Both Schönberg and Hans Keller have speculated on this passage. Schönberg removes the relation between irregular phrase and regular meter by making the meter irregular:

or:

("Brahms the Progressive," reprinted in *Style and Idea*, Philosophical Library, New York, 1950, p. 95). Keller thinks the irregularities result from a compression of the regular

"Principles of Composition" (II), *The Score*, No. 27, July 1960, p. 11.

TOWARD A TWELVE-TONE POLYPHONY*

PETER WESTERGAARD

I T S E E M S to me that there is a serious problem inherent in using
an essentially one-dimensional structural device—a row—to control
intervals in a two-or-more-dimensional situation—polyphony. But
before discussing this problem, I must explain what I mean by polyphony and how I think its intervals have been controlled in earlier
music.

By polyphony I mean not so much a kind of texture as a way of
conceiving of music. To comprehend other people's music—or, for
that matter, to make my own music as comprehensible to other people
as I can—I find that I must be able to form a clear idea of its pitch
structure as a whole. When I try to visualize such an idea, I find it
almost always requires at least two dimensions—a network of intervals in which each pitch in the piece is connected to at least one other
pitch and usually to more than one, and in which the strength of the
connections varies. In deciding which pitches are connected and in
determining the strength of the connection I am guided by two kinds
of considerations:

1. How is the connection projected? Are the two pitches simultaneous? Are they consecutive? Do they come from the same sound
source? Do they have the same timbre, the same register, or the same
dynamic levels? If they are neither simultaneous nor consecutive,
what factors do they have in common that the intervening pitches do
not have, and will those factors be strong enough to project the
connection?

2. Is the interval formed by the connection consistent with intervallic usage elsewhere in the piece (and, possibly, in related pieces)?
If not, is there some other connection which would form an interval
which would be consistent?

For some kinds of music the conventions of musical notation accurately reflect many of these connections. For most Renaissance vocal
music, for example, the appearance of a score is already close to what
I mean by its polyphonic structure. This occurs for two reasons:

---

* Adapted from a talk first given in May 1965 at the Institut für Neue Musik,
Freiburg in Breisgau, Germany.

1. There is a high degree of correlation among the various ways in which connections of the same kind are projected. I know ahead of time that consecutive pitches on the same staff will come from the same sound source, have the same timbre and probably the same register, while pitches written on different staves will come from different sound sources, have different timbres, and will probably be in different registers. In short, I can assume the concept of line as it is generally understood. Furthermore, I have come to expect that pitches already marked for prominence by coming just after or just before a rest, by being higher than the pitches just before or just after, or by having a stronger attack because of the text accent, will also usually be longer than the surrounding pitches. This means that the choice of which pitch is the locally prominent one—and consequently the choice of strong connections between pitches that are neither simultaneous nor consecutive—is relatively straightforward.

2. There is a high degree of consistency in the intervallic usage common to all such pieces. I can assume that I will be able to explain all the consecutive and simultaneous connections in terms of a relatively small vocabulary of two dimensional intervallic patterns. These patterns include not only those involving dissonant simultaneities— passing tones, lower neighbors, and suspensions—but also many more involving only consonant simultaneities—parallel thirds or sixths, 5-6-5's, etc. That is, the patterns would consist of various "ways of getting from one place to another," where place means consonant simultaneity, getting means progress by seconds in at least one line, and way includes the idea of all possible rhythmic dispositions. Furthermore, I would expect connections formed between prominent pitches to favor some intervals at the expense of others. I would not expect tritones between nearby prominent pitches in the same line, and I would expect perfect consonances between opening notes of the various lines participating in an imitation.

What would happen were I to try the same assumptions on a piece written in the early seventeenth century is well known (Ex. 1). Just to begin with, how would I explain that seventh between F and G in the second measure? Obviously, I must either 1) make connections

Ex. 1. Monteverdi: *Lamento d'Arianna*

other than those apparent from the way the score looks on the page, or 2) expand the standard vocabulary of intervallic structures.

Most people have preferred the second approach. The two most popular kinds of explanations boil down to either a) "that seventh is part of a subdominant seventh," implying that the dissonant interval need only be considered part of a permutation of a chord built by piling thirds one on top of another, in order to relate the chord—and with it the dissonant interval—to a vocabulary of chords common to a large amount of music. Or, b) "that seventh is motivic; there it is again in measure 5," implying that anything unusual that happens more than once in a piece belongs to that piece and is self-explanatory. The underlying defect of both these kinds of explanations seems to me the fact that they deal with only one dimension at a time. The great advantage of those ways of getting from one place to another is that they deal with two dimensions at once, which is why I prefer the first approach. I find I can best understand the passage as:

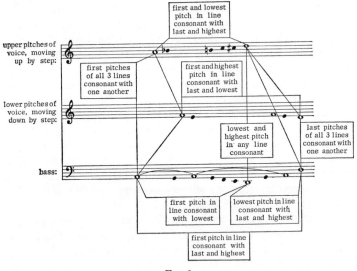

Ex. 2

By thinking of F as the opening pitch of a line, I can relate it to the opening pitches of the other lines. Since the F is consonant with them both, I can understand the F as the stable pitch and the G in the bass as a lower neighbor to the A's. That is, it is as if the F had begun back with the other notes, before the G, so that the three lines could be thought of as involved in a chain of suspensions where the top line beginning its upward motion first moves to B♭ forcing the bass down to G, which in turn forces the middle line to begin its downward motion by moving to E. (This last statement need not be quite so hypothetical if the continuo player provides an actual F in the first measure.)

Obviously such an approach has its dangers. Each step must be carefully questioned. Am I arbitrarily redistributing the lines to fit an established pattern or are there factors other than the internal consistency of the pattern which project this distribution? Is there some other established pattern which would fit as well but require less redistribution?

Nevertheless, such an approach does provide a viable way of comprehending a wide range of music—not just Monteverdi's, but Bach's or Beethoven's, Wagner's or Schoenberg's—in *polyphonic* terms: that is, in terms of both the progress of each individual line and the interaction of the several lines. I can continue to use essentially the same kinds of patterns, although I must be ready, especially for more recent music, to allow for changes in the intervals performing characteristic functions in these patterns. In some of Wagner's music and in most of Schoenberg's, I must assume that the semitone constitutes a more basic kind of step than the whole tone. In some of Schoenberg's music I must even recognize the possibility that two pitches, both of which are treated as stable, may form an interval previously considered dissonant.

For example, in order to understand the fourth piece of Schoenberg's Six Little Pieces, Op. 19, I find I must allow that both B and A are stable pitches. I can then hear a principal line moving from A (with B in the accompaniment) to B (with A in the bass). The motion of this line is supported and clarified by the traditional patterns of parallel thirds and sixths, both in detail (in mm. 1-2, the explicit D♭-C clarifies the implicit B♭-A) and in the large (the entire motion of the secondary line supports that of the principal line).

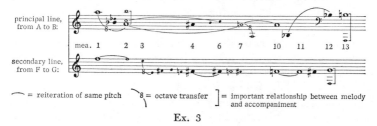

Ex. 3

Many people would argue that this is the hard way of hearing such a piece. They would point to the many motivic correspondences, particularly those between horizontal and vertical intervallic structures.

(For example, the one between the horizontal F-A-F-B♭-D♮ in m. 1 and the vertical

$$
\begin{array}{c}
D \\
B \\
G \\
E♭
\end{array}
$$

in m. 4 or the one between the horizontal G-F-D-C in m. 3 and the nearly vertical

$$
\begin{array}{c}
C \\
\quad G \\
\quad F \\
D
\end{array}
$$

in m. 4.) Obviously such correspondences are essential to an understanding of this piece, particularly of its intervallic detail. Nevertheless while such correspondences do control intervals in more than one dimension, *they control only one dimension at a time*. It seems to me that this is the same kind of situation as that in a work like *Tristan und Isolde*: Tristan may sing "O sink hernieder, Nacht der Liebe," using the pitch-classes from the famous chord in the Prelude, but the chord when it first happens must still be understood as a collision of two stable tones with two unstable tones on their way to slightly more stable tones, and the line for "O sink hernieder" must still be understood in relation to the other lines at that moment.

It is, of course, the advantage of these one-dimensional motivic patterns that they can be turned upside down or backwards, or even sideways, without losing their identity. A suspension cannot be turned upside down or backwards and remain a suspension, and while a passing-tone complex can be turned upside down or backwards, it makes absolutely no sense on its side. On the other hand, passing tones and suspensions and all the other ways of getting from one place to another *do* control both dimensions of the two-dimensional network at once; that, unfortunately, the usual motivic configurations do not.

And that brings us back to the original problem: the use of row techniques to control the intervals in polyphony. For the twelve-tone technique, however systematic it may since have become, was at its inception essentially only a powerful generalization of previous motivic practice. As such it inherited the central problem inherent in that practice: lack of two-dimensionality. While knowledge of the systematic potentials of the twelve-tone technique has increased greatly in the past two decades, so far as I know, this central problem has remained unsolved.

Nor can I offer a general solution. What follows is simply a description of what I think the problem consists of, expressed in the simplest terms I can manage, followed by a few sample solutions with some discussion of their general availability for other intervallic situations.

Consider the two traditional ways of applying the one-dimensional row to a two-dimensional network: 1) One row form controls the network as a whole; the row is *partitioned* into separate lines. For example:

1st line:	1		5	6		8	9		12
2nd line:		2	3	4		7		10	11

2) Each line has its own row form; more than one row is *combined* to form the total network. For example:

1st line:	1		2	3		4	5	6, etc.
2nd line:	1	2	3		4		5	6, etc.

Clearly, in both cases only *some* of the intervals can be controlled by the properties of row order. In the first case, all intervals between simultaneously sounding pitches can either be controlled by row order (e.g. 1/2 or 6/7) or subordinated to a nearby interval (e.g. 1/3 which is subordinated to 1/2 because 1 and 2 begin together and 3 begins after 2, or 9/7 which is subordinated to 8/7 because 8/7 intervenes between the beginning of 9 and the beginning of 7). However, not all of the intervals between consecutive pitches in the same line can be controlled by row order. In the second case, on the other hand, the intervals between consecutive pitches in the same line will all be controlled by row order, while the intervals between simultaneously sounding pitches will not. In each case, methods other than those which follow automatically from the use of classical row technique must be found to control these intervals. However, in both cases, methods are in fact available which share at least some of the properties of intervallic control implicit in classical row technique.

I. PARTITIONING

A row may be partitioned symmetrically so that the various partitions will have the same kind of relation to one another as the various transformations of a row, and will thus afford an analogous kind of intervallic control. This is possible for six partitions of two pitches each, four partitions of three, three partitions of four, or two partitions of six. However, the more pitches per partition, the harder it is to get the right order for each partition.

For six partitions of two pitches each, there is really no problem. The twelve pitch-classes can be divided into six dyads of any interval class except ±4 semitones. The order imposed by the given row creates no new problems in that there are only two possible orders in which the pitches forming the dyad might come, so that the interval itself will not be affected, but only its direction (Ex. 4).

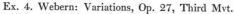

Ex. 4. Webern: Variations, Op. 27, Third Mvt.

Ex. 5. Webern: Symphony, Op. 21, Second Mvt.

In Ex. 4 the dyads are projected by articulation and duration. The same technique can also be used to control the polyphonic substructure of a melody or other textural element (Ex. 5). Here the melody is distinguished from the accompaniment by being concentrated in a single instrument; the dyads in the melody are projected by register, the dyads in the accompaniment by timbre.

The advantage of such a technique is that it will work for any row and for any interval except ±4. The disadvantage is that the "lines" it produces are only two notes long. However, as soon as the number of pitches is increased to three, properties of order begin to intrude. The twelve pitch-classes can be divided into four symmetrical or equivalent trichords of any intervallic content except that of the diminished triad. The only trouble is that for each such trichord there will be six possible orders in which the pitches might occur, and the intervals between consecutive pitches will, of course, be determined by the order. For trichords with an asymmetrical intervallic content this means three different patterns and their retrogrades; for trichords with a symmetrical intervallic content this means two different patterns, one with all four transformations, the other with only two, since $O=RI$ and $I=R$ (Ex. 6).

Ex. 6

This means that the order of the given row must necessarily affect the intervals of the partitions. There is no reason to expect the pitches to appear in the right order. Furthermore, the chances of finding the right order become, if anything, smaller if we try, as in Exx. 4 and 5, to use intervals already emphasized in the row. Nevertheless, a systematic search will usually reveal at least one such partitioning of a given row, and it is even possible to construct rows made up of the four transformations of a three-note pattern which can be partitioned into the four transformations of that pattern (Ex. 7).

For partitions of four or six pitches each, the difficulties increase. In the first place, while almost all intervals or combinations of intervals are available for symmetrical or equivalent dyads or trichords, only relatively few of the many possible combinations of intervals will divide the twelve pitch-classes into symmetrical or equivalent tetrachords or hexachords. In the second place, the number of possible

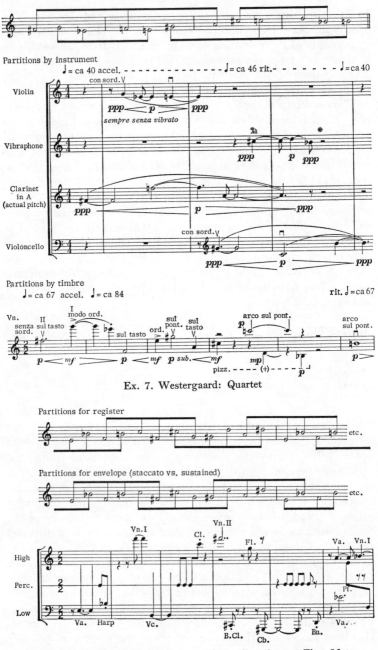

Ex. 7. Westergaard: Quartet

Ex. 8. Westergaard: Five pieces for small orchestra, First Mvt.

orders in which the pitches of a tetrachord or a hexachord can occur (24 and 720 respectively) increases greatly and with it the chance of conflict with the order imposed by a given row. For example, while it is still possible to construct a row which can be partitioned into three transformations of four consecutive pitches of the row itself, it is generally not possible to arrive at the niceties of variety and balance obtainable for four partitions of three pitches each (Ex. 8). Rows which can be partitioned into two transformations of six consecutive pitches from the row itself can be constructed, but I know of no examples of their use. However, it is possible to get the same kinds of results in terms of intervallic control by maintaining content symmetry and allowing changes in order, particularly where the new intervals formed by changes in order appear elsewhere in the row anyway, or are de-emphasized by textural factors (Ex. 9).

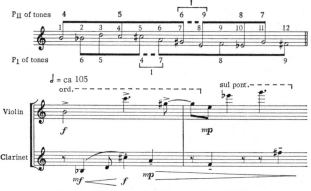

Ex. 9. Westergaard: Quartet, Second Mvt.

The foregoing examples have shown cases of symmetrical partitioning in which the orders of the pitches correspond exactly. This method of intervallic control interests me most because it is closest to the row method itself. But there are other possibilities (see Ex. 10). Here the partitions are asymmetrical; nevertheless the order is such that only two intervals are stressed, ± 4 and ± 1, the intervals between the three pitches that generate the row. The accompaniment is restricted to tones

$$3 \; 6 \; 8 \; 11$$
$$2 \; 5 \; 9 \; 12$$

Thus the simultaneities will automatically be restricted to ± 4 and ± 1, but note that the consecutive relationships 3-5, 3-6, 8-12, and 9-12 are all ± 4, while 6-8 and 5-9 are ± 1. The melody uses only tones 1-4-7-10. Tones 1-4-7 form the inversion of tones 1-2-3, while

Ex. 10. Webern: Concerto, Op. 24, Second Mvt.

tones 4-7-10 form the retrograde. Furthermore, tones 7 and 10 of one row and tone 1 of the next, or 10 of one row and 1 and 4 of the next can also be made to form transformations by choosing the right transposition and transformation for the next row form. Thus melodic continuity can be achieved by the typical Webern means of overlapping patterns.

A profoundly different approach to the problem is seen in Ex. 11:

Ex. 11. Schoenberg: Fourth Quartet, First Mvt.

Here the partitions distributed between the two violins are symmetrical with respect to content, but the correspondence between their respective orders is only partial. The three note groups articulated by the rhythm are nearly, but not quite, inversions of one another: tones 3-4-5 would be the inversion of 8-12-7, not 7-8-12, and 9-10-11 would be the inversion of 2-1-6. However, the correspondence is easy enough to make, since exactly the same three-note groups reappear in the proper order in the very next measure when the I form is partitioned in the same way. Nor are any three-note intervallic successions foreign to the row emphasized; 1-2-6 is a retrograde of 5-6-7, 7-8-12 is a retrograde inversion of 1-2-3, and P_0 :12-I $_5$:1-2 is a retrograde inversion of 6-7-8. But more important to the over-all melodic continuity of the passage is the fact that each of the violins completes a succession of all twelve pitch-classes. Where the partitioning remains the same, this is possible only if the partitions are symmetrical with respect to content. Thus, it would not be possible for the lower two lines in this example, would be possible for a continuation of Exx. 4 and 5 (although, in fact, the property is not used), or for Exx. 7, 8, and 9, and would not be possible for Ex. 10.

The method of symmetrical partitioning offers something near to a general solution of the problem of twelve-tone polyphony. The partitioned row can, like any other row, be transposed, inverted, and retrograded without losing its properties of intervallic control. Its partitions can be projected by a variety of means: by timbre, register, dynamics, sound source, or any combination of these. Nevertheless, most composers would, I think, be reluctant to use the same partitioning throughout an entire piece or large section of a piece, if only because of a danger of monotony. While the length of time between the beginnings of any two consecutive pitches in the row can of course be varied, the disposition of the several lines in the total network—that is, the order in which the lines move to a new pitch—cannot. For a varied disposition of lines we must look to methods of combining row forms.

II. COMBINING

Consider the problem of combining a number of row forms so that the pitches of the several forms can be ordered (preferably in several ways) to yield intervallic successions that are related to the row itself. In general, the more row forms that are combined, the easier. For example, it is possible to arrange the pitch-classes of all twelve transpositions of a single transformation of any row in a 12 × 12 array such that each column has all twelve pitch-classes (Ex. 12a).

D	C♯	A	B♭	F	E♭	E	C	A♭	G	F♯	B
D♭	C	A♭	A	E	D	E♭	B	G	F♯	F	B♭
C	B	G	A♭	E♭	C♯	D	B♭	F♯	F	E	A
B	B♭	F♯	G	D	C	C♯	A	F	E	E♭	A♭
B♭	A	F	F♯	C♯	B	C	A♭	E	E♭	D	G
A	A♭	E	F	C	B♭	B	G	E♭	D	C♯	F♯
A♭	G	E♭	E	B	A	B♭	F♯	D	C♯	C	F
G	F♯	D	E♭	B♭	A♭	A	F	C♯	C	B	E
F♯	F	D♭	D	A	G	A♭	E	C	B	B♭	E♭
F	E	C	D♭	A♭	F♯	G	E♭	B	B♭	A	D
E	E♭	B	C	G	F	F♯	D	B♭	A	A♭	D♭
E♭	D	B♭	B	F♯	E	F	C♯	A	A♭	G	C

Ex. 12a

Consequently, each column may be ordered in any of the 48 available forms (as in Example 12b, for instance).

The order in which the several lines enter will vary according to the row form used to order that unit. Nor is it necessary for each line to wait until the next twelve-tone unit for its next note. The row beginning on F is going to go to E anyway. It can always use the E from the row that begins on E, giving back its own E in the next unit, since its E comes before the D♯ of the other row. Example 12c shows a whole chain of such borrowings resulting in a high concentration of notes in the row beginning with C. (See p. 104.)

Such arrays can be transformed or transposed like rows. They need not use only one transformation. This particular row can be combined in six P forms and six I forms as follows (Ex. 12d):

P ⎧ D C♯ A   B♭ F   E♭ etc.
  ⎪ C   B   G   etc.
  ⎨ B♭ A   F   etc.
  ⎪ A♭ G   E♭ etc.
  ⎪ F♯ F   C♯ etc.
  ⎩ E   D♯ B   etc.

I ⎧ G   A♭ C   B   E   F♯ etc.
  ⎪ F   F♯ A♯ etc.
  ⎨ D♯ E   G♯ etc.
  ⎪ C♯ D   F♯ etc.
  ⎪ B   C   E   etc.
  ⎩ A   B♭ D   etc.

Ex. 12d

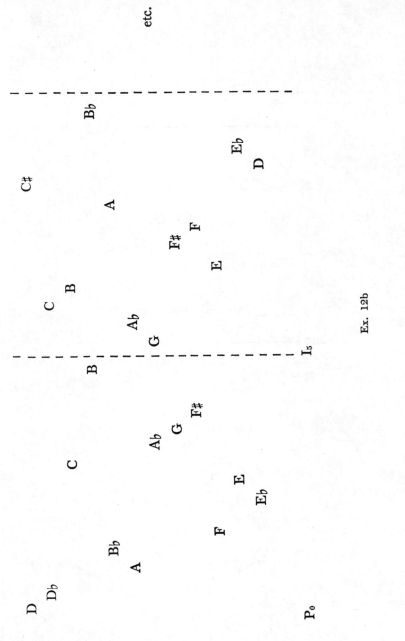

Ex. 12b

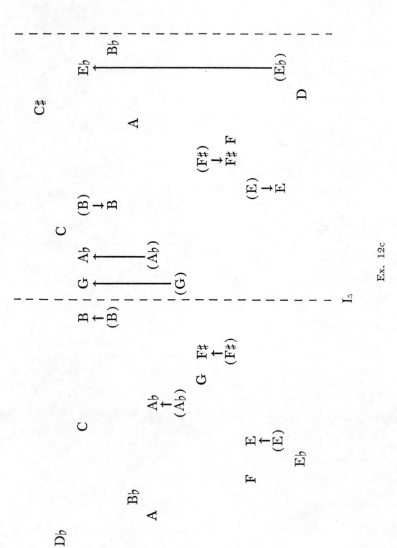

Ex. 12c

	D	C♯	A	B♭	F	F♯	E	C	A♭	G	E♭	B
P	B♭	A	F	F♯	C♯	D	etc.					
	F♯	F	D♭	D	A	B♭	etc.					
	C♯	D	F♯	F	B♭	A	etc.					
I	A	B♭	D	C♯	F♯	F	etc.					
	F	F♯	A♯	A	D	C♯	etc.					
	B	E♭	G	A♭	C	E	etc.					
R	G	B	E♭	E	A♭	C	etc.					
	E♭	G	B	C	E	A♭	etc.					
	C	E	A♭	G	E♭	B	etc.					
RI	A♭	C	E	E♭	B	G	etc.					
	E	A♭	C	B	G	E♭	etc.					

Ex. 12e

And by altering this row only slightly (exchanging the sixth and eleventh tones) we can build a 12 × 12 array with three transpositions of each transformation (Ex. 12e). The advantage of such 12 × 12 arrays is that they combine a total intervallic control in two dimensions with a wide freedom of choice of specific orders. The disadvantage is that they necessarily produce a dense and complex kind of polyphony: it is very difficult for a listener to keep track of twelve lines at once. But the same procedures can also be used in smaller arrays, if the composer is willing to forego the constant circulation of all twelve pitch-classes for a while (Ex. 13). The same 4 × 4 array is being used in all three variations. What is being varied is the transformation of the array, the rate at which its pitches occur, and the textural means by which it is being projected.

If the composer is not willing to forego the constant circulation of all twelve pitch-classes, but still wants less than twelve lines in his polyphony, his opportunities are more limited, but at least they do exist. For example there is a family of rows that can be combined in 6 × 12 arrays. Their structural advantages come from the fact that the four augmented triads can be combined into two sets of two symmetrical and equivalent hexachords (Ex. 14a).

Ex. 14a

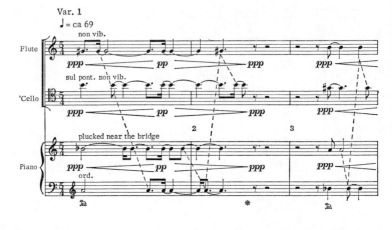

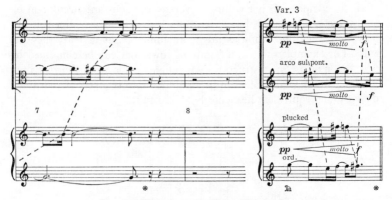

Ex. 13. Westergaard: Trio, Third Mvt.

(Ex. 13 cont'd)

This means that as long as every other interval, beginning with the first, is an odd number of semitones, any row using this hexachordal structure can be reproduced in the columns in a number of possible transformations (Ex. 14b).

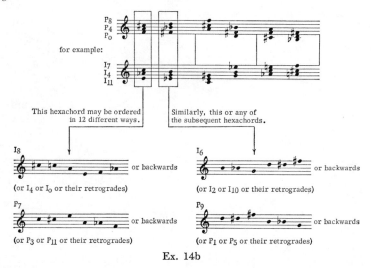

Ex. 14b

Combining four row forms at once is more problematic and necessarily produces a more limited number of possible orders. For example, to make a 4×3 array with four transformations of the same three-note group used in Ex. 14, it is impossible to keep the content of the columns constant, much less have the content agree with that of the row (Ex. 15a).

Ex. 15a

Nevertheless, there are plenty of these three-note successions available; they are just not exclusively in the columns. The problem is to find them and arrive at some satisfactory way of keeping track of all of them in one diagram. A sure way of finding them is simply to try each transposition of the three-note groups on the original array and see if the properties of order conflict (Ex. 15b).

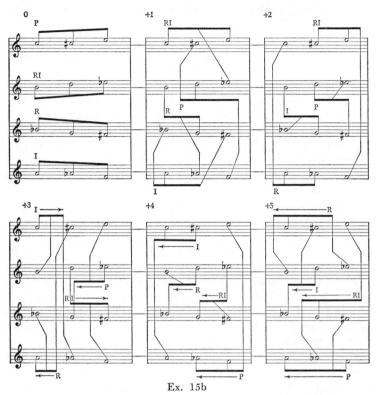

Ex. 15b

The results at +2 and +4 allow six different total orders each, which are summed up as follows (Ex. 15c):

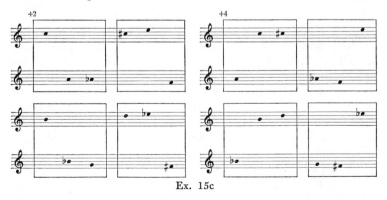

Ex. 15c

Here the order of pitches within each box, and the order of boxes following one another on the same plane are fixed, but otherwise any order will work.

While it is possible to combine as few as three or even two row forms so that the pitches of the several forms can be ordered to yield intervallic successions like that of the row itself, there is usually at most only one such order available. Consequently, the entire advantage of the combining method—its freedom—is lost. However, the combination of two row forms at a time is in fact the combination most frequently used. What composers actually do, of course, is to control intervals between row forms by one or more of a number of essentially different means. These means for the most part represent ad hoc solutions to the problem of intervallic control in polyphony, although there are at least two general principles that are widely used: Schoenberg's combinatoriality and Webern's dyad invariance for I-related row forms.

I will not discuss combinatoriality here, but I would like to point out that, while it is a general solution for pitch-content control for twelve-tone polyphony, it is not a general solution for intervallic control, since the pitches are ordered only by their respective rows. The actual intervals that occur between rows depend on the rhythm of the respective rows—in short on an ad hoc solution. Nor can the principle of dyad invariance be considered a general solution since the rhythmic conditions for its use are so limited. The intervals between like-numbered tones in the two I-related forms (the dyads in question) will be projected rhythmically only if the distance between the beginnings of like-numbered tones is shorter than the distance between the beginnings of consecutive tones in each separate form. This would be true, for example, if the two rows were presented homorhythmically, or where, as is so often the case in Webern, the two forms form a canon in which the lag between the entrance of the two "voices" is shorter than the shortest distance between the beginnings of consecutive notes in a "voice" (Ex. 16). In the lower canon, where the entrance lag is an eighth-note and the voices proceed in half-notes and quarter-notes, the dyads E/F, E♭/F♯, D/G, C♯/G♯, C/A, and B/B♭ are clearly projected. In the upper canon, where the entrance lag is also an eighth-note, but the voices proceed in eighth-notes as well as longer values, the dyads F/F, E/F♯, E♭/G, D/G♯, C♯/A, C/B♭, and B/B are not projected. In this particular case even those dyads which might have been rhythmically projected are completely overshadowed by the perfect fifths and fourths projected by timbre. Here Webern has applied the method of partitioning to a pair of row forms instead of to a single one. (As before, there are distinct advantages to working with partitions of only two

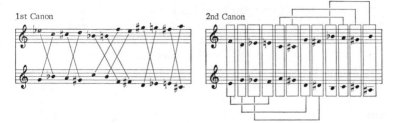

Ex. 16. Webern: Symphony, Op. 21, Second Mvt.

notes each; any interval will work for any pair of rows.) The effect is the same: the selection of certain intervallic connections at the expense of others—indeed, in this case even at the expense of those intervals of the row itself which are not projected by any factor other than the symmetrical disposition of the canon.

In Ex. 16 all the pitches were used to make important connections between row forms. Usually only certain pitches are, as in Ex. 11. There, combinatoriality controls the pitch content so that each half of each measure has all twelve pitch-classes with no repetitions. The two-against-three rhythm stresses the intervals between notes falling on the quarter-note beat. These are in fact all pairs of like-numbered tones. But not all the available dyads are stressed, only those formed by tones 1, 4, 7, and 10. The result is that the relationship D-G is strongly emphasized because it occurs on four out of eight occasions.

This kind of treatment is an elegant example of an ad hoc solution. These two measures cannot serve as a model for what happens else-where in this piece, or even in this section of this movement. While most of the intervals between lines that are emphasized elsewhere are made available by some transposition of this combinatorial scheme, exactly which intervals are projected in any particular passage are the result of the particular rhythm of that passage.

I have been talking about partitioning a single row or combining a number of rows as if these were separate techniques. And so they are, if you start with a given row. But if you start by trying to construct a row whose partitions will have a given intervallic succession or whose combinations will permit a given ordering of the common elements, it soon becomes apparent that the two kinds of two-dimensional schemes are very much the same. In fact, any one of the partitions shown above could be expressed as one possible ordering of a combination of rows or motives and any of the combinations as a set of possible partitions. In both cases, the dilemma remains that the more lines in the network, the easier it is to get it to work both ways. Networks with only two lines are the least available, yet the way to a general theory for twelve-tone polyphony would, I assume, be through an understanding of just such a limited situation.

COMPOSITION WITH ARRAYS*

GODFREY WINHAM

■——————————— ▪▪▪▪▪▪▪ ■———————————

INTRODUCTION

A MUSICAL system, as opposed to a method of composition, consists of a well-defined set of operations upon musical configurations. The latter, however, are not necessarily fully specified musical passages, but may be specified only as to certain features. For example, the tonal system — according, at least, to one plausible construction of it — consists of operations upon configurations specified as to pitch and rhythm, but not as to timbre or dynamics. Moreover, according to H. Schenker, the initially given configurations are not even specified rhythmically (except with regard to order), so that presumably certain operations must, according to this view, consist of specification of rhythmic features; thus the configurations to which the system's operations are applied need not all be of the same degree of concreteness.

Nor is it necessary that the configurations which are resultants of a given system of operations be less than all of the possible configurations of a given degree of concreteness, or even less than all possible configurations specified to any degree. Thus for example, it seems to me that the distinction between tonal and atonal music is best construed not as a difference of whether or not such music is a resultant of some finite succession of operations of the tonal system (given, initially, one tone or chord, etc.), but rather as a difference of the kind of pattern made by the succession of operations (including, for example, such considerations as the number of necessary operations relative to the length of the piece, etc.). In short, the more significant distinctions between systems have little or nothing to do with the totality of their ranges.

From the composer's point of view, indeed, the most useful type of system would be one which did not involve any restrictions on ultimate resultants, but which on the other hand would define some fairly definite kinds and degrees of relatedness among as many configurations as possible, in particular all those which the particular composer has reason to believe he would be likely to want to use. For example,

* This is a dissertation, which was submitted together with a composition for the Ph.D. at Princeton University in 1963.

from a certain point of view it is a major limitation of Schoenberg's system that it does not define any relationships between different twelve-tone rows. It has been suggested that it *implies* the significance of certain relationships, such as identity of total pitch-content of the respective first and second hexachords; and thus composers have based works on sets of rows related in such a manner. However, this procedure, to the extent that it is supposed to represent an extension of the twelve-tone system or a new system, rests on a misunderstanding, because these relationships are not many-to-one and thus no operations are defined which, when applied to one such row, result in another one. What is really being done here is to weaken the degree of specification of the configurations concerned, which become mere unordered sets of six notes; and in the sense in which this "extends" the twelve-tone system, further extension along the same lines would simply lead to the ultimate triviality: a system whose operations are applied to "configurations" not specified in any manner at all, and result in others of the same nature.

This is not an objection to basing works on pairs of complementary hexachords. The objection, rather, is to the description of this as basing them on "sets of rows related by identity of hexachordal content".

Although this is not central to the present paper, the reader may observe how some of the techniques described below could be construed as based on operations which, when applied to a given twelve-tone row, yield another one.

This paper is chiefly concerned, in the first place, with the exposition of a system (called the system of arrays) which constitutes essentially a generalization of the fundamental idea of the twelve-tone system, in a sense which will be explained below. This exposition and explanation occupy Part I. In Part II some uses of this system are shown, with illustrations from the composition submitted together with this paper. The distinction between the operations of the system and compositional techniques is not entirely arbitrary, because of the special nature of this particular system. Partly for the same reason, and partly for the sake of maximal precision wherever possible, the presentation in Part I is *formal*, in the sense that though it is stated in ordinary language (including elementary mathematical terminology), this is done in such a way as to ensure straightforward translatability into a formalized language. The formal presentation is however accompanied throughout by informal commentary on its effects and purposes. In Part II, notwithstanding an attempt to avoid the customary vagueness of musical discourse, informality seemed desirable or even in certain cases necessary, in order not to make arbitrary decisions limiting concepts whose most convenient or useful form was not yet determinable, or because the purpose was to suggest avenues of exploration rather than to make any firm assertions, or for other similar reasons.

In Part I, all terminology is either conventional or explained when used. However, a few notational points should be mentioned here:

(1). X(y) is the *result* of application of the operation X to y; the operation itself is simply X.

(2). (X o Y) is the composite of X and Y, i.e., (X o Y)(z) = X(w) where w = Y(z). XY is also used to mean the same as (X o Y).

(3). The distinctions between numbers and number-signs, triples and triple-notations, tones and notes, etc., are strictly observed; this sometimes leads to some cumbersome locutions, but avoids a major source of confusion.

It seems that little is called for in the way of acknowledgements or references, it being hardly necessary to emphasize the author's indebtedness to the two pioneers of twelve-tone music whose names are mentioned in what follows, and in view of the fact that this paper does not consist of research. Relatedly, I hope it will also be obvious that the numerous references to the author's *Composition for Orchestra* do not in any sense constitute an analysis or explanation of even any part of it, though they do incidentally have the effect of explaining certain aspects of the quoted passages.

It is the author's hope that discussion of compositional technique by those who know something about it "from the inside" will eventually become less rare, inhibited, and apologetic than it is today. He is well aware that to frankly expound one's own methods is to invite suspicions of all sorts, but feels that in the not improbable circumstance of the failure of serious music to survive, it will be those who have preferred concealment and pretended ignorance of their own procedures who will have more to answer for, whether or not there was anything much to conceal.

I

THE SYSTEM OF ARRAYS

1. Let us count as *pitches* only some standard tone and all the tones differing from it by an integral number of (tempered) semitones. This means, for example, that of the tones between any two which are an octave apart, we count only eleven as pitches.

2. A *pitch-class*[1] or *PC* is a set of pitches, containing a pitch x, and such that it contains another pitch y if and only if y differs from x by one or more octaves.

---

[1] Milton Babbitt's term. The non-existence of any traditional term for this concept is remarkable, and highly significant historically (see our historical remark on page 51).

3. A pitch-class x is said to be a *semitone above* another pitch-class y if and only if x contains a pitch a semitone above some pitch contained by y.

For the pitch-classes we shall use the usual names 'C♮', 'C♯', etc. But since there are just 12 PCs and the relation of being a semitone above orders them into a cycle, it is also possible to denote them by the signs and sign-combinations (including '+', brackets, etc.) which usually denote the integers modulo 12, with the convention that '0' denotes C and that '(n + 1)' denotes the PC a semitone above the PC denoted by 'n'.[2] This is possible with consistency in that two of these signs or sign-combinations denote the same PC if and only if in their usual use in mod. 12 arithmetic they denote the same integer.[3]

4. By an *array-form* or *AF* let us mean any non-empty set of ordered triples (x, y, z), of which x is a PC, and y and z are positive integers,[4] subject to the following conditions:

(a) If in some triple (x, y, z), $y = (n + 1)$, then in some triple (u, v, w), $v = n$.

(b) If in some triple (x, y, z), $z = (n + 1)$, then in some triple (u, v, w), $w = n$.

These conditions merely stipulate that the second-elements of the set's triples include all the integers from 1 up to some number; and likewise for the third-elements, the number not necessarily being the same in both cases.[5]

5. In a given triple (x, y, z) of an AF, let y be called the *horizontal order-number* or *H-number*, and z the *vertical order-number* or *V-number*. If a given AF contains (x, y, z) and (x, u, v) only where $y = u$, then y may be called *the H-number of* x *in* that AF; but if there is such a case where $y \neq u$, then y can only be said to be *an H-number* of x *in* that AF, u being another. '*The V-number of* x *in* (the AF) w' and '*a V-number of* x *in* w' are similarly defined. Also, if (x, y, z) is a triple of the AF, x is said to *have the H-number* y and to *have the V-number* z *in* that AF.

---

[2] In this sentence 'n' is a *syntactical* variable, ranging over the numerals '0' through '11'.

[3] Mod. 12 arithmetic itself is of course demonstrably consistent in the strongest sense of "demonstrably". This is important with regard to the possible formalization of our presentation, since the effect of this paragraph is to incorporate mod. 12 arithmetic into our *syntax*.

[4] To avoid any mistake: here we mean the ordinary positive integers (*not* mod. 12, and excluding zero). Hence the following conditions (a) and (b) presuppose that $(n + 1)$ cannot be 1.

[5] It is more convenient to begin these numbers from 1 rather than 0 for several reasons that will become obvious as we proceed (see, for example, the definition of 'R' on page 48, or that of 'nth chord' on page 49).

If it is clear from the context that a particular AF is concerned, the phrase 'in w' in all these usages may be omitted; and the usual grammatical variants of ordinary language may be applied to all these terms. For example, we may speak of 'all the H-numbers which x has in (the AF) y', meaning 'each z such that x has the H-number z in y'.

A particular AF may be designated by writing out the notations for its triples, in any order, but this method is less useful than the presentation of an "abstract" music-example, as follows: (1) Notes are used to represent the PCs to which belong the pitches usually denoted by these notes; (2) the H-numbers of the PCs increase as the example is read from left to right, PCs having the same H-number being represented by vertically aligned notes; (3) similarly, the V-numbers in general increase as the example is read from bottom to top,[6] but here notes denoting different PCs having the same V-number cannot be horizontally aligned, hence (4) in addition, notes denoting PCs having alternate V-numbers will be blacked-in notes. This notation at any rate suffices to distinguish all the AFs discussed below, provided it is understood that anything suggested by such a music-example which is not part of the definition of the AF must be disregarded (e.g., the registration, contour, or spacing of the tones denoted by these notes in their usual sense).[7]

This notation is of course suggested by the simplest musical interpretation of the AF, horizontal and vertical order-numbers indicating relative positions in time and pitch. But the whole matter of interpretation will be discussed separately below.

Note also that there is one respect in which this musical notation is less likely to mislead than the direct notation of the triples. For while, e.g., the second half or upper half of such a music-example still designates an AF, the corresponding half of the triple-notations does not, because the order-numbers denoted do not then begin from 1.[8]

6. A *unary standard* array-form is one in which each of the twelve PCs occurs in just one triple. A *binary standard* AF is one (1) in which each of the twelve PCs occurs in just two different triples, (2) which has a

---

[6] We choose this convention rather than the opposite in order that "lower" note may represent "lower" number.

[7] Example 1 is an illustration of this notation.

[8] Also if the triple-notations are written out, one must write them out in some order, but this order has no significance and might be another source of misunderstanding.

It would be possible and indeed desirable from some points of view to introduce all our terms as descriptive of musical notations of this kind rather than of relations among numbers, etc. But there are more convincing reasons against it: not only would one have to introduce various further notational conventions to secure a one-to-one correspondence of AFs in this notational sense to AFs in our sense, but the definition of the various operations on and relations among AFs would be extremely complicated.

unary standard AF as a subset, and (3) in which the H-numbers in the triples of this subset do not recur in the remainder. A *ternary standard AF* is similarly defined (with a binary standard subset) and so on. For any n, an n-ary standard AF is called simply a *standard AF*.

The simplest interpretation of an n-ary standard AF is thus a "succession of n aggregates".[9] The concept could be extended to cover vertical combination of aggregates also, but this is complicated and will not be required in the following discussion.

7. Two array-forms x and y are said to *have the same specific shape* if and only if there is a one-to-one mapping of the set of all 12 PCs on itself which maps x on y; and a *specific shape* is the set of all AFs having the same specific shape as a given one.

The specific shape of an AF is thus the configuration in which its PCs are ordered, regardless of what they are except for being the same or different from one another. For example, we may regard the concept *twelve-tone row-form* as a specific shape (all V-numbers being 1), since all such row-forms — i.e., all forms of all twelve-tone rows, not merely all forms of any one such row — have the same specific shape and nothing else has this specific shape.

8. The operation of complementation of H-numbers (mod. n + 1 where n is the highest H-number in any triple of the AF), is called *retrogression* or *R*. The analogous operation on V-numbers is called *vertical retrogression* or *V*.

Both of these operations clearly preserve the property of being an AF,[10] and moreover of being an n-ary standard AF with the same n. R is familiar under the same name from Schoenberg's system, and V functions precisely the same way with respect to the vertical order-numbers. But these operations do not preserve specific shape in all cases.

9. Let two AFs x and y be said to *have the same shape* if and only if x has the same specific shape as either y or R(y) or V(y) or RV(y); and let a *shape* be the set of all AFs having the same shape as a given one.

---

[9] An *aggregate*, in Milton Babbitt's terminology, is any set of 12 pitches (or occurrences of them in a composition) of which each pitch belongs to a different pitch-class.

[10] I.e., the set of triples R(x), for example, is an AF if and only if x is an AF. By definition, if R(x) exists, x is an AF; but it does not follow from this alone that R(x) itself is one.

This incidentally raises the question of the formal legitimacy of our method of defining operations, in view of the fact that under these definitions X(y) may not exist, even though the result of substituting constants for these variables appears to be a constant-form and thus to necessarily have some denotation if our language is to be consistent. Our suggestion for avoiding such an inconsistency in formalization would be to treat pitch-class names and numerals, etc., as denoting sets, letting X(y) be the null set wherever no resultant of the application of X to y is otherwise provided.

10. By a *chord of* an AF we mean the set of all PCs having a given H-number in that AF; and by a *voice of* an AF, the set of all PCs having a given V-number in that AF (as usual, the phrase beginning 'of' will be omitted where unambiguity is otherwise secured). We shall not use other senses of these terms in what follows except where specifically comparing senses. Note that under these definitions the same voice may contain more than one element of the same chord, as is also true in tonal theory (when continuous octave-doublings are counted as one voice).[11]

11. The chord of an AF whose elements have the H-number n will be called the *nth chord of* the AF; and the *nth voice of* an AF is the set of PCs having the V-number n in that AF. Thus for example R has the effect that the nth chord becomes the $((m + 1)-n)$th where m is the highest H-number, and V has a similar effect on the voices. And both R and V preserve the partition of the AF into both chords and voices.

12. The *transposition n semitones*, or Tn, of an AF x, is the AF resulting from the substitution of the PC $(m + n)$ for the PC m in each triple of x.

The *inversion*, or I, of an AF x, is the AF resulting from the substitution of the PC $(0 - m)$ for the PC m in each triple of x.

The *circle-of-fourths transform*, or $M5$, of an AF x, is the AF resulting from the substitution of the PC $(m \times 5)$ for the PC m in each triple of x.

Of these operations, transposition and inversion are again familiar from Schoenberg's system, but M5 is less well known. The justification of the compositional use of this relationship, and its similarities to and differences from the Schoenbergian ones, will be discussed later.

13. The *proper* operations, or the operations of the system of arrays, are all and only the following:
   1. R, V, Tn for each n, I, and M5.
   2. (X o Y) where X and Y are proper operations.

---

[11] We define 'chord' for example, so that chords consist of PCs rather than triples, in order to allow different AFs to have a chord in common without having to present it in the same horizontal position or vertical order. Note that this definition also has the effect that the triples of an AF containing a given H-number may determine a chord having fewer or more elements than the number of such triples.

The observation that it is also true in tonal theory that the same voice may contain more than one element of the same chord is not intended to draw any significant analogy, but merely to invoke a verbal precedent without which this might seem an awkward consequence of our choice of terms. Since the elements of our voices are PCs and those of tonal theory are pitches, there is obviously no such analogy here.

There are 192 proper operations.[12] For convenience in speaking of these, the following abbreviations will be adopted:

1. Since (I o M5) is equivalent to the substitution of (m × 7) for m in each triple, we denote this by '*M7*'.
2. The expression 'some X' will be used for '(X o Tn) for some n' where X is an operation other than a transposition.

14. Array-forms are said to be *forms of the same array* if there is a proper operation which, when applied to one of them, results in the other; and an *array* is the set of all AFs so related to a given one.

The proper operations form a group (with respect to (o)), of which the operations of Schoenberg's twelve-tone system are of course a sub-group.

Forms of the same array have the same shape, so we may speak also of the shape of an array, meaning the shape of each of its forms. Moreover, if two AFs x and y have the same shape, there is an AF z which is a form of the same array as x and has the same specific shape as y.

15. We have already described the relation of two AFs such that the PCs are permuted with respect to their order-number pairs, and called it 'having the same specific shape'. Now somewhat analogously, the H-numbers may be permuted with respect to the pairs (PC, V-number), or the V-numbers permuted with respect to the pairs (PC, H-number).[13] Let us say that two AFs related in the former way are *vertically similar*, and in the latter way *horizontally similar*.

Now if two arrays have respectively two forms which are vertically similar, then every form of one is vertically similar to some form of the other. Hence we may speak of vertically similar arrays, meaning arrays standing in this relationship. AFs which are forms of the same array may be vertically similar, or they may not. E.g., R(x) is always vertically similar to x, since R is a permutation of the H-numbers. Analogous remarks hold for horizontal similarity, V(x) being always horizontally similar to x, etc.

---

[12] Operations X and Y are identical only if X(z) = Y(z) for *any* z. The number of proper operations which have distinct resultants on application to a given AF may be as few as *one*, since there is an AF—namely, that in which each of the 12 PCs is assigned to just one triple with H-number 1 and V-number 1—such that all the proper operations upon it are equivalent to the identity operation, i.e., have this same AF as resultant. There seems to be no reason to complicate our definitions to exclude this or any of a number of other degenerate types of AFs, and indeed they might conceivably have some compositional usefulness in some context.

[13] This is only "somewhat" analogous because only H-numbers or V-numbers occurring in the given AF are permuted, whereas the permutation of the PCs mentioned above was a permutation of *all* PCs (which might not preserve the AF's PC-content).

16. The forms of vertically similar arrays will be said to belong to a *vertical array-family*, and '*horizontal array-family*' is similarly defined.

The foregoing sequence of definitions may be regarded as a complete generalization of the fundamental idea of Schoenberg's twelve-tone method, in a sense which we will now explain.

The "fundamental idea" which I mean is that of considering the *order-relations of pitch-classes* in abstraction from other relations.

In as much as "development" in any kind of thought perhaps consists of progressive abstraction, one may reasonably consider this a stage in the development of musical thought in general; particularly if this idea is not considered to "inevitably" involve the specific and personal limitations of Schoenberg's own techniques.[14]

The completeness of this generalization consists in the following three propositions:

1. Any musical passage whatsoever, provided it uses only the tempered chromatic scale,[15] may be regarded as a direct representation of a *single* and *unique* AF, in an obvious manner (lower H-number for earlier attack-point, lower V-number for lower pitch). This point is trivial enough, and is made only to show that no constraints at all are imposed by the decision to use AFs in composition, and moreover it does not even mean anything to "restrict oneself" to one AF.

2. Only two musical dimensions exist in which there is a well-defined linear order of qualities. The operations R and V respectively preserve order (in the directionless sense of order) in these dimensions. Thus while the introduction of V is immediately suggested by the obvious rationale of Schoenberg's R, there are no further operations of this kind and the system is complete in this sense.

3. The set consisting of the operations T_n for each n, I, M5, and their combinations, is exhaustive in another sense. Substitution in each triple of $(m \times x)$ for m where x is not 1, 5, 7 or 11 does not generally preserve distinctness of PCs, nor even the total number of PCs

---

[14] This issue has been persistently confused by statements to the effect that the adoption of the twelve-tone method by composers does not involve any stylistic commitments. The main reason for this apparent situation is that most adoptions of Schoenberg's method are superficial, in that the use of rows has little to do with any other aspect of the compositions concerned.

[15] I.e., provided no essential distinctions are prevented by this interpretation of its notation. Thus quarter-tone music, for example, is excluded; but traditional tonal music is not, because the essential distinctions between the sometimes allegedly different tones represented by "enharmonic" notions have to do with their functions in different contexts, and are in no way compromised by the assumption of pitch-identity between them.

in the AF (substitution of (m × 11) for m is equivalent to I, since for any m, (0 − m) = (m × 11)). Other operations than additions and multiplications fail to preserve the differences and ratios which constitute the significance of these operations.[16]

II

SOME USES OF ARRAYS

The following discussion is devoted to the use of the system of arrays in composition, i.e., with actual compositional techniques. We will enlarge particularly on techniques already used (by the author) in *Composition for Orchestra* and another work (incomplete at present), not because of any prior objection to "speculative theory" but simply because the author is not much interested in merely speculating, but rather finds himself regarding as most theoretically interesting the same techniques as those he is most interested in compositionally exploring. Among the various techniques used in *Composition for Orchestra* which could be discussed, we will speak only of those that seem applicable in at least some other contexts than those in which they are there applied. We will not lay down any rules of method in general, but will from time to time hazard remarks as to what methods seem more or less appropriate in what circumstances. Emphasis will be on the *result* of the application of devices to specific material, and on the *cooperation* of various musical factors rather than their separate "organization" (whether or not according to similar principles).

Since our illustrations will all be drawn from *Composition for Orchestra*, it seems worthwhile to make a preliminary general survey of the AFs used there and some of their chief properties and relations.

The AFs basic to *Composition* are all related in some way described in Part I to Ex. 1. They may be divided into the following categories:

1. Forms of the array of which Ex. 1 is a form.
2. Forms of arrays horizontally similar to that array.
3. Forms of the array of which the first half of Ex. 1 is a form, and horizontally similar forms; and likewise for the second half.

---

[16] This, of course, is by no means to imply that other operations on AFs are uninteresting or useless; on the contrary, Part II of this thesis is devoted mostly to examining such operations. The point is merely that other operations are best not regarded as part of the system of arrays, and involve essentially different ideas rather than extension or completion of Schoenberg's system.

We have also chosen to classify the other operations considered later as methods of compositional interpretation of AFs, but these two distinctions are not necessarily parallel, as can be seen from the fact that even the horizontal and vertical similarities are not counted as proper operations.

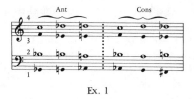

Ex. 1

The separate use of the horizontal halves of Ex. 1 reflects, in the first instance, the fact that it is a binary standard AF; and the use of horizontally similar forms but not of vertically similar forms ensures that these halves are kept discrete from one another.

For convenience, the first half of Ex. 1 may be called its *Ant* (antecedent), and the second half its *Cons* (consequent). These terms may then be extended to all the related AFs; but it must be noted that if its relationship to Ex. 1 involves the operation R, such an AF will have its Cons as its *first* half, etc. 'Ant' and 'Cons' may be regarded as names of horizontal array-families.

Let us also adopt the term '*total form*' to mean any form of the same horizontal array-family as Ex. 1 or any AF resulting from the replacement of the Ant of such a form by a horizontally similar Ant, or an analogous replacement of its Cons. Thus each total form has an Ant and a Cons. But far from every succession of an Ant and a Cons is a total form; for while permutation of voices within one half preserves the property of being a total form, other operations within one half in general do not.

The first general remark we may make about *Composition for Orchestra* is that if 'divides into' is understood with a certain liberality, this piece divides into temporally contiguous total forms. In other words, Ant and Cons are always used in association with one another to make up a total form. The liberality required may be illustrated as follows:

1. The first movement begins with an Ant-form in long held tones, accompanied by sixteenth-notes which together with the former make up various total forms; there follows a passage in which the same Ant-form is given a different kind of representation, and only after that does an associated Cons, i.e., one making up a total form with this Ant, appear.

2. The second movement begins with an Ant-form, followed by T1 of this form; there follows a Cons-form making up a total form with the immediately preceding Ant-form, and then T11 of this Cons-form, so as to make up a total form with the opening form.

Despite these liberalities, one might think that this divisibility into total forms (which are not even combined vertically except for special

cases like the one mentioned in 1. above) would lead to excessive uniformity. This would indeed be so if the representations were all of the
fairly direct type in which one triple of the AF corresponds to one
tone, or elementary extensions of this type by repetition of segments,
etc., as in Schoenbergian twelve-tone music. However, this is by no
means what happens in this piece nor what I conceive to be the general type of appropriate AF-representation, as will be seen shortly.
But before proceeding to the general question of interpretation or
representation of AFs, let us mention a few more properties of the
specific AFs used in *Composition for Orchestra*, since it is the effect of
such properties on features of the musical representations which constitute the point of the procedures of representation.

   1. The voices of Ant- and Cons-forms are all three-element segments of the chromatic scale, or of the circle of fourths.

   2. The four voices of the Ant and the four voices of the Cons of any
total form are the same four sets.

   3. In Ex. 1, the first chord of Ant differs by one PC from the first
chord of Cons; and the *second* chord of Ant differs by one PC from the
third chord of Cons, and vice versa. Only 3 PCs (F♯, G, and A♭) are involved in these differences, and they form a voice in each of Ant and
Cons. Similar properties hold for all the other total forms.

Direct Occurrences

   By a direct occurrence of an AF let us understand an interpretation
of the kind suggested by our abstract music-example notation, i.e., if
this is now understood as an ordinary music-example; except that it
is not necessary that the chords be vertically aligned provided they do
not horizontally overlap with other chords, and that such other
changes be made (such as putting in note-stems, etc.) as are necessary
to make the example correct musical notation. A direct occurrence of
a twelve-tone row form would then be simply a succession of 12
pitches from different PCs. Now of course such direct occurrences
are relatively rare in Schoenbergian twelve-tone music. More usually,
the row-form is divided into segments, each of which is assigned to a
registral or timbral part or set of parts, the order being maintained
within these parts but not necessarily between them; and also any sub-
segment is liable to be repeated, etc., etc.

   Now while on one hand, direct occurrences of closely related AFs
are no more acceptable as the exclusive events of a piece than direct
occurrences of forms of the same row would be, on the other hand,
"free" distributions (analogous to Schoenberg's distributions of
twelve-tone row-forms) are in general no more appropriate. The
voices and chords of the AFs would become mixed up with various

other kinds of vertical and horizontal associations, the voices are generally too short for repeats of sub-segments to allow related forms still to be distinguishable, etc., etc. What are required, in order to obtain variety without nullifying the sense of the AFs, are methods of distribution which constitute orderly processes; methods, in effect, which reinterpret the H- and V-numbers to mean something else than they mean for direct occurrences, without coming to mean nothing at all.

The Method of Reduction to Sequences

If an AF can be reduced to a linear order of PCs by some rule applied to the H- and V-numbers, at least some of the Schoenbergian representation-types may then become appropriate, depending on the nature of the resulting order. Such a reduction, applied to a unary standard AF, produces a twelve-tone row-form. By the rule we will suggest, a binary standard AF is reduced to a succession of two twelve-tone row-forms, and so on. However, the object of such reduction is not supposed to be just to reincorporate all the Schoenbergian possibilities, as will be seen.

Let a *consistent sequence* of a given AF be a succession of PCs such that

(1) Each PC occurs in the succession the same number of times as the number of different triples of the AF which contain it.

(2) For any two PCs x and y such that there is an H-number of x in the AF which is lower than some H-number of y in the AF, an occurrence of x precedes an occurrence of y.

(3) Suppose two PCs x and y have the same H-number in the AF. Then if, among the triples containing x and y and this H-number, there is a V-number of x lower than some V-number of y, an occurrence of x precedes an occurrence of y.

The motivation of this rule should be clear; it constitutes an interpretation of the order-numbers in which the V-numbers determine horizontal (temporal) order within the chord, while the H-numbers continue to have the same sense as for direct occurrences. Except for cases in which two or more PCs belong to the same intersection of a voice and a chord, there is a *unique* consistent sequence of a given AF.

Note that if we compare the sets of consistent sequences of unary standard AFs which are forms of the same array with the sets of row-forms which are forms of the same Schoenbergian twelve-tone row, we may observe a significant difference, *which remains even if M5 is added to the twelve-tone operations*. Namely, consistent sequences of V-related unary standard AFs are *not* necessarily forms of the same twelve-tone row, since they are related by R *within each discrete segment representing a chord of the AF*.

Also observe the effect of reducing horizontally similar unary standard AFs to consistent sequences. Each discrete chordal segment has the same content, but the order differs. This difference, however, is according to a pattern: the PCs of a given voice *always precede* or else *always follow* the PCs of another voice, within the respective discrete segments.

Thirdly, observe that reduction to consistent sequences has a special point in relation to certain AFs, among which are all those having the same shapes as the AFs used in *Composition*; namely, that between PCs belonging to the same voice, the same number of other PCs always intervene.

Finally, note that within the limits of the AFs used in *Composition, the AF is uniquely determined by its consistent sequence* as well as the converse. This would *not* hold in general even for horizontal array-families (which are of course smaller sets of AFs); this is another property ensured by the *shapes* of the AFs of *Composition*, although it *could* also hold for arrays or families with more irregular shapes.

Now by an *inconsistent sequence* of a given AF let us mean a succession for which (1) and (2) of the definition of 'consistent sequence' holds, but not (3).

A given AF clearly does not in general determine a unique inconsistent sequence, but may have many different ones, since the definition specifies the order only between elements of different chords. Also, among the AFs of *Composition* the inconsistent sequence clearly does not determine the AF, since horizontally similar forms all have the same group of consistent and inconsistent sequences, and differ only as to which is their consistent one (this being determined by a purely conventional association of upward vertical order in the AF with forward order in the sequence). For this reason, inconsistent sequences are only appropriate in special circumstances (if we are to stick to our statement that the order-numbers should mean something), perhaps only when the context suggests an analysis regarding them as deviating for some particular reason from a particular consistent sequence (we will shortly illustrate this).

By the *consistent dyad-sequence* (or simply *dyad-sequence*) of a given AF let us mean a sequence of dyads (pairs of PCs in a determined *vertical* order) formed from the consistent sequence of the AF thus: The 1st, 3rd, 5th, etc., PCs are placed in that order below the 2nd, 4th, 6th, etc., respectively (if the AF has no unique consistent sequence it has no dyad-sequence).

The formation of dyad-sequences would have no particular relevance to AFs in general, but is rather a device especially appropriate to AFs like the ones in *Composition*, not only because of their tetrachordal shape but especially because of the combinatorial properties and relations of their voices. Evidently, it constitutes a kind of compromise between the direct occurrence and the consistent sequence.

In view of our sense of "chord", it will be seen that reduction to sequences is a kind of "arpeggiation technique". But from the illustration which we will now give, it will also be evident that the result need not resemble at all what that term probably suggests.

Example 2 is an AF which belongs to the same horizontal array-family as Ex. 1 (voices 1, 2, 3 & 4 of Ex. 1 are respectively some RM7 of voices 3, 2, 1 & 4 of Ex. 2).

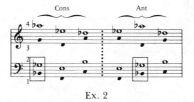

Ex. 2

Example 3 is a piano-reduction of mm. 2–3 of *Composition for Orchestra*, based on Ex. 2 in the following manner:

1. The dyad B♭-G♭, which is fixed in the same two adjacent voices in Ex. 2 (circled there), is held throughout. This is an example of suggestion of a rhythmic feature by a "harmonic" feature of the AF.

2. Together with the held tones, the others present the consistent sequence of Ex. 2, except for one deviation (the order between the pairs F-E and A-E♭ is reversed, so that we have a consistent sequence of Cons followed by an inconsistent sequence of Ant). This deviation compensates for the extraction of the held fixed-dyad from Ant's middle chord, in the following sense: *it restores the moving part's separation of the three tritones (belonging to one pair of voices) by other dyads*, which separation would have occurred in a straightforward consistent sequence. This is an example of the fact that inconsistent sequences may, in certain circumstances, clarify rather than obscure the voice-structure of the AF.

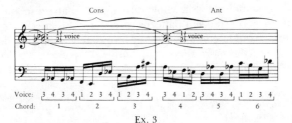

Ex. 3

3. The *repeated* pairs of tones are those which *make up chords of the AF with the held fixed-dyad*. The effect is in a sense to assign one quarter-note's value to each chord; similarly, at least one reason why the tones are repeated in pairs rather than individually is to prolong the chord as such rather than emphasize the individual tones in it.

To illustrate the *dyad-sequence*: Ex. 4 shows another form of Ant, namely T9 of the first half of Ex. 1; and Exx. 5 and 6 show the dyad-sequences of Exx. 1 and 4 respectively. These two sequences stand in the remarkable relation that the discrete *linear* dyads of Ex. 5, in forward order, are the *vertical* dyads of Ex. 6, in downward order (arrows on examples). This gives rise to the possibility of a variational relationship in two simultaneous senses, viz., transposed and untransposed. Such a relationship holds between mm. 3–10 and mm. 31–39 of the second movement of *Composition for Orchestra*.[17]

Ex. 4

Ex. 5   Ex. 6

The Method of Rotary Distribution

This method is applied in the first instance to sequences, including dyad-sequences, and hence indirectly to AFs. The result is a new AF in which each of the units of the original sequence occurs several (the same number of) times, according to a pattern. It is difficult to specify exactly what patterns should be counted as "rotary", but we have in mind patterns in which each unit in turn occupies one of a series of positions which correspond in some sense, so that the original AF is reflected in the new AF as a whole rather than in any discrete proper part of it. Various different patterns could have this effect, and different patterns would be more or less appropriately applied to different sequences; but the more regular or simple the pattern, the less need for it to be justified in terms of its relation to the specific sequence.

[17] The process relating the bases of these two passages is described in "Godfrey Winham's Composition for Orchestra" by J. K. Randall, in PERSPECTIVES OF NEW MUSIC, Vol. 2 No. 1, pp. 102–113.

The pattern of a rotary distribution may be shown by a diagram similar to our "abstract music examples" except with numbers (representing the order-positions of the units in the original sequence) instead of notes, as in Ex. 7. Example 8 should make clear the sense in which Ex. 7 is rotary. The pattern discontinues where it does because continuation in the same manner would repeat itself.

Ex. 7

1	2	4	3	5	6		2	1	3	4	6	5	
6	3	5	2	4	1		3	6	2	5	1	4	
5	4	6	1	3	2		4	5	1	6	2	3	

Ex. 8

Now Ex. 9 shows the first half of the result of application of the rotary-distribution pattern Ex. 7 to the dyad-sequence Ex. 5, except that each dyad is vertically reversed. The second half (not shown) simply reverses the order between the chords of each discrete pair, as can be seen from Ex. 7. It is because of this duplication that when this pattern is used in *Composition*, the individual dyads of Ex. 5 are vertically reversed *in the first half only* (this actually is not part of the technique of rotary distribution as such, since its effect is only within the individual units).

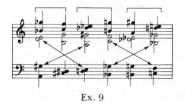

Ex. 9

The particular appropriateness of the application of Ex. 7 to Ex. 5 (and related sequences) derives principally from two properties of Ex. 5 not so far mentioned. Both of these properties have to do with the effect of rotation of the order of its dyads (i.e., addition of a constant mod. 6 to the H-numbers of Ex. 5, considered as an AF); this is evidently a critical factor, because of the rotary nature of the distribution, which (as can be seen most easily from Ex. 8) could be indifferently regarded as based on any of the six such rotary "forms" of Ex. 5.

The first property is that each of these six forms has discrete forms of the same three tetrachords, namely, the chords of Ex. 1. The second is that one of these, Ex. 10, is some RIV of Ex. 5. The six tetrachord-forms concerned in the first property are bracketed on Ex. 10 (the three brackets *below* the example indicate the *discrete* forms in Ex. 5, for instance). It will be observed that the upper line of dyads in Ex. 9 presents the chords of Ex. 1 in order as discrete pairs of dyads (see brackets on Ex. 9); similarly, the lower line of dyads presents the chords of an Ant-form of which Ex. 10 is the dyad-sequence. This was the reason for beginning the pattern with 5 rather than 6 or 1 (see Ex. 8); i.e., in this way the two rotary "forms" of Ex. 5 which are dyad-sequences of Ant-forms (viz., Ex. 5 and Ex. 10) are given an emphasis denied to the other four, by the registral lines. But at the same time the entire configuration derives from either of them, or any of the remaining four, so that just these two are represented in a double sense.

Ex. 10

All of the previous discussion would suggest that Ex. 9 is rather strongly demarcated into two-chord units. However, a demarcation into three-chord units is suggested by the interchanges of dyads between the lower voices, shown by arrows on the example (in the second half of the rotary distribution, analogous interchanges occur between the upper two voices). These interchanges can be emphasized by rhythmic factors, etc., so as to obtain a fluid harmonic motion across the segmentation into aggregates. Indeed, it is by no means necessary that the aggregates formed by the discrete pairs of chords should actually be temporally discrete, for there are many other ways in which these aggregates can have some more or less background influence on the passage.

In the first movement of *Composition*, this one *pattern* of rotary distribution — Ex. 7 — is applied many times, to various forms of Ant and Cons and in various rhythmic settings. Of these the first and simplest case uses the form given as Ex. 9, and is mm. 12–13 of the movement. Here the registration is literally as shown in Ex. 9, with division into six parts in the obvious manner, of which the lower five run parallel, forming a block-chordal accompaniment to the top part. The following observations on this passage will help to explain the more complex setting which will subsequently be examined.

1. The relation of the two rhythmic lines is such that any tone of the top part sounding together with the five-part chord below is al-

(C score)

ways either the one suggested by Ex. 9, or one immediately horizontally adjacent to it.

2. The phrasing clearly follows the demarcation after three chords suggested above, both in the sense that here occurs the only gap of two unattacked sixteenth-note points, and in that here occurs the only octave-simultaneity (E♭s at the end of m. 12 and beginning of m. 13).

3. Since the lower four parts all run rhythmically parallel with the second part from the top, the main effect of this rhythmic setting on the pitch-structure of the passage is on the two-part shape made up by the upper two parts alone (this is emphasized by the orchestration, which places strings on the upper two lines but not the middle lines, so as to isolate the former to some extent).

Now in mm. 91–94 we have the same pattern of distribution, applied this time to some I of Ex. 5, namely Ex. 11. In contrast to the previous example, the rhythmic setting here differentiates all the six parts and even involves simultaneous meters, in the sense that the rhythmic shapes present are augmentations of those of mm. 12–13, to

Ex. 11

twice their original length in two of the parts and 1½ times their original length in the other four parts. The faster-moving parts here are extended (from 3 measures to 4) over the length of the slower ones by means of the devices of (1) entering them canonically, (2) changing over the leading voices to following voices and vice versa half-way through. This changeover arises naturally at this point in view of the phrasing (discussed above).

The two slower-moving parts correspond to the upper two parts of mm. 12–13; here they dominate the passage in the different sense of being present continuously. The other four parts, however, are divided into pairs presenting the rhythm of mm. 12–13 not according to the pairing suggested by the dyads of the rotary distribution, but instead in such a way as to present the interchanges of dyads corresponding to those indicated by arrows on Ex. 9 as interchanges of single tones. Thus the basses proceed Eb-(Ab)-G while the violas proceed G-(E)-Eb; the bassoon has D-(Bb)-A while the clarinet has A-(C)-D; and so on throughout. In view of the repeated figures, etc., that this pairing nevertheless never gives rise to actual octave-simultaneities might appear as a mysterious fortuity, unless we remember from the above discussion that two tones sounding together in this two-part rhythmic setting were always either from the same chord or from horizontally adjacent chords, while the interchanges here are across an intervening chord in each case. (The one octave-simultaneity which does occur in the passage has a function similar to that of the octave in mm. 12–13, and does not involve one of these interchanges.)

It will be observed that the timbral treatment of this passage is to isolate the two halves of the chromatic scale by assigning alternate parts to strings and wind. While the resulting three linear, vertically separate statements of each hexachord are obvious, this also helps to separate to some extent three horizontally distinct statements of each of the same hexachords. Thus for example, the first measure (approximately) of this passage (m. 91) immediately refers back to the whole top part of mm. 12–13 (in several other ways besides the mere total PC-content), thus preparing locally for the (systematically predetermined) inversion of this top part which follows, etc.

The whole passage mm. 91–94 shares with mm. 12–13 the literal identification of melodic instrumental parts with the registral parts suggested by the rotary distribution, while breaking down the division of the distribution into chords and aggregates (or rather, allowing it to recede into the background). It should be mentioned that the opposite possibility of elaboration equally exists: to hold relatively strictly to the chordal demarcations, while making up instrumental lines from notes from different voices, etc. Whether both aspects could be elaborated at once without the rotary distribution receding so far into the background as to be of dubious meaning is another question, though there seems to be no a priori reason why this should not also be possible if some orderly method of selecting the instrumental parts be adopted. But here we reach the frontier of speculation.

Uses of the Circle-of-Fourths Transform

Although sufficient reasons are given in Part I for the inclusion of the circle-of-fourths transform among the proper operations, it is obvious that it fails to preserve an important property preserved by the familiar Schoenbergian operations. It would not be adequate to describe this as failure to preserve "interval-class", since the placing of the intervals of, e.g., 1 and 11 in the same "class", but not 1 and 5, must be previously assumed in order to support this description, which is therefore circular. The significant difference is that 1 and 11, being complementary, may hold between the same two pitch-classes, while this can never be so for 1 and 5. Thus any pair of tones may correspond to itself under the correspondence between two passages determined by their being some I, some R, some V, etc., of each other, while this holds only for certain pairs if M5 is involved. However, it should be noted, first of all, that this formulation shows that there is an equally basic difference between transposition and the other operations. Secondly, this point, while differentiating M5 from the rest, does not in any way do so to its disadvantage as a compositional tool, but merely suggests that its manner of usage should be correspondingly differentiated. And thirdly, it would not even be correct to say without qualification that I is a "closer" relation than M5 or M7. For while M5 preserves the intervals 3 and 9 while complementing 2, 4, 8 and 10, and M7 does the opposite, I complements all of these and preserves none; so that in one sense I is the least "close".

The last consideration, i.e., that M5 preserves some intervals and complements others, is one of the keys to its possibilities. Thus, for example, a conception of M5 purely in terms of the multiplicative aspect of it might lead to some surprise on the realization that this relation holds between mm. 75–77 and mm. 162–163 of the second movement of *Composition*, the near-identity of these passages being accomplished by the not too difficult procedure of arranging for the preserved and complemented intervals to hold between the same pairs of pitch-classes in the two cases, while the difference between intervals of 1 and 5 at the same time yields an element of contrast. Among several other respects in which the relation of these passages illustrates the specific possibilities of M5, there is the fact that although each proceeds horizontally in minimal intervals (i.e., of less than an octave) and with essentially the same contour, there is a great difference in their total vertical spans, with the result that they can begin from quite disparate registral areas to arrive at final simultaneities having two pitches in common (the E and D). While the use of M5 gives rise to considerable problems of registration, simply because the contour-equivalent of a chromatic scale under M5 spans 5 octaves (so that in general the literal transformation of whole passages by exact multiplication is not practicable), it also, and by the same token, suggests possibilities of registral organization by taking advantage of this predetermined distinction (rather than by imposing unrelated registral distinctions on the pitch-class material).

When Schoenberg builds a hexachordally combinatorial row, he sets up a specific relation between forms related by I o Tn for some particular n, which not only distinguishes this transposition of I from the rest, but also establishes pairs of forms which are in one sense more closely related than pairs which are simply transpositions of one another; and of course other possibilities of this kind besides combinatoriality exist (including some used by Schoenberg). Such possibilities similarly occur with M5, including, of course, hexachordal combinatoriality itself (thus for example among Babbitt's "all-combinatorial source-sets" there are some which are super-all-combinatorial in that they admit of M5-related orderings, and others not so; and in general the consideration of M5 leads to a more ramified classification of the types and orders of combinatoriality). Combinatoriality, however, from the point of view of the system of arrays becomes only a special case of the more general concept of the standard array (binary, in the case of hexachordal combinatoriality); and Schoenberg undoubtedly moved in the direction of this concept by his emphasis on the note-against-note counterpoint formed by the combinatorially related forms, especially in his String Trio, where there is no longer any

unique row and for certain passages an explanation in terms of arrays
would actually be more efficient than any less radical extension of the
twelve-tone "assumptions". (But even in much earlier works of
Schoenberg the relevance of this note-against-note conception is clear;
and also in his uniquely non-combinatorial third string quartet, the
row itself is essentially a succession of dyads rather than single pitch-
classes, from the point of view of both its structure and its use, as regards most considerations not of a quite local character.) Once this
tendency is made explicit and the basic configurations of a piece are
conceived in the first place as two-dimensional, vertical combination
of such configurations themselves becomes a superfluity, and its use
as a determinant of a special transposition of I or M5 appears superficial in the light of much more specific and relevant determinants
which can be found, of which, however, combinatoriality may be an
incidental by-product. Thus, for example, Ex. 5 is hexachordally
combinatorial with some M7 (as well as with some RI — namely Ex. 10;
and hence with some M5); thus some RM5 has the same ordered pair
of discrete hexachords. Now in *Composition*, this transposition of RM5
is indeed assigned a special status, but not for that reason. The actual
reason can be most easily seen by comparing the beginning (mm. 1–11)
and the end (mm. 148–158) of the first movement, as regards the
wind and string parts respectively. At the beginning Ex. 5 is treated as
shown in Ex. 12 (i.e., with overlapping of alternate dyads), while at
the end approximately the same is done with the RM5-form con-

Ex. 12

cerned (see Ex. 13). The point is that *the same four simultaneities of intervals of 4 (or 8) occur in the same order*, but those which are simultaneously
attacked in Ex. 12 (G♭-B♭ and G-B) occur obliquely in Ex. 13 and vice
versa (A-C♯ and E-G♯). These intervals (including the oblique cases)

Ex. 13

all have the same kind of function in relation to the accompanying shorter tones as was explained with reference to Ex. 3 — hence this particular consideration of them, rather than others. But note that exactly the same relation also holds between the ordered quadruples of simultaneities of interval 2 *(or 10)* in each example. Finally, it should perhaps be mentioned that the idea of overlapping the dyads in the first place comes from the circumstance (mentioned earlier) that chords of forms of Ant are made up by each successive pair of dyads, and relatedly, that in view of the origin of Ex. 5, i.e., its being a consistent dyad-sequence, the distinctions between attacked and oblique occurrences of intervals here derive essentially from the distinctions between different pairings of the voices of Ant.

NORTON PAPERBACKS ON MUSIC